The Secure Child

Timeless Lessons in
Parenting and Childhood Education

The Secure Child

Timeless Lessons in
Parenting and Childhood Education

edited by

Richard Volpe

University of Toronto

Information Age Publishing, Inc.
Charlotte, North Carolina • www.infoagepub.com

Library of Congress Cataloging-in-Publication Data

The secure child : timeless lessons in parenting and childhood education / edited by Richard Volpe.
p. cm.
Includes bibliographical references and index.
ISBN 978-1-60752-389-5 (pbk.) -- ISBN 978-1-60752-390-1 (hardcover) --
ISBN 978-1-60752-391-8 (e-book)
1. Child rearing. 2. Parenting. I. Volpe, Richard.
HQ769.S393 2010
305.231--dc22
2009047646

Dedication

This volume is dedicated to the memory of Professor Betty M. Flint, a scholar whose deep caring brought her to rescue an entire cohort of deprived orphaned children. After that her careful scholarship enabled her to tell their life stories using security theory in four books that became career milestones: The Security of infants (1959); The Child and the Institution: A Study of Deprivation and Recovery (1966); New Hope for Deprived Children (1978); Pathways to Maturity: Insights from a Thirty-Year Study of Deprived Children (1996).

CONTENTS

ACKNOWLEDGMENTS

This work began with the encouragement of Nick Laidlaw, which eventually led to financial support for the Blatz project from the Laidlaw Foundation. Along the way Rita Del Cotto, Kendell Sokoloskie, and Alison Gilbert supplied much needed assistance in bringing the collection into its final form. Finally, Christine Davidson, Coordinator, Academic Support, Dr. R.G.N. Laidlaw Research Centre, Institute of Child Study, University of Toronto provided invaluable editorial, bibliographic, and indexing expertise that increased the value and usability of this book.

CHAPTER 1

CONSCIOUSNESS AND CONSEQUENCES ACCORDING TO BLATZ

Richard Volpe

INTRODUCTION

This is a collection of original papers by former students and colleagues of W. E. Blatz MD., PhD. He was a pediatrician/psychologist known as the Dr. Spock of Canada. Blatz was the first director of the Institute of Child Study, University of Toronto, and a researcher/scholar who became a well-known radio and television personality in the 1960s. Several opportunities enabled those interested in his work to come together to discuss and write about him. All of the resulting papers were circulated among the authors with the aim that they would eventually be published. Ainsworth and Grapko, former students of Blatz, and Wright were close colleagues of Blatz. By contrast, Gamlin, Winestock, and I never met him. The manuscripts provided by Ainsworth and Wright were used in writings about their own careers and relationship to Blatz. The institutional affiliations of the authors at the time the papers were written have been retained in the chapter "About the Authors." In whatever way we arrived at our

The Secure Child: Timeless Lessons in Parenting and Childhood Education, pp. 1–13
Copyright © 2010 by Information Age Publishing

appreciation of Blatz, we all agreed that a collection of reflections on his work was long overdue as the field of child psychology had changed and again become more focused on stage independent ways of understanding personality and mental health.

This edited work makes an important contribution by bringing forward Blatz's insights about children in the context of contemporary ideas about human development and parenting. I expect the book will be of use in courses on personality theory, socialization, parenting and child development.

The compilation also includes an edited version of a previously unavailable guide to parenting written by Blatz and other members of the parent education team called "The Expanding World of the Child." This draft manuscript appears to have been used in parent education classes. This insightful work captures the current applicability and appropriateness of Blatz's work in understanding children and supporting their parents.

Much about the Institute has changed over the years but the child centeredness and set of beliefs about human development and security have survived through many transformations. One of the many triumphs of the Institute is its endurance. Of all the research centres established by the Rockefeller Foundation, the Institute is the only one that has remained fully intact. Much of this legacy is attributable to the life and work of William "Bill" Blatz.

The presence of William Blatz nearly a century after establishing the research program that became the foundation of the Institute of Child Study is still detectable. More specifically, it is evident in a sense of purpose that attempts to interrelate academic study and various forms of social, psychological, and educational practice. Many aspects of Blatz's work are, however, puzzling, and much of its potential has yet to be realized. The papers in this book give some insight into both Blatz and his work.

EARLY CHILD STUDY AT THE UNIVERSITY OF TORONTO

In the early 1900s, two Toronto psychiatrists, Drs. Charles Clarke and Clarence Hincks, moved the accomplishments of public health in preventing disease to the field of mental health. Eventually they came to embrace the idea of child study as a way to provide preventative interventions early in life. Both were supporters of the newly emerging discipline of psychology. With resources provided by The Rockefeller Foundation they approached Professor Ned Bott who was in the Department of Philosophy to pull together an academic group to engage in child study and eventually take what was learned into practical interventions. As the first head of psychology at the University of Toronto and a prominent member of the Canadian Mental Hygiene Committee, Professor Bott had a central role in developing child study. Project grants awarded in 1924 by the Laura Spelman Rockefeller Memorial Foundation and the Canadian National Mental Hygiene Committee enabled Bott to set up an interdisciplinary project administration board.

This opportunity prompted Bott to leave philosophy and begin work on establishing a Department of Psychology. Bott established an amazingly diverse advisory committee to administer the work of a school of scholars interested in advancing child study. This founding group was thoroughly interdisciplinary and interprofessional, consisting of representatives from psychology, pediatrics, psychiatry, and education. Its objective was to advance mental health through application derived from the human sciences. For their laboratory they first established a nursery school and later a full elementary school. They hired Dr. William Blatz, a pediatrician and psychologist, to direct and coordinate research. Blatz was born in Hamilton, Ontario in 1895 and obtained his BA (physiology, 1914) MA (physiology, 1917), and MB (medicine, 1921) from the University of Toronto and a PhD (psychology, 1924) from the University of Chicago. Dr. Blatz was appointed as an assistant professor, Department of Psychology in 1924 and retired as professor of psychology in 1963. Over his career he published 7 books and over a 100 articles in scientific and professional journals. Under the direction of Blatz, child study provided the practice and policy research base for many of Canada's postwar advances in work with children and families.

Interestingly, for Dr. Blatz, the school was established as much for parents as for children. In fact, there was actually a period early in the history of the child study program at the University of Toronto that in order to enroll your child in the school you had to agree to mandatory parent education classes.

In 1925 Professor Edward Bott officially established the St. George's School for Child Study at the University of Toronto. The School eventually became known by its present name—the Institute of Child Study—and from its inception combined youthful enthusiasm, scientific zeal, and the optimistic belief that the human condition could be positively changed through the study of children. Although the Institute has changed over the years in response to various challenges, it has retained its core "child centeredness." This value has been a protective factor and source of the Institute's resilience over the years.

Bott hired Dr. William Blatz to direct all child study related projects, which included implementing a longitudinal study of children's social adjustment in public school, setting up a laboratory nursery school, and creating a parent education program. The nursery and parent education programs became the two major divisions of the School. (In a university, the term "school" refers to a group of scholars that share a point of view.)

The functionalist psychology which Bott and his young protégé Blatz ascribed to played a major role in shifting the focus from biological factors in human development to environmental (educational) influences. "Adjustment," the establishment of an optimal relationship with the physical and social environment, became the organizing concept for research at the School, and evolved into Blatz's "Security Theory."

In 1924, the Canadian Mental Hygiene Committee asked the Toronto Board of Education to authorize a series of studies examining the mental health of school children. The first Toronto project was a longitudinal study of children's adjustment in Regal Road Elementary School. The proposed project coincided with longitudinal projects undertaken at Berkeley, Yale, Minnesota, and Iowa. The Toronto study looked at the ways children adjust to school life and the effectiveness of preventive interventions.

The nursery division doubled in size from 4 to 8 children between September and January. The parent education division grew rapidly from 20 to 30 mothers and eventually from 2 to 6 courses. Parents of children in the nursery school were expected to enroll in these courses. Although nursery schools had been in existence for a decade, the idea of someone other than a mother taking care of a young child was still considered radical. Blatz was quick to point out that the Toronto nursery was not experimenting with these children. Rather, the children played and socialized, while researchers engaged in close but unobtrusive observation. The focus of the Toronto School was on studying normal children at home and in school, and the Toronto projects flourished.

In 1930 the Windy Ridge Day School came under Blatz's direction, and the Regal Road and Windy Ridge projects gave the St. George's School for Child Study an unprecedented base to advance its educational research. The 1930s saw the School come into national and international prominence for its role in the early education of the Dionne Quintuplets and the School became an important contributor to Canada's war effort, helping to establish the war nurseries in England. By 1939, the School's work with children was recognized throughout the world. Wartime nurseries were also needed in Canada, and Blatz and his team were called upon as experts.

After the war, the St. George's School for Child Study became the source for legislation enabling nursery schools to be set up in Ontario. The parent education program had achieved such a reputation that professionals in education and social work began to look to the School for in-service opportunities.

In 1938, the Ontario Department of Education recommended the School be granted autonomy from the Department of Psychology. The School name was changed to the Institute of Child Study, a separate governing committee of the Academic Senate was established, and the budget was assumed by the University of Toronto's President's Office. In 1944, the Institute started offering its own graduate degree, a 1-year postgraduate program leading to the graduate diploma in child study.

The Institute became one of the most prominent points of interdisciplinary study within the university. In 1951 Sidney Smith, President of the University of Toronto, claimed the Institute had "helped to make the ideal of the university as a community of scholars a reality." Few divisions within the university, he observed, had so many strong interdepartmental and interdisciplinary relationships.

In 1953 the original nursery division combined with Windy Ridge School to form the elementary school called the St. George's School and later the Laboratory School. This consolidation enabled an expansion of programs, the development of an in-house journal, and an increased use of radio and television to share the Institute's collective wisdom. It was during this period that Dr. Blatz became the Dr. Spock of Canada. His work was eventually recognized as a distinctly Canadian approach to understanding child development.

AN OVERVIEW OF REFLECTIONS ON BLATZ

The chapter by Wright chronicles the evolution of Blatz's influence and the impact of his advocacy on behalf of children. Further, she examines Blatz as the producer of a system of thought that resonates with certain contemporary intellectual themes. Wright concludes that Blatz anticipated many modern ways of thinking about personality and child development.

The appreciation by Ainsworth attests to the influence of Blatz as an inspiring teacher. The intuitive insights afforded by security theory allowed an unfettered and imaginative amalgamation with object relations theory and ethology to produce the basis for modern attachment theory.

Grapko then outlines some of the basic language associated with security theory. The chapter by Grapko is based on a dissertation written under Blatz's direction. Much of his test development, research, and writing involved the application of security theory.

Winestock's chapter, also based on her dissertation, approaches Blatz from the perspective of "presentism," a standpoint that analyzes current issues and ideas in the study of human development through interpretations of the past. Winestock argues that presentism can be a useful tool as historical analysis as long as it is used along with sufficient attention to the context in which ideas emerge and not as a means of using the past to narrowly justify present dominating ideas. She asserts that Blatz was clearly a transitional figure in the evolution of developmental psychology from an early version of child psychology.

The chapter by Gamlin also makes a strong presentism case for the value of Blatz's insight into learning and the similarity of his views to those of Heider and Vygotsky. By viewing learning, thinking, feeling, and relating to others as unified constructs, both of these chapters emphasize the active, problem solving, intentional dimensions of children's adaptations to their increasingly complex worlds.

The final section presents an edited version of an unpublished manuscript by Blatz and his two early colleagues, Edward and Helen Bott. Although clearly a collective undertaking, this manuscript contains many of the insights that have come to characterize the Blatzian perspective.

In many ways, all of these papers illustrate the enigmatic nature of Blatz's contribution. His intuitive genius was obviously inspiring. His insights appear more right than wrong. His writings are almost prophetic. His positions on education, reward and punishment, prevention, and mental health can be mistaken for contemporary statements. To some, he is sage, seer, scholar, and scientist. Despite this reverence, he left few easily testable propositions and conceptualizations that have experienced anything more than minor refinements. His followers have used his concepts and have been stimulated by his insights, but there has been little growth and elaboration of his conceptual scheme. However, a number of scholars have reviewed his work and have acknowledged its social impact and practical significance (Gleason, 1999; Raymond, 1991; Richardson, 1989; Sutherland, 1976).

HUMAN SECURITY AND SCIENTIFIC THEORY

In the remainder of this introduction, I examine this enigma by uncovering some of the sources of security theory and some of the directions it might take. In this era of practice, scientific theory is more important than ever if we are to evolve and refine beyond intuitive wisdom our thinking about children.

The view of scientific theory adopted here assumes that its value lies in its ability to abstract and provide an overview and interrelation of experience. In Popper's (1965) words: "theories are nets cast to catch what we call the world to rationalize, explain, and master it. We endeavour to make this net finer and finer" (p. 59.) Rational arguments are used to criticize attempts to solve problems using theory. Theories grow by meeting problems with tentative solutions that are controlled by criticism. Thus, knowledge grows by correcting mistakes. Through this process, both theories and problems are known better (Popper, 1968). In the world of practice, theory grows from unorganized everyday impressions based on implicit or explicit assumptions, and then returns to concrete experience in the form of testable propositions. Reflective practice is vital to this process (Schon, 1983). Reflection, however, is only part of the process. As Dewey (1938) argued, reflection should not be confined to raw experience but extended to conceptualize experience made meaningful within a structure of interrelationship with abstract concepts subsuming the less abstract and extending beyond them (Volpe, 1981).

The root metaphors of security theory need to be examined in order to make its core conceptions and assumptions clear and scientifically useful. This is important if security theory is going to survive as more than an oral tradition (Wright, chapter 2). Scientific theory provides a way to facilitate communication and to accumulate and verify information. The knowledge base of child development involves the maintenance of a fragile consensus made possible through some agreement about current descriptions and explanations.

Blatzian notions have not received the attention they deserve in the scientific community. The career path followed by Blatz—as outlined in this volume by Wright and detailed by Raymond (1991)—makes it understandable why his contribution was more provincial than cosmopolitan. Blatz also reinforced this situation by refusing to allow his work to be pigeon-holed and labeled. He made few connections between his work and that of others. He made no effort to connect his thinking to sources and antecedents. This stand of his makes the task of explicating his ideas more difficult but not impossible.

SECURITY THEORY AS THEORY

As Wright (chapter 2) notes, Blatz's style of theorizing was in the "system building" of the 1930s. In contrast to a formal or axiomatic theory, a system is a coherent, inclusive, and yet flexible organization. This style is more like current theorizing that attempts to capture what is found to be the essential insights of such diverse areas as object relations theory or rationales for primary prevention. For Blatz, the concept of security was used as a construct, a single symbol used to represent a host of observations.

Bear in mind that Blatz was not eclectic, that is, he did not attempt a reconciliation of a number of views by obscuring their differences. Rather, Blatz was very consistent in building a logical edifice on his core conception of security. This consistency is the key to his root metaphor and the first step in enhancing the scientific status of security theory. For Blatz, the source of his consistency was the functionalist tradition in psychology, and the core metaphor was that of consciousness.

CONSCIOUSNESS AND CONSEQUENCES

Prior to the establishment of the School of Functionalism, it was James who recognized the biological role of consciousness as a phenomenon reflecting the need for making choices and guiding action. He contended that the study of mental processes or functions and not the static elements of consciousness were necessary in order to illuminate important utilitarian and common sense issues in psychology (James, 1890). Dewey, Angell, and Harvey Carr (Blatz's dissertation supervisor at the University of Chicago) were among the most systematic proponents of this view. It was Blatz's allegiance to "functional" conceptions of consciousness that enabled him to align his physiological and psychological studies. The common features of functionalism (Boring, 1950) are briefly outlined below:

1. Psychology should deal with mental functions (including physical functions) rather than mental content.
2. Psychological functions are adaptations to the environment.
3. Psychology should be utilitarian, applicable to areas of practice such as education and public policy.
4. Psychology need not make a distinction between stimulus and response because mental activity is part of all activity, psychological and physiological.
5. Psychology is closely related to biology; understanding anatomic and physiological functions is helpful in understanding mental phenomena.

The functional tradition evolved to become the study of mental operations, the utilities of consciousness that are employed in mediating between the needs of the organism and the environment. Mental operations were seen not as isolated events but as part of a larger functioning organism. The organism's mental functions enabled the organism to survive through adaptation to the environment. The metaphors of philosophy and biology combined in the centrality of consciousness.

Blatz's early scientific work was in the area of physiology. His very first publication was a report by the Hart House Team (see Wright, chapter 2) on the denervated mammalian muscle; it supported the observation that blood flow and temperature increase in denervated limbs (Hartman, Blatz, & Kilborn, 1920). In 1925, Blatz published a report on his doctoral dissertation, done under the direction of Harvey Carr. In this work, he studied the cardiac, respiratory, and electrical phenomena involved in the emotion of fear. He found that subjects who expected to fall in a collapsing chair evidenced less physiological arousal (fear) than uninformed subjects. Important here was Blatz's interpretation that consciously informed subjects were better able to accept the consequences of the experiment.

In 1933, Blatz published a paper titled "The Physiology of Appetites" in Karl Murchison's second *Handbook of Child Psychology*. I believe this to be Blatz's most important paper and the basis for security theory. Blatz divided human needs into three areas: cultural, emotional, and the most basic appetitive. In this work, Blatz examined the appetitive aspects of organic life. He asserted that because children are reacting at all times to their environments, the appetitive factors that determine the specific forms of this reaction could be known. In his framework, appetites are not impelling motives. Rather they are secondary directing motives that are necessary to satisfy a need. The organs of the body are functionally integrated to manifest a rhythm in continuously successive cycles that are consciously experienced and represented in overt behavior. This behavior needs to be directed at some point in the lives of children by an educational plan that helps them adapt to their environment.

The six appetites are hunger, thirst, elimination, change, rest, and sex. Each of these evidences a rhythmic pattern: first, a restlessness accompanied by crying and other evidence of dissatisfaction; then a recognition of need and a seeking of satisfaction; this is followed by acts such as suckling and swallowing that are aimed at obtaining gratification; and finally a period of repletion or rest. Hunger in the newborn provides a good example of this rhythmic pattern: first a restlessness, crying, and evidence of dissatisfaction; second, obvious patterns of suckling and swallowing become apparent; third, a phase involving postfeeding quiescence and eventually sleep. With the exception of the appetite for change, all appetites operate in similar ways. The desire of an individual to change the focus of his or her attention, however, usually involves all sense modalities and directs attention toward new phases of experience.

The point of this brief summary is to illustrate how Blatz came to employ some of the metaphors from his depiction of the appetites and their rhythmic pattern in security theory. Restlessness and the recognition of need parallel the state of insecurity that an individual must deal with by learning or expending effort. The satisfaction gained produces new levels of security. This state of rest or repletion can be likened to serenity (see Grapko, chapter 4). The insecurity-security rhythm continues, as does the cycle of biological appetites. Unlike biological rhythms, serenity becomes boring and the individual consciously recycles by seeking new experiences and moving to a new situation. As a consequence, change comes about and growth occurs. These are Blatz's root metaphors as they emerged from his first physiological studies. My contention is that with the end of this scientific phase in Blatz's thinking came a series of successful applications of these metaphors with little alteration or evolution of content.

Consider Blatz's (along with Bott) almost contemporary definition of "prevention" published in 1928:

> On the side of mental hygiene, interest was first aroused in relation to severe mental disorders ... in this whole field such study as was given ... remained therapeutic or ameliorative in outlook; the idea of prevention— the keynote of mental hygiene in our generation—had not yet arisen ... the shift of emphasis from therapeuses to prevention with an objective that is educational in terms of hygienic principles ... is ... radical and important.... The natural history point of view ... brought a new flood of light through its emphasis upon an understanding of genesis as being essential both to diagnosis and prognosis as well as treatment. But the forward-looking direction of study has proven incomparably the most illuminating. And not only has this latter longitudinal plan furnished a method of investigating the anomalies of behaviour, but also of studying all behaviour in its developmental aspects. In the latter sense mental hygiene with prevention as its aim is no longer to be conceived as meaning various therapies designed for end stages and extreme forms; its first and fundamental interest is to understand normal processes of individual adjustment and their variations in all stages in life, extreme cases being merely special instances ... the forward-looking conception has led to a new emphasis upon the importance of environmental factors as contributing, if not the original causes, at the occasions and determining conditions of many mental disturbances ... the emphasis on environmental factors tended to break down the vicious and artificial distinction between "normal" and "abnormal"... it is now recognized that in the life of any individual so called normal and abnormal trends were always blended. (pp. 5-6)

Next note Blatz's (1930) definition of the field of mental hygiene:

> Mental hygiene as a method is educative rather than therapeutic. It is essentially preventative rather than ameliorative. There are several factors, which must be kept in mind if the above is true. In the first place it will be years before the true worth of any procedure may be judged at all. The methods of control used in other fields of scientific investigation are here useless.... In the second place it is much easier to create a demand and stir up an interest in any newly attired formula than it is to satisfy this demand. Before this need can be satisfied a great deal more work and research are necessary, and more data are essential than are presently at hand. (p. 1)

This writing was followed Blatz in 1934a with a description of the practice of teaching:

> The teacher is dealing with the child in terms of a learning situation. The more we stress teaching, the less there will be learned. The teacher is not really a teacher, but a learner.... If she has confidence in the learning situation, she will present this to the child in such a way that the child will see that it is intrinsically interesting ... there is only one way to motivate learners —the teacher must be interested in what she is teaching. (pp. 3-4)

Blatz (1934a) also made his first published statement on security:

> This discussion is an attempt to strike at the root of social living and to try to bring out its first principle—security.... Security is not safety, because as soon as we desire safety we thereby show that we have not achieved security ... security is something you cannot buy or borrow. It is something you must learn and earn. The secure individual is one who when presented with a problem chooses an alternative and then is willing to accept the consequences, whatever they may be.... The standard of security may be achieved in two ways. The first way is through the mechanism of dependence.... Individuals grow toward the goal of maturity ... being born dependent, we achieve independence.... Independence is the end result of emancipation from all those persons or things upon which we are dependent since birth.... How do we achieve this independence? The mechanism is that of learning.... As you know how to do something, you are increasingly secure ... every individual may be regarded as striving for security in four phases of his social milieu ... a purpose in life ... vocation ... avocation ... social intimacies. (pp. 3-4)

For our analysis, the final quote from a 1939 article employs the biological sense of the term adaptation to characterize the relation of the individual and his or her environment:

> All behaviour may be described and explained in terms of the individual's adaptation to his environment.... The individual adapts to two main types of environments: (a) the physical and (b) the social.... It has been found helpful to seek to analyze the early behaviour of individuals rather than to try to untangle the complexities of adult adjustments.... There is never just social action but always social interaction. Thus in a social situation the relationship is always dynamic. Each response is determined not only by what has gone before but also what is expected in the future. (p. 829)

These statements outline the core conceptions of Blatz's work and laid the ground-work for security theory and 3 decades of service, education, and research at the Institute of Child Study.

Security was considered by Blatz to be a first principle, the basis of social living and a means of unifying theory and practice. He contended that it was the basic goal of all human beings and was fleetingly manifest as "a state of mind which accompanies the willingness to accept consequences of one's own acts" (Blatz, 1966, p. 15). Although acknowledging Freud's insights, Blatz (1951) was concerned that the centrality of the concept of the unconscious had been an explanatory wastebasket. By contrast, the concept of security, based on the role of consciousness, presented a largely positive, objective, and life span relevant view of human nature. In the Functionalist tradition, consciousness embraces both immediate awareness and knowledge that encompasses the past, present, and anticipated future (Boring, 1950). Consciousness is, therefore, fundamental to change in behavior and learning. Consequences are events that accompany or follow events. They are a moment of consciousness that is linked to another moment of consciousness. Moreover, they are a source of feedback to the individual as to cause and effect—which adaptations to the environment are working and which are not—and what skills and knowledge are needed at a given time.

REFERENCES

Blatz, W. E. (1930). *The mental hygiene of childhood*. Chicago: The Metropolitan Life Insurance Company.

Blatz, W. E. (1933). The physiology of appetites. In K. Murchison (Ed.), *Handbook of Child Psychology* (pp. 723-770). Worcester, England: Clarke University.

Blatz, W. E. (1934a, December). *Human needs and how they are satisfied* (Bulletin 44). Des Moines: State University of Iowa.

Blatz, W. E (1934b, December). *The importance of failure* (Bulletin 45). De Moines: State University of Iowa.

Blatz, W. E. (1939, May). The individual and the group. *The American Journal of Sociology, XLIV*(6), 829-837.

Blatz, W. E. (1951, Winter). Freud and the Institute. *The Bulletin of the Institute of Child Study. 48*, 1–4.

Blatz, W. E. (1966). *Human security: Some Reflection*. Toronto: University of Toronto.

Blatz, W. E., & Bott, H. (1928). *Parents and the pre-school child*. London: J. M. Dent & Sons.

Boring, E. G. (1950). *A history of experimental psychology*. New York: Appleton Century-Crofts.

Dewey, J. (1938). *Experience and education*. New York: MacMillan.

Gleason, M. (1999). *Normalizing the ideal: Psychology, schooling, and the family in postwar Canada*. Toronto: University of Toronto Press.

Hartman F. A., Blatz, W. E., & Kilborn, L. G. (1920). Studies in the regeneration of denervated mammalian muscle. Ottawa, ON Canada: Medical Services.

James, W. (1890). *The principles of psychology* (Vol 1). New York: Dover.

Popper, K. (1968). *Conjectures and refutations*. New York: Harper Torchback.

Popper, K. (1965). *The logic of scientific discovery*. New York: Harper Torchback.

Raymond, J. (1991). *The nursery world of Dr. Blatz.* Toronto: University of Toronto Press.

Richardson, T. (1989). *The century of the child.* Buffalo: SUNY Press.

Schon, D. (1983). *The reflective practitioner.* New York: Basic.

Sutherland, N. (1976). *Children in English-Canadian society: Framing the twentieth century consensus.* Toronto: University of Toronto.

Volpe, R. (1981). Knowledge from theory and practice. *Oxford Rev. of Education,* 41–51.

CHAPTER 2

W. E. BLATZ

The Person and His Work

Mary J. Wright

Dr. Blatz is one of the most sparkling figures in the history of Canadian psychology. He had a keen and perceptive mind and was "probably the brightest member of the Department of Psychology at the University of Toronto from 1925 until his death in 1964" (Myers, 1982, p. 85). He was dynamic and full of energy, drive, and new ideas. In his public life, he was a fearless and formidable exponent of reform.

The ideas Blatz brought to Toronto in the 1920s and 1930s may now seem commonplace, but at the time most people regarded them as shocking. He challenged all of the most sacred precepts of conventional wisdom about child rearing, especially authoritarianism in all its forms. He taught that children should be given freedom to develop their own ideas, make their own decisions, and learn from experience. He spoke out against punishments of all kinds, including shame and spanking, and he ridiculed the use of rewards such as stars, prizes, and praise. He pointed out the dangers inherent in the use of competition to motivate children and advocated doing away with examinations and "marks." He argued that "consistency" rather than love was the essential component in parental

The Secure Child: Timeless Lessons in Parenting and Childhood Education, pp. 15–41
Copyright © 2010 by Information Age Publishing
All rights of reproduction in any form reserved.

infant care and that "fathering" could be as effective as "mothering" in meeting an infant's needs. One of his talks on this latter subject inspired the writing of a hilarious parody for *Saturday Night* entitled "I can't give you anything but consistency, baby" (Ross, 1947).

To suggest that Blatz was a controversial figure is an understatement. He has been aptly described as "a general all-round disturber of the intellectual peace" (Berton, 1977, pp. 118-119). He was controversial not only for what he said but for how he said it. His style was provocative. He deliberately shocked to arouse and alert, and he did so with mischievous delight and a good deal of humour. He was also clever. His reasoning was cunning and convincing. He was *not* an opponent who could be easily bested. As a result, some declared him a prophet and a radical by others, idolized by the former and denounced by the latter.

As an advocate for children, Blatz was highly effective. He changed public opinion not only in Ontario but also across the nation and abroad. He influenced the parents who sent their children to his schools, requiring them to attend parent education classes. Through his teaching at the university, he shaped the thinking of the soon-to-be leaders in the country. As a result, government began paying attention to Blatz, and his work profoundly influenced public policy. In 1946, it was Blatz and his colleagues who set the standards for day nurseries in Ontario, legislated into law in the Day Nurseries Act. Also in this post-World War II period, the Ontario government funded a province-wide parent education program directed by a member of Blatz's staff. The "bibles" used in this program were products of Blatz and his colleagues. Although the name Blatz had become a household word in Toronto long before the war, it was now heard throughout the province. In Canada, he was the Benjamin Spock of his time.

But Blatz was more than a "mover" and a "shaker." He was a scientist, a scholar, and the author of seven books and many papers. The child-rearing practices he advocated were based firmly on his studies of children and his theory of personality development. As a pioneer in this field, he made significant contributions to the literature. He was highly insightful and anticipated many of the concepts which are commonly accepted today. His security theory, outlining the nature of mental health and how it is attained, was an original and useful theory. It yielded testable hypotheses and inspired innovative applications. The contents of this book are testimony to that.

Finally, Blatz was a warm and sensitive human being. He was deeply fond of the children he studied and served. He enjoyed his students, and they enjoyed him. His undergraduate classes typically overflowed with visitors eager to listen to this challenging and stimulating teacher. His graduate seminars were debating sessions where he provoked but did not instruct. To spar intellectually with students in class or in private was one of his greatest delights. True to his beliefs, Blatz set no examinations. When forced to assign grades, he gave everyone a "B" unless they complained, and then he would just as cheerfully assign "A"s.

As director of the Institute of Child Study, he was a leader but never a boss. He had great respect for and faith in his staff. He offered them responsibility and the freedom to innovate. He worked alongside them and inspired in them both affection and loyalty. When he came to occupy the chair reserved for him in the Institute's coffee room, he was the centre of everyone's attention.

With his friends at home, he was a genial host. He was also a polished raconteur, widely informed and able to relate a tale with maximum embellishment. He liked good food, and he liked to cook. He is said to have published some of his recipes. He enjoyed having small numbers of his friends around him for quiet talks. He also loved large parties, and those he gave were always great fun with much singing and merriment; some of the most memorable were held at his farm in the Caledon hills, a place in which Blatz found much peace and joy.

THE PREPARATORY YEARS

Blatz was born and raised in Hamilton, Ontario. He was the youngest of nine children in a family which was warm and close-knit. His father was a tailor who came to this country from Germany in the 1860s. His German extraction is noteworthy, for it was to play a part in determining the course of his career.

Like many others of his time, Blatz became a psychologist more by accident than design. When the First World War broke out in 1914, he was an undergraduate at the University of Toronto. There he obtained a BA (1916) and an MA (1917), the latter in physiology with a thesis on the functioning of the adrenal glands. He then applied to become a probationary flight officer in the Royal Navy Air Service. "He was accepted for entry and was about to leave for England when it was ascertained that this gentleman was of German extraction."[1] As a result, he was disqualified as a security risk. He had also applied for entry as a surgeon probationer with the Royal Navy, but was again declared unacceptable for the same reason. After these rejections, Blatz met "by chance, a man who was to have a large part in my future career, Professor E. A. Bott" (Blatz, 1966, p. 4). According to Myers (1982),

> Bott liked to tell the story of how he met this young medical student wandering disconsolately across the campus because he had been turned back at

the gangplank of a troopship in Halifax Harbour due to his German-sounding name. (p. 95)

Professor Bott was to become the head of the first separate Department of Psychology at the University of Toronto and to guide its destiny for 30 years. He had also been disqualified for service in the armed forces—in his case, for poor eyesight. He had, however, promptly plunged into civilian war work—the rehabilitation of wounded soldiers. He started this work in the psychological laboratories, but it soon occupied the whole second floor in the west wing of University College, and, in 1917, was transferred to even larger quarters in the newly constructed Hart House. Bott invited Blatz to join his rehabilitation team. Blatz did so and learned that "in our work we were dealing with a phenomenon more elusive than any other—consciousness." He discovered that the literature of the day, especially in psychology, was not illuminating and decided that "this was to be the area of my vocation" (Blatz, 1966, p. 4). Shortly after he joined the Hart House enterprise, it was incorporated into the Canadian Army Medical Corps. So, in the end, Blatz did get into the services. As he said: "I found myself a staff sergeant in the military hospital, nominally in charge of research in the field of mental illness" (Blatz, 1966, p. 4).

When the war was over, Blatz went back to school at Toronto to finish the last year of his clinical work in medicine and obtained his MB in 1921. He wrote: "Included in my clinical year were four lectures in Psychiatry, none in Psychology... Thus my decision was strengthened to find out exactly what psychology had to offer in the understanding of human beings" (Blatz, 1966, p. 4). Sponsored by Bott, he obtained a scholarship for advanced studies in psychology at the University of Chicago. He qualified for the PhD there in 1924. His thesis was titled "The cardiac, respiratory and electrical phenomena involved in the emotion of fear" (Blatz, 1925).

In those days, Chicago was the place to go to study psychology. Dewey was no longer there, but his younger colleagues, Angell and Carr, were championing the cause of what was to become known as functionalism (as opposed to structuralism and behaviorism) and their work, especially that of Harvey Carr, influenced Blatz's thinking in fundamental ways. Although Blatz did not describe himself as such, he clearly came away from Chicago a functionalist.

While Blatz was in Chicago, important events of great significance for his future were occurring in Toronto. Dr. Clarence Hincks, the founder and Director of the Canadian National Committee for Mental Hygiene, had persuaded the Laura Spelman Rockefeller Foundation and some local insurance companies to provide funds for the establishment of a child study centre at the University of Toronto. Furthermore, with the help of E. A. Bott, he had persuaded the University that it should accept funds for this purpose. Bott, now the Head of the Department of Psychology, assured the University of his department's support. He also knew just the right man for the job of director—Blatz. According to Mary Northway (1973), Hincks had never met Blatz and could not vouch for him, and when the representatives of the Rockefeller Foundation finally met Blatz, they had serious misgivings. Apparently he impressed them as a brash young upstart. However, Bott's assurances were effective, and Blatz was invited back to Toronto as assistant professor in the Department of Psychology to direct the child study project. Blatz accepted the offer, took up his appointment in 1925, and helped open a nursery school, the laboratory of child study. The school was located first in a house rented by the Canadian National Committee for Mental Hygiene at 47 St. George Street. Five years later it was moved to larger quarters at 96-98 St. George Street. It was named simply the St. George's Nursery School. It did not become the Institute of Child Study until 1938, and the Institute did not move to its present quarters at 45 Walmer Road until 1953.

THE PHASES OF HIS CAREER

The period between 1925 and 1964, the span of Blatz's career, can be roughly divided into three phases, each lasting about a dozen years. These phases reflect changes in his personal objectives and changes in the external demands made on him by the events of the times. From 1925-1938, Blatz's work focused mainly on his duties at the University: organizing the child study centre, doing research, developing his theories, working out and testing their implications for practice, writing, and teaching. These activities established his reputation as a scientist, scholar, teacher, and administrator and culminated in the creation of the Institute of Child Study. From 1938 to 1950, his endeavors were greatly influenced by World War II and its aftermath. Finally, between 1950 and his death, he was occupied with the establishment of an expanded Institute in its new quarters at 45 Walmer Road and the consolidation of his life's work in his final book, *Human Security* (Blatz, 1966).

Phase I: 1925-1938

The new Child Study Centre at Toronto was set up under the general sponsorship of the University of Toronto with a management committee representing several interested departments. Professor Bott chaired this committee and the staff meetings in the Centre. However, Blatz appears to have been given a fairly free hand in staff selection, staff training, and program development with the full support of his colleagues in the Psychology Department. Bott's interest embraced even the practical affairs of the nursery school and equipment for the playground. Helen Bott, his wife and a talented person in her own right, also played a significant role both as a parent educator and as a proponent of scholarly efforts during the early years.

The mission of the centre as outlined by the Laura Spelman Rockefeller Foundation was the advancement of mental health goals through research and service. On the research side, the initial plans followed the model of several other North American child study centres established in the early 1920s, notably the one at the University of California at Berkeley. A longitudinal study was immediately launched. Parents were required to register their children for admission to the nursery school at birth so that they could be studied during their infancy as well as later. The children were then to be followed up at regular intervals until they were young adults. Some were followed up until they were 24. In addition, methods for obtaining normative data on the children in the preschool were developed. Entering records on carefully designed sheets was a daily chore for the teachers. Data were gathered on personal care behaviors such as eating, sleeping, and toileting, as well as social interactions, emotional episodes, and reactions to discipline. On the service side, the Centre was organized from the start into two divisions: the Nursery School and a Parent Education Division, each with its own supervisor.

The initial methods used in the nursery school and the content of the parent education courses taught are not entirely clear. However, Blatz seems to have been sure of his educational objectives, to have developed the main outlines of his theory, to have adopted an educational philosophy not unlike that of Dewey, and hence to have had a vision of what all this meant for practice. Therefore, after the first year, he refused to hire any trained teachers. Instead, he selected local bright young women for the staff of the preschool and collaborated with them on the task of implementing a program and developing educational and management methods. He gathered together a team of workers, gave them highly effective leadership, and induced in them a remarkable degree of dedication.

The thinking of Blatz, however, was soon revealed not only through his teaching but also through his published works. In collaboration with Helen Bott, two of his books were produced and published in the first 4 years. These were *Parents and the Preschool Child* (Blatz & Bott, 1929) and *The Management of Young Children* (Blatz & Bott, 1930). Both were addressed mainly to parents. Next came a book for nursery school teachers, *Nursery Education: Theory and Practice* (Blatz, Millichamp, & Fletcher, 1935). About this time, an in house journal titled *The Parent Education Bulletin* was also launched. Research in the first few years was published in scientific journals such as the *Genetic Psychology Monographs* and the *Journal of Genetic Psychology*, but in 1933 the University of Toronto Press established a special Child Development Monograph Series for that purpose. The first was titled "Methods in Social Studies of Young Children" (Bott, 1933).

All of this creativity and productivity earned Blatz a reputation abroad as well as at home. He was much in demand as a lecturer at universities in the United States and in Canada and as a teacher during summer sessions. In anticipation of loss of funds from the Rockefeller Foundation, Lawrence Frank and others had persuaded the National Research Council (NRC) in the United States to establish a committee on child development. This committee sponsored an annual conference on research in which Blatz regularly participated. The third of these conferences was held in Toronto in 1929. Among those in attendance were John Anderson, Lawrence Frank, Arnold Gesell, Florence Goodenough, and Harold Jones. Blatz presented a paper on juvenile delinquency. During the depression, finding sufficient funds to finance both his research and the operations in his center became an onerous part of Blatz's job. This was his task until 1958 when a more prosperous university finally assumed financial responsibility for the day-to-day operation of the Institute.

Also during his early years at Toronto, Blatz had extended his work far beyond his duties in the Psychology Department. Through his efforts, psychology became part of the medical curriculum at Toronto. He delivered lectures on mental hygiene to second-year medical students and offered a seminar for graduates in psychiatry at the Toronto Psychiatric Hospital. In the community, he became consultant to the Juvenile Court and, in the early 1930s, the director of the Windy Ridge Day School for children aged 2 to 8 years. These two positions provided him with an opportunity to study school age children, an interest he also pursued as a member of the team conducting a public school study referred to as the Regal Road Project.

The recognition Blatz had achieved in the 1920s and early 1930s grew to international fame in the late 1930s as a result of the birth in 1934 of the Dionne Quintuplets[2] and his work with them. As Pierre Berton (1977) put it,

> To Blatz, the quintuplets, landing virtually on his doorstep must have seemed sent from Heaven especially for his benefit. No social scientist had ever been faced with such a unique and intriguing challenge—here he had children who sprang from a totally different background (from those studied in Toronto) and not only that: there were five of them, all alike. Moreover, they were confined in a controlled environment, twenty-four hours a day, away from their parents. (p. 118)

For about 2 years, from when the Dionne "quints" were eighteen months until they were close to four years of age, Blatz had the opportunity of planning and directing their daily routine and their play opportunities,[3] with the approval of the medical management committee. Blatz and his Toronto colleagues gave their caretakers, who were all nurses, training in the nursery school in Toronto and on-the-job-training. During this period, the children were studied by Blatz and by others at the University of Toronto such as Norma Ford Walker who was interested in the genetics of these identical sisters. Blatz and his colleagues observed various aspects of their behavior: for example, their social interactions, emotional responses, and language development. In October 1937, a conference was organized in Toronto to present the results of this research. It was a gathering of distinguished scientists from both Canada and the United States, including R. H. Judd, G. D. Stoddard, F. N. Freeman, and H. H. Newman. Blatz arranged for them to travel to Callandar in a private coach to observe the "quints." Then they met at the Royal York Hotel for sessions and discussions. A collection of the papers given at these sessions (Blatz et al., 1937) and a book titled *The Five Sisters* (Blatz, 1938) were published. The latter was written for the lay reader. It drew on information derived from the research and described the plan of training used with the children and their responses to it.

The work with the Quintuplets finally persuaded the University of Toronto to create the Institute of Child Study. For some years, Blatz had been trying to convince the university that his centre should not be part of any one department, but an independent unit to facilitate interdisciplinary research. The collaboration across departments in the studies of the "quints" had demonstrated the value of interdisciplinary research. The Institute was considered an "experiment"—the first Institute in the University of Toronto's history. Thus, said President Sidney Smith, "an important area of study is removed from any rigid departmental or faculty pattern and is made the subject of a free and diverse approach" (Northway Bernhardt, Fletcher, Johnson, & Millichamp, 1951, p. vii). In 1958, the Institute was made an independent unit in the university, and its affairs became the responsibility of a committee of the Senate with representation from the faculties and departments concerned.

Blatz's security theory was conceived during this first phase of his career. By the mid-1930s he was discussing it in his classes and capturing the interest of bright young graduate students like Mary Salter (later Ainsworth). Mary wrote:

> It was a theory of personality development, and that was what I had been waiting for! I was honoured when, having completed my master's thesis (in

1937), Blatz proposed that I undertake my dissertation research within the framework of his security theory. (Ainsworth, 1983, p. 203)

So, in 1937, research on the theory began in earnest. Salter's dissertation was devoted to the construction of self-report scales to assess the security of young adults. She studied the balance between security and insecurity (defensive behaviors) in certain major areas of life. One of the first statements of the security theory appeared in Salter's 1940 PhD thesis, and that same year, in *Hostages to Peace* (Blatz, 1940), the theory was described and interpreted in the context of the outbreak of war.

The Second Phase: 1938-1950

By 1941, the exigencies of war redirected Blatz's attention from research, as they did Mary Salter's who joined the Canadian Women's Army Corps. Blatz was invited, along with C.M. Hincks and Stuart Jaffrey of the University of Toronto's Department of Social Work, to visit Great Britain to confer on the protection of children and Canada's assistance in providing for their wartime care. After returning to Canada, Hincks organized the Canadian Children's Service and, in 1942, sent three groups of workers to England: elementary school teachers, social workers and nursery school teachers, with Blatz in charge of the latter.

Blatz's job was to establish in Birmingham a training school for child care reservists to staff the many wartime day nurseries and nursery classes in infant schools. All able-bodied women in England had been mobilized, and provision for the care of their children had become a necessity. During Blatz's 1941 visit to England, he had stressed the need for "trained" teachers for preschool-aged youngsters and had offered to help provide appropriate training.

Early in 1942, Blatz visited Birmingham to arrange for the school. The site was chosen—an abandoned, bomb-damaged infant school in the city's core. In May, when the school was ready, he and five helpers proceeded to England, and "Garrison Lane Nursery Training School opened its doors on July 1st 1942 to forty-two children between the ages of two and five and forty student child care reservists, much older" (Blatz, 1944, p. ix). The school included a demonstration day nursery for working class families living under extremely difficult conditions in bomb-damaged homes in the centre of this big industrial city. Classrooms and other facilities for the teachers-in-training were located on the second floor. Dr. Blatz's office was in a turret on the third floor, a room in which he took great delight.

Initially, Blatz's five helpers included three senior members of the Institute's staff: Dorothy Millichamp, the Assistant Director in charge of student training; Margaret Fletcher, the Director of the nursery school; and Anne Harris (later Blatz). The other two were juniors: Mary McFarland (later Smith) and Mary Wright (author of this paper). The full-day program in the day nursery was an adaptation of the shorter preschool program at the Institute in Toronto, and the students were taught the Institute's theory and methods. By the end of the first summer, the school was well established, and Blatz and his three senior staff returned to Canada to deal with wartime demands developing there. But Garrison Lane continued its work until the summer of 1944, with student training in the trembling hands of Mary Wright and the day nursery restaffed by a second contingent of teachers who arrived from Canada in late August.

On the way home in 1942, Blatz decided to write another book on nursery school theory and practice for publication and use in England. It had not been possible to obtain a supply of the Institute's publications for the Garrison Lane library, and this made teaching Blatz's system, which was different from that used in England, difficult. He started the book immediately and completed it during the summer of 1943 when he returned to Birmingham. *Understanding the Young Child* (Blatz, 1944) was published in England, but too late to be much help at Garrison Lane. However, it was republished in Canada and served its purpose there where new training programs were being developed to meet an escalating demand. This book reports the impact of the program on children's Binet IQs. The test results were impressive, with most of the children making large IQ gains (Blatz, 1944, p. 251).

It is difficult to assess the impact of Blatz on early childhood educators in England, but there is reason to believe that it was substantial. His ideas were disseminated widely. At Garrison Lane, training programs were offered to school administrators as well as to child care reservists. These programs were a week long and were fully enrolled. Also, visits from VIPs were an almost daily occurrence. And beyond the school, Blatz was in much demand as a lecturer, often appearing on the platform with the most significant educators of the time. Among these was Anna Freud who, as a refugee, was operating child care centres in the London area and forcefully disseminating her own ideas about child guidance. Although Blatz's style abroad was somewhat more constrained than it was at home, he did not fail to challenge "sacred cows" or to express his views in his usual witty, challenging, and forceful manner.

The informal early education in English nursery classes and schools since the publication in 1967 of the Plowden Report has much in common with the type of education promoted by Blatz. In describing the English system, Lillian Weber (1971) uses many of Blatz's favorite terms.

"There are many similarities, both philosophically and psychologically, between new infant school practice and the American progressive education of the 1930s" (Evans, 1975, p. 322). It is very likely that Blatz sowed the seeds of these ideas in Britain.

In the fall of 1942 when Blatz and his senior colleagues returned to Canada, they found that the need for wartime day nurseries had been recognized at home. The Welfare Council of Toronto and district had found that many mothers recruited for essential work in war-related industries were unable to secure adequate care for their children. The Council called on the Provincial and Federal Governments to rectify this situation (Stapleford, 1976, p. 2). As a result, by July, Ontario and the Federal Government signed a cost-sharing agreement for the establishment and support of day-care facilities. Ontario initiated this cost-sharing program and was the only Canadian province that took advantage of it on a large scale. A few wartime day nurseries were also established in Quebec, but none in any other province. Perhaps this was because it was only in Ontario that people were sufficiently informed (by the Institute) of the value of early education; or perhaps it was because only Ontario had the resources (the Institute) to develop appropriate facilities.

"The Provincial Government indicated its concern that day care service provide a program of the highest standard aimed at the full development of the child" (Stapleford, 1976, p. 2) and turned to the Institute for direction. Dorothy Millichamp was seconded to the Department of Public Welfare to direct its new day nurseries branch, and she recruited several early trainees of the Institute to help her. Thus, the first public day nurseries in Ontario were placed in the province's most capable hands. These women pressed for an educational program for the children (rather than custodial care) and teachers trained to implement it. Trained teachers were, however, in short supply, and so emergency training programs had to be planned and launched. The early trainees at the Institute were graduate students in psychology working on 2-year, MA programs. The new programs, emphasizing teaching rather than research, were shortened. The first (emergency training program) was to run for 18 months, but was cut to 6, then to 4, as needs in the field increased. In 1943, a 1-year, post-BA diploma program was instituted, but the 4-month program continued for the duration of the war and for some years later.

The programs for the children in the day nurseries were modeled after the one developed at the Institute. Thus a definable Ontario "traditional" early education program was established that endured for more than 2 decades, enshrined in legislation. At the end of the war, the Federal Government withdrew its support for the day nurseries, but in Ontario (unlike Quebec) they were not closed because of the hue and cry of mothers who had found them so beneficial. The Ontario Government agreed to continue support on condition that, if this was to be a permanently established program, it must be regulated. The first Ontario Day Nurseries Act was drafted in 1946 and passed into law the following spring. It required that day nurseries and nursery schools meet specified standards for mandatory licensing. Blatz and his colleagues were asked to establish the standards. Everybody was so busy that meetings to discuss the Act were held at night. "We did fairly well on space and equipment, but when it came to program, Dr. Blatz, who was very tired, said 'just tell them to do what we do at the Institute' " (Millichamp & Northway, 1977, p. 14), and that is exactly what they did. The Act read that "each procedure on the timetable shall conform to the standards currently accepted by the Institute of Child Study of the University of Toronto," and this statement appeared in every subsequent revision of the Act until 1968.

The 1946 Ontario Day Nurseries Act was one of the first of its kind in North America and the first in Canada, and the standards it set were unequalled. It provided a model for similar acts passed in other jurisdictions for many years. The Government also ensured that the requirements of the Act were implemented by hiring a well-qualified graduate of the Institute to succeed Dorothy Millichamp as director of the Day Nurseries Branch. This was Elsie M. Stapleford. A forceful child advocate, Stapleford had done her doctoral studies in psychology and worked for her master's at the Institute. She continued as director for some 30 years, until her retirement in the mid-1970s.

The postwar upsurge of interest in parent education led to the Institute's province-wide parent education program, launched by the Ontario Government. Leaders for parent study groups were trained in great numbers in both large and small cities throughout the province. Frances Johnson, who was in charge of the Parent Education Division of the Institute, was hired by the Government to direct the program. Those who had training at the Institute were recruited as instructors. The instructional materials and the "bibles" for group leaders were a series published by the Institute in the early 1940s. They enunciated Blatz's philosophy and his plan for guiding the development of young children.

After the war, research on the security theory was resumed. Blatz obtained grants from the Defense Research Board to support several graduate students, and he organized an enthusiastic research team. Blatz and Mary Salter, who returned to her academic post at Toronto in 1946, codirected the research program. The work continued to focus on developing scales to measure security in different aspects of life and at various stages of development. The most complete description of the studies of this period is provided in a publication by Ainsworth and Ainsworth (1958).

Phase Three: 1950-1964

In 1951, the Institute of Child Study celebrated its 25th birthday with a grand party and the presentation to Dr. Blatz of a magnificently bound copy of *Twenty Five Years of Child Study* (Northway et al., 1951). The whole staff of the Institute cooperated in the production of this book, describing the Institute's history, organization, place in the community, goals, and research.

Blatz was now 56 years of age, but he had yet to fulfill a major goal—to bring into the Institute the private elementary school, Windy Ridge Day School, of which he had been the director for many years. He wanted to study longitudinally the growth of security in the age group 9 to 12 years when, he believed, moral and ethical principles were developed.

To achieve his goal, the Institute needed a much larger building, one which could house classes up to the sixth grade as well as an expanded teaching and research staff. Blatz had long been pressing the University for such a building, preferably located near the projected new Arts building on St. George Street. He even had architectural plans drawn up for it, but the University resisted. Finally, however, in the spring of 1953, Blatz was offered the Leighton McCarthy mansion, which the University had inherited, at 45 Walmer Road (Millichamp & Northway, 1977, pp. 19-23). The exterior of this house was most attractive, but its interior was both unsuitable in design and inadequate for space. Extensive reconstruction and a major addition were required. Its location so far away from the main campus was also a disadvantage. Nevertheless, since it appeared to be the best the University was likely to offer, Blatz accepted it and moved everyone into it almost immediately. By the fall of 1953, Walmer Road was home to the staff and students of both the "old" Institute and the former Windy Ridge School.

This move ushered in a period plagued with administrative headaches. For 2 years, overcrowding and the noise and confusion of construction added to the tensions of integrating two formerly independent staffs, each with its own hierarchy of authority. In spite of the difficulties, significant progress was made, especially in research.

In 1953, Blatz was awarded a major Federal Health grant to support both his research and the operation of the Institute. The thrust of the research continued to be his concept of security and its growth and measurement at various age levels. The results of work already completed were integrated with new data, and the theory was developed into its final form (Northway, 1959). The work of the Ainsworths was published during this period (Ainsworth & Ainsworth, 1958). Their most important finding was a significant positive relationship between independent security and mature dependent security, suggesting that both had a common base in immature dependent security. Their results generated greater interest in the development of mature dependent security and in the relationships children formed with peers at different age levels (Ainsworth, 1960, p. 10-11). Mary Northway's method of studying peer relations using sociometric techniques was now considered a promising approach, and she became part of the security research team. Northway's developmental sociometry used fictitious social situations (e.g., the "Birthday Test") for measuring changes with age in the choice of adults or peers in situations which varied in the amount of help and support the child needed (Northway, 1971, pp. 28-31). During this period, Grapko was working on the development of a method of measuring security in school age children. He produced a test for 9- to 12-year-olds called "The Story of Jimmy" (Grapko, 1957) and later one for 6- to 8-year-olds called "The Story of Tommy" (Grapko, 1965). In addition, Betty Flint was working on a scale for measuring the mental health of infants (Flint, 1959). It was a highly productive 5 years for research on security as reviewed by both Mary Northway (1959) and Mary Ainsworth (1960).

Immediately after the move to Walmer Road, Blatz hoped to initiate a longitudinal study in the elementary grades. However, this had to be postponed mainly because of difficulties in program development. Blatz wanted to implement an educational program which his theory predicted would promote the development of mental health (security). The necessary consistency from grade to grade required changes in the style and approach of some of the teachers that were not easy to bring about. Another reason for the postponement was Blatz's failing health. During the Christmas season of 1955, he developed pneumonia, from which he never fully recovered. He did not resume his duties until the fall of 1956, and he lacked his former energy and drive. The new longitudinal study of school-aged children did not begin until 1962 (Northway, 1964), but Blatz, who had by then retired, was deeply involved in planning the work, and he participated during the first 2 years.

During the 1950s, the training and service demands made on the Institute greatly increased. After 1954, the Institute ceased to train master's students in psychology, but the diploma programs were expanded. Mental health officers for the school system were trained, including a group from Thailand. Additional special courses were developed at the request of several different faculties such as graduate psychiatry, public health, social work, dentistry, food science, and education. For example, students training as primary specialists did part of their work at the Institute. Staff members, particularly in the Parent Education Division, were in constant demand as lecturers and consultants. In addition, clinical facilities were established. Blatz's Institute had earned an enviable reputation and exercised a tremendous influence on the community. As the president of the University put it:

> The influence of the Institute of Child Study has not been confined to the University. Child study is not simply an affair of the classroom and the seminar. By its program of parent education, it has transformed the abstractions of research into wise counsels for home and school. (Northway et al., 1951, p. viii)

In 1960, Dr. Blatz resigned as director of the Institute. He was made its honorary director and continued to participate in research planning. However, he retired to an office in the Department of Psychology and there began work on his final book *Human Security: Some Reflections* (Blatz, 1966), an integrated statement of his ideas about child rearing and the theory on which it is based. His health was failing and the final chapters were produced with great difficulty with the help of Mary Northway. The book was published posthumously.

William Blatz passed away on All Saints Eve, October 31, 1964. As he so often pointed out, it is the achieving, not the achievement, that matters. "Life is not fulfillment, but fulfilling" (Blatz, 1944, p. 165). A complete life is never finished.

It is difficult to estimate the full impact of this man on our society. As Karl Bernhardt (1961) said:

> His contributions to educational theory and practice, to child rearing and family life, to parent education and to an understanding of human development have had a profound influence on the life of his country and have extended beyond its boundaries to other parts of the world. (p. 2)

BLATZIAN THEORY

As a pioneer in his field, Blatz maintained an independent stance. He felt no obligation to admit indebtedness for his ideas to anyone, and this has led to some debate about the "school" of psychology and the "stream" of educational thought he represented. He was, however, quick to criticize, and so it is useful to begin with his analyses of his contemporaries.

Blatz was opposed to the fierce empiricism of his time as it was reflected in behaviorism. He never abandoned the conviction that consciousness, although difficult to study, was the primary subject matter of psychology (Blatz, 1966). He respected Freud, of whom he wrote "all of his guesses were shrewd and many of them correct" (Blatz, 1951), but he rejected the concept of the unconscious as scientifically untenable. Blatz stressed the role of learning in development, rather than biological determinism, and this brought him into conflict with both Freud and Gesell. Blatz accepted the notion of maturation, but preferred to emphasize cultural demands and child-rearing practices to explain Gesell's ages-and-stages behavior. About Piaget's work, which at the time was in its early formulation, Blatz seems to have had little to say except to criticize it (as did many others) on methodological grounds.

Blatz's "school" of psychology was definitely functionalism. In conversation with him on this topic, the writer wrested from him a twinkle-eyed grin of acquiescence. As a student at Chicago he was influenced by Harvey Carr, for whom he had the highest respect, and he was impressed by Carr's theory of sensory consequences. As a functionalist, Blatz was biologically oriented, viewing learning and development as adaptation and consciousness as fundamental to the adaptation process. Man, he argued, is a conscious, striving being and "as long as he is alive, he will be seeking something every moment of his life" (Blatz, 1966, p. 21). For him, the essence of consciousness was *selection*: making choices between behavioral options and making predictions about possible outcomes of those choices. Selection depended on motivation—the ebb and flow of physiological appetites (hunger, thirst, elimination, rest, change, and sex)—the "tastes" associated with the appetites, and acquired attitudes and emotions. Motivation was, he insisted, always conscious: "we cannot conceive of an unconscious wish" and "with us the emotions are the most highly conscious aspects of our lives" (Blatz, 1951, p. 3). Learning, he said, began with a challenge. It occurred when motivated individuals were goal-seeking but felt inadequate because they had no readily available responses for achieving their goals. Emotion played a fundamental role in this process. Dependent on the degree of inadequacy felt, responses focused attention on the problem and produced the energy needed to deal effectively with the challenge. Thus, he emphasized the facilitating function of emotion as opposed to its disruptive potential, pointing out the importance in child rearing of helping children develop the ability to utilize their affective responses productively rather than allow them to get out of control. Blatz viewed specific emotions in cognitive terms. He considered them to be a function of the child's appraisal of a situation. If the "emoting" child judged the challenge to be masterable the response was approach/attack (e.g., anger); if judged not masterable, the response was withdrawal/flight (e.g., fear). As the child acquired knowledge and skill, his/her appraisals of specific situations changed, as did his/her behavioral responses to them and the emotions they engendered.

Kohlberg (1968) suggested that educational thought could be differentiated into three streams: the first regards children as active, the second as reactive, and the third as interactive in their dealings with the environment. Blatz belongs in the last of these three streams, the cognitive developmental one, along with Dewey, Piaget, and Kohlberg himself. "Learning can never be mechanical," said Blatz, because of "the active, conscious participation of the individual.... There is always a future reference in learning.... The past provides the means, the future reference determines the end" (Blatz, 1944, pp. 46-47). Blatz stressed the role of the learner as a change agent, emphasizing the person's perception of a situation as the primary determinant of action. Thus, each child interacted with the world, modifying it as well as being modified by it. A teacher who understood a child's motivation and past experience could create for that child a learning situation (i.e., set up conditions calculated to start adaptive, problem-solving striving)—but could not make the child learn. It was the child, Blatz insisted, who must initiate the action if real learning was to occur.

Blatz was opposed to formal education and pointed out that direct instruction and authoritarian methods of control produced superficial and temporary change but no real learning and development. His schools at both the preschool and primary grade levels were, therefore, play-oriented (i.e., organized around children's interests). He assumed that children were intrinsically motivated to be active and exploratory, and he postulated the appetite of change. "The appetite of change 'demands' satisfaction in the form of new perceptual or ideational imaginative content of consciousness" (Blatz, 1944, p. 100). Man strives to induce as well as to reduce tension. The child seeks novelty and variety. No extrinsic rewards are needed to produce active learning, said Blatz; indeed, the use of such rewards can be highly destructive. Blatz's over-all goal was to help children "learn how to learn." He endeavored to set the stage for children to become exploratory (curious discoverers), constructive (planful and purposeful), creative (flexible, innovative problem solvers), and considered (reflective). His schools offered challenges hard enough to induce tension so that the child would experience the thrill of overcoming tension when the challenge was met. The challenges were, however, always selected by the children themselves. Hence the teacher's role was to set the stage for the child to find challenging, growth-producing activities but otherwise to maintain a low profile. Blatz's teachers even wore inconspicuous apparel (blue smocks) so that during free play periods they would fade more effectively into the background.

Some have suggested that it was social learning, rather than cognitive-developmental theory, which Blatz espoused. This is in part because Blatz did not focus, as did Piaget, on genetic epistemology, the comprehension of reality, and cognition at successive stages of development. Blatz accounted for all behavioral change and development in terms of growth in knowledge and understanding and the resultant modifications in the way the child regarded a situation. This is well illustrated in his conceptualization of the growth of social cognition:

> A child, born conscious, catalogues and classifies his experiences and evaluates them in terms of his needs and wants…. A child's first conscious experience must be one of discrimination…. He classifies events into "stable" and "unstable" experiences. The unstable may be divided into … experiences which are regular … and those which occur irregularly…. The irregular group are then classified into those over which he can exercise some degree of control and which, hence, become in some measure predictable, and those which are uncontrollable and unpredictable…. The experiences in the predictable class are then classified into those over which he seems to have some direct control, e.g., objects, and those over which he seems to have only a kind of indirect control, e.g., people, and the nature of this indirect control is highly mysterious. (Blatz, 1944, pp. 150-151)

He traces children's acquisition first of a concept of self and then of a concept of others like themselves whose vagaries, needs, and wants must be understood and considered if effective social skills are to be acquired. Blatz says that if a child has clearly shown an interest in directing the behavior of others and frequently attempts to do so, this is not by itself evidence of satisfactory social development. To determine how well children are developing socially, Blatz says, we should look at how their peers respond to their attempts to direct. If their peers usually acquiesce, this means the children are developing the social knowledge which produces consideration and are becoming leaders whom others enjoy following. If, on the contrary, their peers usually resist (and especially if coercion is applied to gain compliance), this means the children have not acquired the needed social understanding and are inconsiderate "bosses" or "bullies."

THE CONCEPT OF SECURITY AND THE PLAN OF DISCIPLINE

In 1925 when Blatz became the Director of the Child Study Centre at the University of Toronto, he was given a specific mission to promote mental health. But what was mental health? There was no agreement about how it should be defined. Clearly, Blatz's first task was to produce a working definition of it, and his concept of security was the result. The concept delineated what Blatz concluded were the most fundamental characteristics of those who were robust from a mental health point of view. Having specified these characteristics, he was ready to determine the conditions that would foster their development.

Blatz's concept of security underwent some revisions in the 1950s, but it is important to understand his earlier ideas for they influenced his teaching about child-rearing practices. The fullest statement of these occurs in chapter 9 of *Understanding the Young Child* (Blatz, 1944).

Blatz postulated "security" as the primary goal of human beings and the promotion of security as the primary objective of parents and educators. However, security in the sense in which he used the term should not be equated with "safety." Being safe, he said, was a static and insecure state, derived from dependence on an agent and always subject to crisis. Security, on the contrary, was a dynamic state which facilitated the functioning of a human being as a constantly striving creature. It was a state of mind characterized by serenity based on inner strengths. It grew out of trust in one's ability to manage the future. It was accompanied by:

(a) a willingness to make decisions and tolerate the insecurity and anxiety that decision-making entails; and

(b) a willingness to accept the consequences of one's decisions and assume responsibility for them. Achieving security meant learning to cope with consequences because confidence in one's ability to handle consequences rendered one willing to make decisions.

From the beginning, Blatz had a great deal to say about discipline. This was not because he was interested in obtaining immediate control of behavior. His goals were aimed at setting the stage for children to develop independent security, to acquire the ability to make decisions, and to deal with consequences. He defined discipline as a *plan* for guiding the development of children (Blatz, 1944, p. 57). Specific objectives included the development of self-management skills, the acceptance of responsibility, and the ultimate emancipation of the children. In the earlier phases of Blatz's thinking, developing independence or "independent security" was the ideal, even though he recognized that this could never be fully achieved.

In Blatz's plan for guiding development, children were given as much freedom as possible to make their own decisions, discover the consequences of those decisions, and sharpen their knowledge of cause-and-effect relations. Limits to their freedom were, however, necessary to protect them from catastrophic consequences and to facilitate essential learning. Children were to be *instructed* about requirements and limits by objective, nonauthoritarian *statements*, never commands. Statements conveyed information that children could use to direct their own behavior. Commands depended on the presence of a commander forcing the child into a dependent role in an unpredictable and uncontrollable situation. *Consistency* of caretakers was of fundamental importance. Consistency in the requirements was essential to insure that the child accepted them as necessary and not the whim of some particular individual.

To promote the development of self-management skills, children were given the freedom to conform, or not conform, to the requirements. They were offered a *choice*. Children had to experience the consequences of both options to acquire the knowledge for making accurate predictions and for governing their behavior to produce the most desirable results. The consequences that the children were to experience were carefully planned. If children chose not to meet a requirement, the consequences had to be *logical*, if possible naturally occurring, or at least instructive, meaningful, and related to the real reasons for the requirement. (Punishments were never logical, and so they were never used.) Consequences had also to be *consistent*, hence predictable, and if an adult were involved, *objectively* administered in a nonjudgmental way with no reprimands of any kind. This objectivity was essential to prevent the child from blaming the adult for the outcome and thus avoiding personal responsibility and losing the opportunity to learn from the experience. Caretakers, Blatz said, must respect children as learners who inevitably make mistakes. Their role was not to save or protect the young from unhappy consequences but to support them emotionally and help them see that a mistake was not a disaster that could not be handled. As children gained in knowledge and ability, the limits to their freedom were to be systematically expanded until, eventually, they were managing all of their own affairs and assuming full responsibility for the outcomes of all of their actions.

Blatz described how these principles could be applied at every stage of the child's development—through early childhood, adolescence, and young adulthood. For example, in the development of responsibility in the management of money, Blatz said that a child must be given an allowance to manage. The amount would depend on the age of the child and what expenses the child agreed to cover. Then the child was to be given complete freedom to spend the money. If it was all spent immediately, the child was not to be scolded, but allowed to suffer the natural consequences which were, in this case, being "broke" until next allowance day. If the allowance included money for a special event, the child would miss that event. The parents' job was to help the child accept the consequence. They could feel sorry with the child that the event had to be missed. They could offer suggestions about alternate activities that did not cost money. The one thing the parents were not to do was save the child from the consequences by providing additional funds. Blatz said the allowance should never be "docked" for neglect of duty or misbehavior because, to be in a position to manage it, the child needed to know for sure how much money to expect. As the child's ability to handle money increased, the amount of money and the range of responsibility for purchasing was to be gradually increased.

PERSONALITY DEVELOPMENT

Blatz delineated three overlapping phases through which persons progressed in attaining security. The first was a phase of immature dependent security, followed by growing independent security and, finally, mature dependent security.

Immature Dependent Security. Dependent security is a condition in which an agent accepts responsibility for the consequences of an individual's actions. This, said Blatz, is the only kind of security possible for immature infants and young children. For them, being "safe" in this dependent state is not only healthy but also essential for their future development. The caretakers of children in this phase must be consistent, predictable, and dependable so that they can be trusted. This safe, stable, environment eventually bores the child, facilitates a search for novelty and variety, and gives the child the courage to venture forth and learn— because retreat to a safe and trusted haven is always possible. Experiencing good quality immature dependent security sets the stage for the development of independent security.

Independent Security. In 1944, Blatz wrote about independent security as follows:

> Independent security can be attained only in one way, by the acquisition of a skill through learning. Whenever an individual is presented with a situation for which he is inadequately prepared or whenever he is striving for something and finds that his preparation is inadequate, he must make one of two choices, either to retreat or to attack. This situation is emotionally charged, but there is more than the emotional content in such situations. The individual must, if he is to attack, emerge from the security of a dependent sort and accept the state of insecurity. His attack, of course, will result in learning; the degree of skill which he acquires will depend on his persistence. But once having learned, he will meet this situation in the future with assurance, because now he possesses a behaviour pattern which makes it possible for him to adapt himself satisfactorily. Furthermore, he has become familiar with the consequences of his advance and is willing to face them. Such a skill, having been acquired through his own effort cannot be subject to the same kind of crisis as the other agents which have been described. (p. 167)

The "other agents" to which Blatz referred were ones used by individuals who felt insecure but who were not prepared to gain independent security through learning. An agent might be a previously satisfactory agent (such as the parent) or a deputy agent. Deputy agents were described by Blatz as devices an individual uses to carry him over a period of insecurity until he is willing to accept the consequences of a genuine decision. They work by freeing him of his insecurity at least temporarily, but they lead to no adequate permanent solution (Blatz, 1966, p. 93).

In the later phase of his theory, he labeled them postponement, re-interpretation, re-direction, and denial. He considered them healthy problem-solving devices if they were used with insight and employed only as a temporary expedient, but they were seriously maladaptive in their extreme and solidified forms.

Postponement of a decision represented good judgment if more information was required, if more time to consider was needed, and if the individual could accept the insecurity resulting from the delay. However, postponement to avoid decision-making could become procrastination fraught with anxiety. *Reinterpretation* in its healthy form could be reasoning about alternative solutions to a problem but, if no decisive action followed, the reasoning could turn into rationalization or a "fantasy of lies" and obliterate the reality of the situation. *Redirection* was attributing the cause of one's insecurity to others or blaming someone else for one's predicament. It was, Blatz suggested, commonly used to avoid the consequences imposed by an unjust authority. Resentment was induced, and this justified the blaming. If carried to its extreme, resentment could become feelings of persecution. *Denial* was maintaining that there was no problem to be solved and hence no decisions to be made. Being ill and forgetting were the two most common forms. In their extreme, they became hypochondria and amnesia.

Mature Dependent Security. Blatz recognized that independent security could not be fully attained. As social beings mature adults were necessarily dependent on others for the satisfaction of at least some of their basic needs. Furthermore, in a complex society they were dependent on others in many ways for the achievement of personal as well as group goals. He also recognized that learning had its limits, that there were unknowables which must be dealt with in some anxiety-reducing way. Mature dependent security was the goal for the adult, and Blatz analyzed it in four overlapping compartments: philosophy, vocation, avocation, and intimacies. In each of these compartments, a person might be secure dependently or independently. If insecure, the individual might have reverted to a former agent, accepted a new agent, acquired a deputy agent, or be putting forth effort to attain independent security.

To Blatz it was obvious that an individual could not carry on without a *Philosophy of Life*. As children grow up, they begin to inquire into the meaning of significant events beyond their comprehension. They ask about death and the purpose of living. They may find refuge in an orthodoxy provided that they have complete faith in its tenets, but this is a dependent response. The orthodoxy is an agent subject to the crisis of doubt if some aspect suddenly appears untenable in the face of scientific or other kinds of evidence. To attain independent security in this area, the individual must be allowed to question, explore, and seek experiences that will enable him/her to formulate a personal view of the universe and a working plan for living and dealing with the incomprehensible. This kind of philosophy of life will not be subject to crisis.

In the *Vocational* area persons are considered independently secure if they accept the responsibility for their own survival and for cooperating within the social community. Blatz suggested some vocations provided more independent security than others. Many persons are dependently secure because the jobs which provide their living depend upon the stability of the firm for which they work. Independent security is best attained by developing special skills that are needed by society for its preservation. Thus, a physician or a farmer or an artisan may attain independent security. Blatz warned against narrow vocational training for youth, arguing that an educational philosophy should be independent of industrial expediency. In a changing society, children need generic training, not a specific skill, to enable them to contribute to society in more than one way.

In the *Avocational* area persons are independently secure if they have acquired sufficient interests and skills to occupy their leisure time fully and happily. Blatz believed that the development of leisure interests should be an important aspect of modern education. He pointed out that too many people were dependently secure in this area, relying on entertainment and inevitably becoming bored.

Intimacies may be discussed under two headings: familial and extrafamilial. The former deals with social development in the family, the latter with social development in the community. Stable familial intimacies provide children with an ideal kind of dependent security. It was the stability, Blatz said, that was important. Later on, as children experienced more independent security, they would accept the insecurity of unfamiliar nonfamily members and gradually become comfortable with them. The sign of familial independent security was acceptance of extrafamilial associates. The kinds of companionship which develop between children at various age levels depend on both their needs at the time and the growth of their independence. When they become adults, emancipated persons look for qualities in peers that will give them a different kind of dependent security. They look for a person in whom to confide and who will not reveal their confidences, whose interests are similar, and whose experiences are different enough to be exciting. Such extrafamilial intimacies may develop between companions of either gender.

THEORETICAL REVISIONS

A reformulation of the theory occurred in the 1950s. In the mid-1940s Blatz's colleagues became critical of his stress on the attainment of independent security as the ideal. They insisted that such extreme independence was unhealthy. To them, children who were developing in wholesome ways were those willing to accept help from others and able to share in decision making and accepting responsibility for consequences. The revisions resulted from Blatz's discussions with his staff and from findings of his research associates (Ainsworth & Ainsworth, 1958). The Ainsworths had studied the security of young adults in the four areas delineated by Blatz (philosophy of life, vocation, avocation, and intimacies) and had found a high correlation between independent and mature dependent security, suggesting an interrelation, and probably a common core. As Northway (1959) put it, it appeared that:

1. dependence was not cast off and replaced by independence; rather, that the two grew in balance together; and
2. the form dependence took developed from a primitive to a complex sophisticated one, the extremes of this change being designated as "immature" and "mature" dependence, but the variations within the developmental pattern being much more subtle than a division into two types. (pp. 2-3)

In the final phase of the theory, the quality of the immature dependent security enjoyed by infants and young children was seen as the basis from which both independent and mature dependent security developed. If the quality was high children would develop a basic trust in their caretakers, in the world in general, and in themselves that they would carry with them throughout life. Trust would determine their expectations and influence their actions. Their trust in others would generate effective interpersonal relations, and their trust in self would lead to effective learning and accomplishment. As Blatz (1966) put it:

> During the first years, the agent must supply a jumping off platform. The *trust* the child learns to place in his early agent remains throughout life as the prototype of the confidence he will place later on in other agents and ultimately himself. And, by the same token, a lack of opportunity to develop such trust will be reflected in his later contacts with others. (p. 39)

Mature dependent security in adult personal relations was always considered to be based on mutual trust. But now something else was added. Mature dependent security was conceptualized as an interdependent state in which intimates formed mutually satisfying, reciprocal relationships where responsibility was shared. Neither partner shirked responsibility because each was independently secure. Such close, equally contributing fellowship was highly rewarding. Blatz's final discussion of an ideal mature dependent relationship included both a description of its characteristics and the difficulties inherent in developing it. This development required social skills and the ability to accept people and their peculiarities as they were. In this partnership,

> neither will assume the right of ascendancy over the other.... Who is the boss in a mature dependent relationship is a meaningless question.... A high degree of trust is developed between two people only over time.... To achieve it communication is essential. (Blatz, 1966, pp. 86-87)

The final chapter of Blatz's (1966) last book deals with the scope of the security theory. It begins:

> The concept of security is all-inclusive and all-pervasive. By "all-pervasive" I mean that the actions of all individuals in all places and at all times can be viewed in the scheme of security theory. It is a system of psychology which meets the criteria of being both comprehensive and consistent. (p. 112)

The frame of reference is indeed internally consistent. There are no contradictions in the way in which Blatz deals with the nature of human nature, how learning and development occur, and how effective maturity is attained. He produced a tight exceedingly useful model. In summary:

> Consciousness is the stuff we use to get what we want. We select our goals and we decide on the actions we will take to reach them. If we are willing to accept the consequences of our actions, our state of mind is said to be secure. The feeling accompanying this state may be called serenity, which is the basic goal of all living beings. (Blatz, 1966, p. 122)

NOTES

1. Quotation from a letter, signed by the vice admiral of the director of the Naval Service of Canada, sent from Ottawa on March 17, 1917, and published in a W. E. Blatz memorial paper titled *W. E. Blatz; His Family and His Farm: Some Personal Reflections*. Victoria Carson and Margery de Roux. Margery de Roux (formerly Blatz) is Dr. Blatz's daughter.
2. The quintuplets were born in Ontario, South of North Bay, on a farm east of Lake Nipissing, near the village of Callander.

3.   The political events which followed the birth of the "quints" and the circumstances that permitted Blatz to work with them are described by Berton (1977).

REFERENCES

Ainsworth, M. D. (1960). The significance of the five year research program at the Institute of Child Study. *The Bulletin of the Institute of Child Study, University of Toronto, 22*(1), 3–16.

Ainsworth, M. D. (1983). Mary D. Salter Ainsworth, 1913-. In A. H. O'Connell & N. F. Russo (Eds.), *Models of achievement: Reflections of eminent women in psychology* (pp. 201–19). New York: Columbia University Press.

Ainsworth, M. D., & Ainsworth, L. H. (1958). *Measuring security in personal adjustment.* Toronto: University of Toronto Press.

Ainsworth Salter, M. D. (1940). An evaluation of adjustment based upon the concept of security. *University of Toronto Studies, Child Development Series*, No. 9. Toronto: University of Toronto Press.

Bernhardt, K. S. (1961). Dr. Blatz and the Institute of Child Study *The Bulletin of the Institute of Child Study, University of Toronto, 23*(1), 1-4.

Berton, P. (1977). *The Dionne years: A thirties melodrama.* Toronto: McClelland and Stewart.

Blatz, W. E. (1925). The cardiac, respiratory and electrical phenomena involved in the emotion of fear. *Journal of Experimental Psychology, 8*, 109-132.

Blatz, W. E. (1938). *The five sisters: A study of child psychology.* Toronto: McClelland and Stewart.

Blatz, W. E. (1940). *Hostages to peace*. New York: Morrow.

Blatz, W. E. (1944). *Understanding the young child.* Toronto: Clarke, Irwin, & Co.

Blatz, W. E. (1951, Winter). Freud and the Institute. *The Bulletin of the Institute of Child Study, University of Toronto, 48*, 1-4.

Blatz, W. E. (1966). *Human security: Some reflections.* Toronto: University of Toronto Press.

Blatz, W. E., & Bott, H. (1929) *Parents & the pre-school child.* New York: Morrow

Blatz, W. E., & Bott, H. (1930). *The management of young children.* New York: Morrow.

Blatz, W. E., Chant, N., Charles, M. W., Fletcher, M. I., Ford, N. H. C., Harris, A. L., et al. (1937). Collected studies on the Dionne quintuplets. *University of Toronto Studies, Child Development Series*, No. 9. Toronto: University of Toronto Press.

Blatz, W. E., Millichamp, D. A., & Fletcher, M. (1935). *Nursery education: Theory and practice.* New York: Morrow.

Bott, H. M. (1933). Method in social studies of young children. *University of Toronto Studies, Child Development Series*, No. 1. Toronto: University of Toronto Press.

Evans, E. D. (1975). *Contemporary influences in early childhood education* (2nd ed.). New York: Holt, Rinehart & Winston.

Flint, B. M. (1959). *The security of infants.* Toronto: University of Toronto Press.

Grapko, M. F. (1957). *The story of Jimmy.* Toronto: Institute of Child Study security test, University of Toronto.

Grapko, M. F. (1965). The construction of a primary form of the Institute of Child Study security test "The Story of Tommy." *The Bulletin of the Institute of Child Study, University of Toronto, 27*(4), 3-12.

Kohlberg, L. (1968). Early education: A cognitive–developmental view. *Child Development, 39*, 1013–1062.

Millichamp, D. A., & Northway, M. L. (1977). *Conversations at Caledon: Some reminiscences of the Blatz era.* Toronto: The Brora Centre.

Myers, C. R. (1982). Psychology at Toronto. In M. J. Wright & C. R. Myers (Eds.), *History of Academic Psychology in Canada.* Toronto: C. J. Hogrefe.

Northway, M. L. (1959). Studies of the growth of security. *The Bulletin of the Institute of Child Study, University of Toronto, 21*, 1-7.

Northway, M. L., Bernhardt, K. S., Fletcher, M. I., Johnson, F. L., & Millichamp, D. A. (Eds.). (1951). *Twenty-five years of child study.* Toronto: University of Toronto Press.

Northway, M. L. (and the research staff). (1964). The research programme and the longitudinal study. *The Bulletin of the Institute of Child Study, University of Toronto, 26* (1), 5-13.

Northway, M. L. (1971). The sociometry of society: Some facts and fancies. *Canadian Journal of the Behaviourial Sciences, 3*(1), 18–36.

Northway, M. L. (1973). Child study in Canada: A casual history. In L. Brockman, J. Whiteley, & J. Zubek (Eds.), *Child development: Selected readings* (pp. 2-3). Toronto: McClelland & Stewart.

Ross, M. L. (1947, March 15). "I can't give you anything but consistency, Baby." *Saturday Night*, p. 10.

Stapleford, E. M. (1976). *History of the Day Nurseries Branch.* Toronto: Ontario Ministry of Community and Social Services.

Weber, L. (1971). *The English Infant School and Informal Education.* Englewood Cliffs, NJ: Prentice Hall.

CHAPTER 3

SECURITY AND ATTACHMENT

Mary D. Salter Ainsworth

Throughout my entire career the underlying aim has been the understanding of intimate interpersonal relationships, especially the earliest of
these, and how they influence subsequent personality development.
Undoubtedly it was this interest—then half-recognized—that led me to
choose to study psychology when an undergraduate at the University of
Toronto in the early 1930s. This core interest became overt after having
attended Professor William Blatz's courses in genetic and abnormal psychology, in which he introduced us to his "security theory." At the same
time, an experimental project directed by Professor Sperrin Chant taught
me that research could be fascinating. These experiences, especially, led
me to stay on at Toronto as a graduate student.

Theoretical and research interests were happily combined in 1936
when Blatz suggested that I undertake dissertation research relevant to
his security theory under his and Chant's supervision. My dissertation was
completed in 1939 and published in the following year (Salter, 1940). I
believe that it was the first publication stemming from Blatzian security
theory. Blatz and I intended then to assemble a team to continue and
expand this research, but the outbreak of war intervened. Blatz became
involved in the establishment of wartime nurseries in Great Britain. I
remained in the department for 3 years as a member of the faculty, but

The Secure Child: Timeless Lessons in Parenting and Childhood Education, pp. 43–53
Copyright © 2010 by Information Age Publishing

43

then joined the Canadian Women's Army Corps and was assigned to the Directorate of Personnel Selection. Then in 1945-46 I became Superintendent of Women's Rehabilitation in the Department of Veterans Affairs.

These services experiences led me to perceive clinical psychology and its assessment procedures as a way to implement my interest in personality development. Thus after I returned to the University of Toronto in 1946 my teaching focused on personality theory and appraisal, and Blatz and I finally undertook team research guided by security theory.

In 1950 personal circumstances led me to London where by good fortune I obtained a research appointment at the Tavistock Clinic in a project directed by Dr. John Bowlby on the effects on personality development of separation from the mother in early childhood. Bowlby, a psychoanalyst, had become impressed with the adverse effects on young children's personality development that could follow the distortion or disruption of their relationships with their mothers. He had chosen specifically to study major separations since, unlike other adverse experiences, their occurrence could be readily established. While his research team gathered data relevant to this problem, he explored the theoretical implications of our findings. The upshot was a new theory of personality development—attachment theory. This is an open-ended, eclectic theory, stemming from psychoanalytic "object relations" theory, but drawing heavily on contemporary biology (especially evolutionary theory and ethology), systems theory, and cognitive psychology.

I became engrossed first in the research and then also in the theory itself. When I left the Tavistock in 1953, I spent 2 years in Uganda, and then went to the Johns Hopkins University in Baltimore. In both places my research focused on the development of attachment of infants to their mothers. Almost from the beginning, I found myself guided by both Bowlby's attachment theory and Blatz's security theory. To me, the two positions were mutually enriching. In the partnership that John Bowlby and I have had in developing attachment theory and research over the years, certain of Blatz's concepts became focal.

I would like here to focus on these aspects of Blatzian security theory and show their relevance to attachment concepts.

HIGHLIGHTS OF BLATZ'S THEORY OF SECURITY

Although I first learned about Blatz's security theory as an undergraduate, this was expanded later by my later close research association with Blatz. He did not record or publish many of his insights. Even in his last book titled *Human Security* (Blatz, 1966) he said relatively little about what had first captured my interest. Security theory was largely an oral tradition and there was plenty of scope for one listener to focus on some aspects and other listeners to focus on others. What I can tell you about it is what came through to *me* as most important.

Security theory is essentially a theory about personality development. It can be characterized as an open-ended theory, in that Blatz anticipated that it would be expanded and refined through research. He was a brilliant hypothesizer, but I believe that he did not think of research so much as a way of testing hypotheses as a way of reformulating old hypotheses and discovering new ones. He did not attempt to spin a theory to encompass all of personality and its development. He did, however, think that the concept of security could guide the exploration of this rich and confusing field.

When Blatz first conceived of security theory, Freudian theory and its several variations dominated views of personality and its development. I believe that Blatz was basically influenced by these theories, although he never publicly acknowledged this, and indeed his views differed very much from Freud's on several points. Blatz specified two emotions (anger and fear) and several "appetites" as the sources of motivation, but his theory is not a drive theory like Freud's, with all drives having a common pool of libidinal energy. The appetites included hunger, thirst, elimination, sex (although he did not focus on infantile sexuality), rest, and change. The appetite of change was original and of particular value. His notion was that from infancy onward people are intrinsically interested in changes that take place in the world around them, for their own sake and not necessarily as a derivation from some other motive—whether such changes result from their own activity or otherwise. It is the appetite for change that leads to exploratory activity, and thus to learning and the acquisition of skill and knowledge. Blatz's notion of appetites and emotions is less elaborated than the concept of behavioral systems that Bowlby's attachment theory borrowed from contemporary biology, but compatible with it.

Blatz's differences with Freud centered on the issue of the unconscious. He thought it was logically ridiculous to talk about unconscious thoughts or wishes. Thoughts and wishes *had* to be conscious. This belief, in my opinion, resulted in difficulties especially when he came to deal with defensive processes, which he recognized as essential for an understanding of individual differences in personality development. The cognitive research that demonstrated how cognitive processes may operate unconsciously was useful to John Bowlby when he came to account for defensive processes in attachment theory. Had that body of research been available also to Blatz he might have given more credence to the role of unconscious cognitive processes.

What of "security," which formed the core of Blatz's position? He usually spoke of security as willingness to accept the consequences of one's own behaviour, or being able to rely upon someone else to accept them on one's own behalf. This statement refers more to the definition of conditions that make for security than constituting a definition of security itself. In 1939 when I was drafting my dissertation, it was drawn forcibly to my attention by Professor Edward A. Bott that the word is derived from the Latin *sine cura*, that is, "without care"—or, if you like, "without anxiety," "without fear," or indeed "free from insecurity." This definition implies that security is a feeling. Blatz, too, thought of security as a feeling, for he distinguished between *safety*, objectively defined as being free from harm or danger, and *security*, defined as a subjective feeling of being safe whether one actually was or was not. By the time I published my dissertation, I wrote:

> Security as defined by Blatz and Chant implies two things: (1) the immediate experience of adequacy in any given situation—that is, the individual feels capable of dealing with the situation whether he actually is or not; (2) a feeling of adequacy to meet the future consequences of the immediate response, as anticipated by the individual, whether this anticipation be a clear-cut foreseeing of possibilities or merely a vague expectation of results. Thus security as experienced has an immediate and a future reference. (Salter, 1940, p. 6.)

Thus Blatz seemed to equate feeling secure with feeling confident or effective, even though one's feeling of efficacy might stem from reliance on something or someone other than oneself.

BASES OF SECURITY

According to Blatz, security rested on several bases: immature dependence, independence, mature dependence and, to some extent, defensive maneuvers that he called "deputy agents" or "compensations."

Immature dependent security. Infants, and to a decreasing extent young children, can achieve security only through depending on others (primarily parents) to take care of them, fulfill their survival needs, and take responsibility for the consequences of their behavior. The appetite of change leads children to be curious about the world around them, however, and to explore it, and to learn about it. But learning itself involves insecurity. Blatz's notion was that if and when children get into some kind of frightening situation—perhaps only "in over their depth"—they have to feel free to retreat to a parent figure for comfort and reassurance in order to derive security enough to be able to venture forth again to brave the insecurities of exploring and learning. I cannot remember whether Blatz used the term "secure base from which to explore the world" or whether this is my own phrasing. In any event the concept of a secure base had captured me.

> Familial security in the early stages is of a dependent type and forms a basis from which the individual can work out gradually, forming new skills and interests in other fields. Where familial security is lacking, the individual is handicapped by the lack of what might be called a secure base from which to work. (Salter, 1940, p. 45)

To the extent that children can rely on parents to provide this kind of base they are secure, and to the extent that they can not, they are insecure. To Blatz this kind of dependent basis for security was characteristic only of the earliest phase of life, and both impossible and inappropriate as a continuing sole basis for security. The concept of the secure base is also a key concept in attachment theory.

Independent security. As children explore the world from a secure base they gradually gain knowledge about it and skills to cope with it. This body of knowledge and skills gradually forms an independent basis for security. Children rely increasingly upon themselves, and thus less upon their parents. Indeed Blatz assumed that by the time children reach maturity they should be fully emancipated from parents and not dependent upon them any more. Thus any substantial continuation of "immature dependent security" was to be viewed as undesirable.

Mature dependent security. However, Blatz pointed out that one cannot be secure solely on the basis of independence. He conceived of "mature dependent security" as a state in which people depend on one or a few others to supplement whatever independent security they have managed to achieve. He thought of this as occurring in a reciprocal give-and-take relationship, in which each partner on the basis of his or her knowledge and skills can provide security to the other. Thus, a relationship characterized by mature dependent security is contingent upon each partner having achieved a modicum of independent security. Of course, the prototype of a good relationship of this kind is a good marital partnership.

Bowlby's attachment theory counterpart to mature dependence is what he called the "goal-corrected partnership." However, Bowlby conceived of this partnership beginning to develop as early as the fourth year of life, when newly acquired cognitive abilities (such as perspective-taking and improved communication through language) enable a child to understand a parent's perspective, motivation, and plans well enough to negotiate to achieve common plans mutually agreed upon. Thus, under favorable circumstances, the nature of a child's attachment to the parent undergoes developmental change and continues to do so. It is this capacity for "goal-corrected partnership" that carries forward to enable secure attachments to other partners to be formed later in life.

Thus an "attachment," although first developed to a primary caregiver in infancy, is not synonymous with immature dependence. Secure attachment almost from the beginning tends to foster the development of self-reliance (cf. the secure base concept). Thus attachment is not antithetical to self-reliance, whereas dependence and independence are indeed considered polar opposites. Blatz's distinction between immature and mature dependence went a long way toward correcting the notion implicit in the dependence-independence polarization that dependence is an undesirable characteristic beyond infancy. However, Blatz held that a young person could not have a healthy relationship with parents except through having become independent of them; he did not conceive of a parent constituting a maturely dependent secure base for an offspring. Nevertheless, his concept of mature dependent security is one of his most important original contributions to an understanding of personality development.

Deputy agents. Blatz's theory includes defensive processes, termed deputy agents. This term implies that when persons can neither accept the consequences of their own behavior nor rely on other agents (such as parents) to do so, they have to resort to other substitute or deputy agents. He likened these "agents" or processes to analgesic drugs that reduce pain without coping with the cause of the pain—an apt characterization of defenses. As such, they provide some illusory security. The more that people rely on deputy agents as a source of security, and the less they rely on other sources, especially on independent and mature dependent security, the more fragile is their adjustment. Nevertheless, Blatz attached some value to these defensive processes in their analgesic role. If they temporarily assist people to overcome insecurity enough to get on with the acquisition of knowledge and skills relevant to the problem at issue, they can gradually shift the basis of security to confidence in their own resources, and dispense with the defenses provided by the deputy agents.

Some common deputy agents, as I recall them, were intolerance of the views of others, and blaming others for one's own shortcomings. I now think that Blatz arrived at his list in a purely *ad hoc* fashion in the course of his clinical experience, and never claimed that it was complete. He rejected Freud's notion of using libidinal energy to banish painful experience to the unconscious, but apparently did not attempt to discover another explanation for the mechanisms through which defenses operate. In considering deputy agents in scale construction I felt handicapped by multifarious particulars without any basis for grasping the underlying processes. I do not believe that one can cope with defenses in personality assessment without a theoretical basis for understanding them, and indeed I believe that such a basis must acknowledge the existence of unconscious processes. Current attachment theory has gone a long way toward handling this problem.

Security versus insecurity. Blatz's theory does not hold with a simplistic dichotomy between secure and insecure. The degree to which children are secure can be assessed through an examination of their confidence in others, especially parents, to provide comfort, reassurance, and protection when needed, and their confidence in being able to cope with the world on the basis of their own skills and knowledge. Similarly for an adult, it would be largely the combination of the contribution of mature dependent and independent security that would tell the story. This then would be balanced against the incidence and strength of feelings of insecurity in making the judgment of how secure in comparison to how insecure the person felt.

But there is also the issue of the security contributed by immature dependence on others beyond childhood and by deputy agents. One can not arrive at a single security-insecurity score, but should instead consider the *patterning* in a comprehensive assessment. This patterning was implicit in the assessment research that Blatz directed, even though I do not recall him ever being theoretically explicit about this matter.

AREAS OF SECURITY AND INSECURITY

It was Blatz's emphasis on close interpersonal relations—intimacies, as he called them—that I found compelling. In retrospect, it is quite extraordinary how both psychological theory and research at that time shied away from scientific exploration of interaction between intimates, especially between sexual partners. Even Blatz, who attached much importance to marriage in his security theory, did not propose to assess security in marriage—at least in what was then the foreseeable future—because of the danger of arousing consternation in the general public, which could jeopardize further security research.

Although dependent security, both immature and mature, implied close interpersonal relationships, Blatz conceived of security as pertaining to other areas of life as well. Specially, he mentioned not only familial intimacies (children and their parents) and extrafamilial intimacies (age peer intimacies in close friendships and later in sexual partnerships), but also vocations (jobs and money), avocations (hobbies and interests, with boredom implying insecurity) and philosophy of life. In this Blatz's theory spreads its net more widely than does attachment theory. In focusing so closely on intimacies some attachment researchers have come to conceive of them as the only source of security—which is a pity. However, it is intended here to focus on intimacies, and to refer the reader to Grapko (this volume) for more detail about others areas.

ASSESSMENT OF SECURITY-INSECURITY

My dissertation research, the first assessment of security–insecurity following Blatzian theory, focused on familial and extra-familial intimacies. The subjects were young adults—116 third-year college students enrolled in a course in personality which required an autobiography from each student. I used these autobiographies in my study.

Scales were constructed for each of the two areas, consisting of self-report items administered as a group pencil-paper test. Anonymity was ensured for both scale scores and autobiographies by a student-monitored system using identifying numbers. The scale items were in the form of statements descriptive of feelings and attitudes. The students were instructed to check only those statements they felt to be applicable to them; they were not forced to respond to every item.

Each test had two scales. The two scales for the familial test were security–insecurity and independence-dependence. These items were presented in random order. A scale value was calculated for each item. For the security-insecurity scale items indicating security were given positive scale values, and those indicating insecurity negative values. The algebraic sum of these values gave the security-insecurity score. Similarly for the other scale an independence-dependence score was obtained. Four patterns of scores could be identified on the basis of the two scales: independently secure, dependently secure, independently insecure, and dependently insecure.

The two scales for the extrafamilial test were security-insecurity and tolerance-intolerance—the latter indicative of the extent to which "deputy agents" were used. The score for each scale was the algebraic sum of the scale values. The four patterns of scores were thus socially secure and tolerant, socially secure and intolerant, socially insecure and tolerant, and socially insecure and intolerant.

Care was taken to ensure internal consistency in each scale, and to discard items that did not meet the criterion. The difficult part was the weighting of the various items, for there was preexisting methodology for only forced-choice scales—and I felt strongly that these introduced distortions. My methodology was severely criticized by some.

However, the size of the total scale scores turned out not to matter, because it became apparent that the strength of the method of assessment lay in the patterns of scores that emerged. Thus, for example, those whose scores were clearly secure in the familial area could be divided into those whose scores on the independence-dependence scale were either clearly independent or clearly dependent. There were twice as many who were secure and independent as there were those who were secure and dependent. Nearly all those who were secure and independent in familial relations were clearly both secure and tolerant in the extrafamilial area. (In attachment terms, those who were securely attached to parents but who were also self-reliant tended to have secure relationships with age peers and were free of distortions of social attitudes associated with defensive processes.)

I selected the most extreme cases manifesting each of the most common patterns of scores, together with a few striking uncommon patterns, as illustrations of the usefulness of the descriptions yielded both by the patterning of the scores and the content of the items endorsed. For each of these I summarized the autobiography. I was enormously impressed by the congruence of the score patterns and the autobiographical material. However, at that point I could conceive of no way to analyze 116 autobiographies in order to demonstrate objectively the congruence of these with the test patterns, and had to be content with my own subjective impressions, which scarcely provide acceptable validation.

After the war had ended, Blatz and I codirected a research team to resume scale construction to cover other areas. I myself revised the familial and extrafamilial scales, and constructed scales assessing security-insecurity in the areas of avocations and philosophy of life, and these were eventually published (Ainsworth & Ainsworth,1958). Apart from a study by Leonard Ainsworth, establishing that insecurity as measured by these scales was correlated significantly with rigidity in problem solving, I know of no use that was made of them. In the 1960s I made an unpublished exploration of their diagnostic utility with mental hospital patients, and found that testable depressives scored as strikingly insecure, but that patients diagnosed as having anxiety state, paranoid conditions, or psychopathic character disorders were conspicuous for endorsing very few items that resulted in minimally secure scores. This confirmed dissatisfaction I had already felt about the weaknesses of self-report tests in the case of highly disturbed subjects. I am certain that such tests do a poor job of detecting defensive maneuvers that mask underlying insecurity.

When I joined Bowlby's team at the Tavistock Clinic, I became wholly enchanted with the notion of prospective research in the natural environment, relying on direct observation of behavior beginning in infancy, rather than upon retrospective inferences from paper-pencil tests for adults. Meanwhile, others of Blatz's team in Toronto went on with security research constructing their own tests, with Grapko studying children and Flint infants. Although their work has been of undoubted value, I shall not attempt to comment on it, for my purpose here is to highlight the contribution that my work with Blatz made to attachment theory and research.

CONCLUSIONS

Among the aspects of Blatz's position that I most valued was the implication that intimacies could be subjected to scientific study, and that the findings of such study were relevant to an understanding of personality development. However, it was the concept of security itself, as a guiding principle to such understanding, that constituted his chief contribution to my subsequent work.

First, his developmental emphasis, with the fundamental concept of a secure base, was perhaps the most important concept that I carried over into attachment theory. In infancy and throughout later life it balances exploration, learning, knowledge, and skills that result in security based on self-reliance with intimacies in which one can rely on one's partners to provide security. Both develop in parallel, but in interacting parallel, each aspect influencing the other.

Second, Blatz's theory holds that a secure base in an intimate relationship, from which one could explore confidently (and achieve), depends on the motivation implicit in the "appetite of change," as well as upon whatever motivation leads one to seek proximity to a caregiving figure. Thus the motivations underlying both seeking and sustaining intimate relationships and exploration, learning, and achievement stemmed from different behavioral systems. In attachment theory these are the attachment and the exploratory systems. Blatz seemed to take for granted that there was some underlying motivation for an infant to seek security, comfort, and reassurance from a parent when feeling insecure but did not specify it.

Third, Blatz's work implies that feelings of security and insecurity are central to an assessment of individual differences in personality relevant to mental health. This has been absorbed into attachment theory and research, and gained widespread acceptance and use.

Fourth, the developmental perspective inherent in security theory begins with the interplay between immature dependent security and insecurity, and continues with the development of both independent security and mature dependent security and may be extended to apply to adult life. Blatz did not sketch in the story of this development across the life span in any detail, but relied on future research to do so. Attachment research began at the beginning and has filled in much detail about the infancy period, but only recently has begun to extend itself into the issue of attachments and other affectional bonds in later years. However, I am optimistic that security theory coupled with attachment theory will do much to expand our knowledge of personality development across the life span.

REFERENCES

Ainsworth, M. D., & Ainsworth, L. H. (1958) *Measuring security in personal adjustment*. Toronto: University of Toronto Press.

Blatz, W. E. (1966) *Human security: Some reflections*. Toronto: University of Toronto Press.

Salter, M. D. (1940) *An evaluation of adjustment based on the concept of security*. University of Toronto Studies, Child Development Series, No. 18. Toronto: University of Toronto Press.

CHAPTER 4

SECURITY THEORY[1]

Michael F. Grapko

Blatz defined security as "a state of consciousness which accompanies a willingness to accept the consequences of one's own decisions or actions." There are three main points in this definition:

1. security is a conscious datum of human experience related to the behavioral response to a decision or action;
2. the willingness to accept consequences presumes the knowledge of the consequences to follow and their likely effect; that is, security can be achieved only after certain causal relationships have been understood and, therefore, learning is central to the development of security;
3. security pervades all human behavior because all activity involves a decision to action followed by the performance or the restraint of the action. (Blatz, 1940, p. 82)

The notion of "consequence" is not new to psychologists. Learning theorists acknowledge the crucial importance of reinforcement as a condition of learning. A particular activity is repeated and remembered when it has resulted in a favorable outcome—either it satisfies some need or it contributes to the satisfaction of a need.

The Secure Child: Timeless Lessons in Parenting and Childhood Education, pp. 55–67
Copyright © 2010 by Information Age Publishing

In security theory, the concept of consequence may assume a broader meaning. Any activity has a consequence: the organism moves from point A to point B, or the hungry animal eats food and is satisfied. Security may also involve a remote consequence arbitrarily related to the activity. A high school student who comes home late one evening and who must forfeit his free evenings for the next week is an instance of a remote consequence. Indeed, in a complex society where social demands become attached to almost all aspects of human behavior, the remote or extrinsic consequences play a great part in determining security.

Security is experienced when two conditions are fulfilled: (1) feeling adequate in the performance of an activity, and, (2) being willing to accept any intrinsic or extrinsic consequences which ensue. Out of the criteria which determine adequacy arises one of the major problems for security theory. Consistent lack of improvement at golf, for example, inspires a variety of excuses for each poor game that follows, and yet the level of performance after four months may be the same. The phenomenon of aspiration level is inextricably tied to feelings of adequacy reflected in performance. At present, however, it is assumed that the ability to accomplish a task within reasonable limits of the individual's expectations and needs bring security. The acceptance of consequences depends in great part upon that performance.

The individual who possesses the necessary skill in a particular task and accepts the consequences is *independently secure*. The degree of independent security is contingent upon the skills acquired. It is expected, of course, that these skills are relevant to daily living, involving such matters as an occupation, getting along with others, managing personal and home affairs, participating in leisure time activities, or working toward a satisfying philosophy of life.

The dependence upon some agent to accept the consequences of one's decisions or actions is defined as *dependent security*. In most cases the agent is another person; however, an insurance company, an institution, or an ideational component may also serve as agents. Given the complexity of social and community life the transfer to agents of responsibility for one's own behavior or for accepting the consequence is a common practice.

The complete dependence upon an agent is known as an *immature dependent security* whereas a partial or shared acceptance of consequences with the agent is known as a *mature dependent security*. The former establishes a uni-directional relationship of help between person and agent (i.e., P→A); the latter is represented by a bi-directional or reciprocal help relationship between person and agent (i.e., P←→A). *Immature dependent security* is illustrated by the young infant who relies wholly upon the mother for his nutritional needs. The relationship between husband and wife, where the responsibility for family and home management is shared, is an example of mature dependent security.

Failure to foresee or the reluctance to face consequences and insufficient skill in making decisions or performing necessary acts are the main reasons for reliance on an agent in an immature dependent security situation. The circumstances tend to be much more complex in mature dependent security situations. The trend in our society toward marked specialization adds to the interdependence of people in a social setting. Democratic trends in family life give further evidence of a shift toward greater shared responsibility. It seems inevitable that as human life becomes increasingly bound by interpersonal relations the security of the individual depends upon the development of mature dependence.

Certain attributes of the agent clarify dependent security. The use of any agent carries with it the threat of removal of the agent. The person employed as agent may die, the company may go bankrupt, and the ideology may change. Thus dependent security is threatened by the potential of insecurity, more marked in immature than in mature dependent security.

Then, the relationship between person and agent must be consistent. This provides a measure of reassurance and predictability. Any doubt about the efficacy of the agent results in feelings of insecurity.

The use of an agent to achieve security in one human activity usually involves restriction of experience in another. The young boy attached to a gang scoffs at the idea of a girl friend, a football player abides by training regulations, a wife shows fidelity, a newspaper writer adopts a particular viewpoint or a young aspirant in politics limits himself to party policies. Whether the agent is retained depends upon the present needs and values of the individual. Shifts in motivation, interest, basic values, and attitudes account for some major developmental changes in security patterns from childhood to adulthood.

The avoidance of consequences through some ideational factor is known as employing a *deputy agent*. Rationalization and procrastination are examples. The male adolescent who is convinced girls are a waste of time or the university student who postpones his assignments because she works better under pressure illustrate the use of a deputy agent. Substitution, compensation and sublimation are further examples.

Achieving security through deputy agents fails to deal directly with the situation. If the activity is essential to the satisfaction of needs, the recurrence of insecurity is inevitable and quite pronounced. Insofar as the individual recognizes their use, deputy agents can serve as an expedient means of resolving insecurity and are not deleterious to mental health.

The persistent use of a deputy agent, however, is a poor way of dealing with problems, and eventually the individual is likely to lose sight of the ineffectiveness of his technique. The paranoid who no longer accepts responsibility finds ample justification for condemning others for personal failures and shortcomings. The projection of blame on others for the consequences of a person's own behavior is no longer a temporary technique but has become a psychological reality. In this case, the person has lost insight into the use of a deputy agent.

The persistent use of a particular deputy agent in early childhood determines the neurotic pattern of behavior in later life. The young child who has learned to blame the chair for his fall later blames the teacher for lack of interest at school and eventually blames society for disappointments in life. Whether neurotic patterns can be traced back to childhood experiences with certain deputy agents is a problem for future research.

The nonacceptance or avoidance of consequences is called *insecurity*, a person may be unwilling to accept the consequences for various reasons. Lack of understanding about the consequences involved in a new experience may result in nonacceptance. The young child who wanders from home ground for the first time may find his experience too new and too fearful. The adolescent who tries his first cigarette may develop symptoms that discourage the act. The young man who tries his hand at square dancing may find the steps too intricate and bewildering to continue.

Insufficient skill may bring consequences which the person is unwilling to accept. Lack of precision in entering the water may discourage the novice from diving. The poorly trained fighter may find the threat of injury too great. The student who enters university may find that his/her preparation and study habits are inadequate.

The reluctance to accept consequences may stem from a disparity between actual achievement and anticipated results. The player who refuses to continue playing bridge because of many careless errors is an illustration. Exceptional demands by parent, teacher, or supervisor may impose standards that exceed the individual's actual level of achievement.

The phenomenon of insecurity is a frequent and inevitable part of human experience. When a person pursues a new activity, lack of knowledge and the consequences thereof will be accompanied by insecurity. From a mental health point of view the emphasis is not on the avoidance of insecurity; rather the important condition is the reaction to insecurity. Readiness to accept insecurity is tantamount to learning.

Adventures into the unknown are exciting and fascinating and, at the same time, fearful. Tolerance for insecurity is essential to learning. A beginner at the wheel of a car is beset with anxious moments while gradually learning to make the proper shifts, gauge distances, and demonstrate care. As the skill increases, insecurity decreases until eventually the individual has full confidence.

Accepting new situations that are too difficult may result in mounting insecurity. The anxious parent may push a child into situations that are too complex and too new for the child to handle. A young man whose ambition exceeds his performance finds a mounting insecurity as he continually fails to breach the gap. Recurrent failure to deal with insecurity leads to feelings of inadequacy and inferiority and eventually reluctance to accept new problems.

The developmental aspect of the theory covers the security patterns from infancy to adulthood. The newborn infant is wholly and immaturely dependent upon the parent for survival. The routine requirements of feeding, washing, and body comfort are accepted by the mother. In a short time, the child learns to take over some of the responsibilities. As skills are developed, the child acquires independent security in those activities.

The set of factors that bring about a shift from an immature dependent to independent security is not quite clear. In some activities, it appears to be a matter of expediency. In others, it seems the dependent situation would persist were it not for inevitable occasions giving rise to insecurity. This is evident in situations where the child feels unable to cope independently and the solution in terms of dependence is impossible or refused by the parents.

A second explanation is that the confinement associated with dependency is restricting and eventually becomes boring. The need for change challenges the individual to explore and investigate. Shifts in interest and attitude accompanying developmental changes demand independent rather than dependent patterns of behavior. The 8-year-olds who join their first gang must learn to stand on their own feet and accept responsibility for their own actions.

A third suggestion is that as the individual is aware of the traces of insecurity inherent in dependency, he/she seeks to achieve independence. The dependence upon an agent that may refuse to accept future responsibility or that is subject to crisis compels the individual to seek a more reassuring form of security. Inasmuch as the attainment of a skill provides the only complete security, the individual strives to acquire this independence through expenditure of effort.

Whatever the circumstances it is apparent that the child seeks independent security in certain activities. Emancipation is the term applied to the process of achieving independent security. Preschool children are dependent upon parental agents for care, nourishment, and shelter. However, they have by now acquired some skill in eating, washing, and toilet routines. They have achieved some skill in getting along with contemporaries and in accepting the consequences of play activities. School-aged children, while still quite dependent, are beginning to expand the limits of their environment. They stay away from home for a longer time, seek more meaningful relations with playmates by organizing gangs or joining clubs, and begin to learn skills that are useful—mowing the lawn, going to the grocery store, taking on a paper route. Adolescents are nearing the final stages of emancipation. While still relying on parents for food and shelter, they learn to accept full responsibility for deportment, begin to form friendships with their own sex and with members of the opposite sex, make plans for their life's work, and are engrossed in the wonderment and meaning of life.

By the time adulthood is reached, the security picture is notably different. The early dependence upon the parental agents has disappeared. The skills necessary for dealing with home and work life have been acquired, and adults accept responsibility for their own decisions and actions. Relationships with companions also change. From a casual interest in all contemporaries at the preschool level, through the organized social activity of the school-age period, to the often serious attachments formed during adolescence, the adult has now established a few close friendships based on mutual interest and affection. The security pattern reflecting the individual's outlook on life and leisure-time activities also shows considerable modification from childhood through to adulthood, changing from immature dependent to independent or mature dependent behavior.

The dynamics of security development define the pattern of security which may evolve. The young boy who tries to make his way to the park alone for the first time is faced with a new situation, beset with insecurity. He may feel that the experience is too threatening and return to wait until his mother can take him. The reaction is known as regression and is common at the preschool level. The boy may, however, accept the insecurity and make his way slowly along the street, taking extra care when crossing and remembering correctly at which corner he had to turn. If he arrives at the park safely, he experiences a feeling of accomplishment and self-assurance. He has displayed the care and skill necessary in this new situation, and he feels independent.

He may, on the other hand, choose to share this new experience with the boy next door. The two may try to make their way to the park together. One boy remembers the correct corner to turn; the other knows when it is safe to cross the street. They both arrive at the park together, each feeling a sense of accomplishment and a sense of dependence on one another. This shared feeling of dependence provides a mature dependent security. They have the skill providing they combine their effort and knowledge.

A fourth way of resolving the insecurity is to use some form of avoidance reaction, viz. to employ a deputy agent. The boy assures himself that there is nothing at the park of interest and that it is much more fun to stay around the yard. He may decide that he will try tomorrow, or (perhaps) be satisfied to play with his truck instead. This form of behavior is common at all levels of development. But its persistent use indicates poor adjustment practices and suggests neurotic behavior.

The insecure individual may choose, then, one of four procedures: withdraw and return to a previously satisfactory agent; make an effort towards independent security through learning; seek to share his experience with a contemporary, accepting partial responsibility for the task and ensuing consequences; or adopt a deputy agent.

For purposes of mental health assessment, it is expedient to classify behavior into four major categories of activity: social life, vocation, avocation, and philosophy of life. This classification is arbitrary, and while the fields are discrete, some overlap is apparent.

SECURITY RELATED TO SOCIAL ACTIVITIES

The social life (or intimates category), is further broken down into: social relations within the home (i.e., familial); social relations outside the home (i.e., extrafamilial); the relations dealing with a sense of belonging; and relations dealing with a sense of competition. It has been found useful to divide the field of vocation into two areas: namely, activities dealing directly with the job, and activities dealing with the handling of money (Blatz, 1944).

Organization of activities into categories has a practical usefulness for diagnosis and prognosis. While the degree of relation among the categories has not yet been determined, the security pattern in one does not necessarily resemble the security pattern in another. At the same time, it has been suggested that security in one may compensate for insecurity in another. Certainly, security measurement in each of the categories provides a more detailed understanding of the individual's security picture.

The familial area in the intimates category involves activities which centre around child/parent relationships. The early dependence of children upon parents has already been discussed. The parents assume responsibility for children until they are ready to fulfill their own requirements. As children learn the skills essential for their own care and welfare, the security picture shifts from dependence to independence.

The child who accepts some responsibility for activities that involve both parent and child develops a mature dependence in the familial area. Seeking parental guidance and advice rather than parental shelter and protection shows a shift toward mature dependent security.

The use of deputy agents arises from lack of balance between the pressure placed on the child to accept new situations and the child's lack of readiness to learn. Conversely, reluctance of the parent to allow the child to take responsibility may lead to the child adopting a deputy agent.

Insecurity in the familial area is represented by inadequate child-parent relationships. A plan of training that is inconsistent, or one that depends heavily upon emotional overtones, often leads to the child's insecurity. Broken homes and homes bereft of parental affection and care result in the child's familial insecurity.

The extrafamilial area encompasses interpersonal relations between contemporaries and near-contemporaries. Because of the nature of the relationship, independent security is denied. Activities which involve the associations formed among people are essentially shared and the consequences necessarily involve all participants. Mature dependent security is based on faith, trust, and confidence. Each individual is psychologically involved and accepts his/her role in the situation.

The immature dependent person leans on others for support and protection, seeking associations that serve the function of a parent surrogate. Having little understanding of other people, such an individual is preoccupied with personal needs, interests, and satisfactions.

The use of a deputy agent in the extrafamilial area arises out of lack of success and satisfaction in interpersonal relations. The individual feels that friendship is not worth the time and effort and finds ample evidence of the insincerity of others.

Feelings of inadequacy and inferiority in interpersonal relations are a manifestation of insecurity. The individual shows little self-confidence and is apprehensive about meeting people and participating in groups.

Security in the area of belonging relates to the individual's feelings about associations with other people and with groups. As the experience of belonging involves the interaction of two or more people, independent security is again denied. Mature dependence in this area is characterized by a trust and confidence of one person for another. The mutual acceptance of responsibility, expressed through interest and concern for the other person, provides the basis for mature dependent security.

The individual who clings to other people and to groups in an effort to feel wanted and accepted while making no attempt to return this feeling to others, is immaturely dependent.

The belief that one lives best when one lives unto oneself reflects the use of a deputy agent. The "lone wolf" who is reluctant to risk lack of acceptance by others argues that one fares best alone. The extreme case is the hermit who chooses to withdraw from all forms of interpersonal behavior. It is clear that an action which refuses to face a necessary part of human life is not an independent state of security.

Insecure people lack faith in themselves as contributing members of society. They feel little sense of personal worth and lack self-assurance. Their perceptions of themselves as they relate to others are underrated. Parents who compete for the affection of their child may engender the child's insecurity in this area.

Competition involves those activities where two or more individuals compare their skill. Generally, specific criteria are set down to determine whose skill is superior. Because competition forms an integral part of human activity in our society, a measure of security in this area is useful in the assessment of mental health.

A person may "compete" with his/her own previous performance—as illustrated by the golfer who aims to improve upon his/her lowest score. While this kind of activity is often referred to as competitive, it is not the kind of competition referred to in this context. The individual who seeks to improve past performance is essentially concerned with the refinement of a skill through practice.

The independently secure person in the competitive area willingly accepts the rules and regulations, seeking to match ability with those of comparable skill, and achieving satisfaction from the thrill of the activity. While the independently secure person is alert to the criterion which represents superior performance, attention is on the activity. The activity has an intrinsic interest.

The individual who compares skill with another must accept the consequences alone. A mutual sharing of consequences with a competitor is a contradiction: thus, mature dependent security in competition is not meaningful.

Team competition, where two or more persons match their combined skill against equivalent numbers, may involve a feeling of belonging as well as one of competition. However, the feeling of security as it relates to competition should not be confused with belonging.

A competitive activity which ends in a draw presents consequences that are common to both competitors. In this case, the criterion which represents superior play has been inadequate to produce a differentiation. Theoretically, an individual experiences the greatest satisfaction in draw play, and as the disparity between one skill and the other increases, the satisfaction for either competitor gradually decreases.

The immaturely dependent person in the area of competition tries to avoid open competition with contemporaries. Satisfaction is derived from competitive play within the family where the consequences are not taken seriously and there is ample support and praise. Immature dependence is further reflected in the spectator who identifies strongly with a team but shares only in the victories.

The person who employs a deputy agent discards losses as unimportant, yet accepts victories with satisfaction and delight. The person who insists on the last word exemplifies a further use of a deputy agent.

Insecurity is exhibited through nervousness and lack of confidence in one's own ability. The person who shows a constant concern about the score in a game indicates signs of insecurity.

SECURITY RELATED TO VOCATION

Activities classified under vocation are divided into two areas: activities dealing directly with work; and activities relating to the handling of money.

The person who possesses the skill and knowledge necessary for the job is independently secure. Satisfaction comes from the work itself and feeling that this effort promotes greater prosperity for the community. It is important, of course, that this skill be purposeful within the existing technological and social structure.

The maturely dependent individual seeks identity with fellow workers, emphasizing the importance of teamwork and group effort for satisfactions. There is reassurance of the worth of this skill and contribution and promise of increasing responsibilities.

The person who derives satisfaction only from the income for work is immaturely dependent. As a result, there is a preoccupation with a stable work situation and a job where the requirements are clearly defined. Such workers avoid any responsibilities beyond those stipulated in the work itself.

The feeling that it is futile to do good work because it is never recognized involves a deputy agent. The insistence that success depends upon "who" one knows rather than "what" one knows is a further illustration. Again, the person who is convinced that advancement and vocational prosperity depend upon "the breaks" and not the quality of work manifests a security achieved through a deputy agent.

Vocational insecurity refers to feelings about present work rather than unemployment. The insecure person feels unsuited to the work, expressing uneasiness because the job holds little promise or because the earnings are not adequate.

Activities which relate to the handling of money are earning, saving, and spending. While it is assumed that a measure of security/insecurity must be based upon all three activities, the relationship between earning, saving, and/or spending activities has not yet been established.

The independently secure person is confident of the ability to function financially without assistance, plans savings in relation to some specific purpose, and spends money without regret and in accordance with needs.

The maturely dependent person feels assured of being adequately paid, can manage to live within this income through careful adherence to a budget, and seeks sound value for money rather than looking for bargains.

Immature dependence fosters the principle of maximum returns for minimum effort. The person who strives to get all that the traffic will bear and who has a grasping attitude towards earnings manifests common signs of immature dependence. For such a person, the best way to save money is to have it deducted at source. There is little concern about running short of money because there is a readiness to borrow from others. The immature dependent person prefers to make purchases where there is assurance of a refund in case of a change of mind. The installment plan, spreading payments over a period of several months, is preferred to cash.

The man who complains that he could work harder and earn more but for the fact that he regards his health as more important than money is achieving his security through a deputy agent. He further believes that he could manage his savings and spending if he were really interested in the slavish adherence to a budget. The purchases that he does make convince him that he never gets his money's worth anyway.

The insecure person in this area feels uneasy about not earning enough money to take care of present needs, and is never satisfied with the amount of savings. Projecting this feeling of inadequacy into activities dealing with spending, the insecure person assumes blame and regret for poor choices.

SECURITY RELATED TO AVOCATION

Avocational activities are considered along two dimensions—pattern of a quadrant—social, asocial and participant/spectator.

The social/participant activities are those which are enjoyed with others and where the person accepts an active part in contributing skill to the enjoyment. Dancing, bridge, games and discussion groups illustrate a few social/participant activities. The asocial/participant tasks provide essentially creative outlets. Such activities as painting, writing, woodworking, and gardening are of this kind.

The social/spectator activities provide the opportunity for group identification where members share in the thrills and enjoyment of an event. Attendance at sports, games, shows and displays are examples. Asocial/spectator activities offer the opportunity for quietness and relaxation. Light reading, listening to the radio, looking at television, watching a movie and sunbathing are in this category.

From a mental health point of view concentrating leisure time into any one of these four areas to the exclusion of the others is unhealthy. There are no exact percentage figures to suggest what may be ideal but any division of leisure time must accommodate developmental shifts in interest and energy as well as individual differences. Presently, with ever-increasing leisure time, the planning and developing of avocational skills and recreational outlets are becoming pressing concerns for the educator and the social scientist.

Measures of security/insecurity are obtained from the distribution of leisure time and from the feelings and attitudes associated with a person's choice of activities. Independent security is reflected in adequate and satisfying outlets for all leisure time. The person who has achieved skills to permit satisfying social play as well as opportunities for creative expression is independently secure. These recreational skills are not used for financial return or to achieve status.

The mature dependent person receives greatest enjoyment from leisure time activities which involve other people, confidence in skills, and being willing to share interests and possessions with others. Leisure pursuits include creative outlets although such interests are secondary.

The person who devotes the greater part of leisure time to spectator activities is immaturely dependent, lacks sufficient persistence to stay at any one thing and, as a result, receives little satisfaction from self-initiated activities. Status is sought through any existing skills. Watching sports events provides thrills and excitement.

Delaying the start of an activity until one has sufficient time to do it properly is a common deputy agent in the avocational field. The person who complains that there just is not time to devote to developing skill in any one hobby achieves security by means of a deputy agent. The belief that it is important to work in one's spare time so that later one can really enjoy leisure moments is a further illustration.

Insecurity in the avocational field is evidenced by boredom. The man who feels undecided and inadequate in planning leisure time is insecure. He possesses few, if any, skills and is dissatisfied with his own efforts when he does engage in social activities or even in activities by himself.

SECURITY RELATED TO PERSONAL PHILOSOPHY

Activities associated with philosophy are perhaps the least understood. The influence upon behavior ascribed to one's philosophy of life is difficult to assess. A measure of security/insecurity in this field has been brought through reference to the serenity permitted within the limits of one's ideology.

Mature dependent security is reflected in the acceptance of and adherence to a system of values determining a course of action. The maturely dependent person feels confident in the ability to maintain and strengthen values through increasing experience, and indicates a willingness to modify values which are achieved through a more mature judgment. There is an acceptance of the challenges of life and contribution toward the betterment of man.

The person who is motivated by self-interest and the need for personal reassurance is immaturely dependent. This reassurance may be achieved by maintaining rigid adherence to a system of prescribed rules and practices which relate to a personal deity. The person who feels content because fate is entirely in the hands of a higher power is a further reflection of immature dependence.

Doubt is the main sign of insecurity. The person who finds previous beliefs untenable and begins to question the validity of certain tenets inherent in the concept of purpose is insecure. This uneasiness makes it difficult for the person to accept a guiding principle to behavior and the person feels helpless and alone in relating to the scheme of things.

The individual's security picture is achieved by studying the measures obtained from each of the above fields. The mental health of the individual is based on the total security and insecurity patterns in place, with the ratio of security to insecurity providing a mental health quotient.

As learning is central to the development of security, the concept is essentially dynamic. As new interests and activities are introduced, the patterns of security and insecurity may shift. The security picture undergoes a shift from a state of predominant dependence to independence as the individual grows from childhood to adulthood.

While security is essentially related to feelings it is also reflected in learning new skills and adjustments. The overview is designed to indicate how the individual meets and accepts new situations and accomplishes skills and adjustments.

NOTE

1.   Chapter abridged from Grapko (1953).

REFERENCES

Blatz, W. E. (1940). *Hostages to peace: Parents and the children of democracy.* New York: Morrow.

Blatz, W. E. (1944). *Understanding the young child.* Toronto: Clark, Irwin.

Grapko, M. F. (1953). *The relation of certain psychological variables to security.* Unpublished PhD thesis, University of Toronto, Toronto, Ontario.

CHAPTER 5

SECURITY THEORY AND THE HISTORY OF DEVELOPMENTAL PSYCHOLOGY

Sheri L. Winestock

In this chapter I will review William Blatz's life and career from the perspective of the historiographical concept of presentism. Presentism in the historiography of psychology refers to a bias on the part of historians who view the history of a discipline from the vantage point of the present rather than within the context of its emergence (Butterfield, 1963; Danziger, 1984, 1990; Leahey, 1986; Smith, 1988; Stocking, 1965; Young, 1966). These historians usually attempt to discover "founding fathers" and to show the historical record as one of linear progress from the "primitive" past to the "enlightened" present. In this view individual psychologists are portrayed as "great men" who anticipated or contributed to currently dominant positions. In the same vein, psychologists whose work does not fit into current categories are little acknowledged even if they were prominent in their time. Further, the lack of context in these histories makes for a singularly insular interpretation of thoughts and ideas (Morawski, 1982). By attending to the social, political, economic, and

The Secure Child: Timeless Lessons in Parenting and Childhood Education, pp. 69–95
Copyright © 2010 by Information Age Publishing
All rights of reproduction in any form reserved.

philosophical context of a period, the historian can avoid this type of account.

William Blatz is an interesting subject in this regard because he falls into both historical categories of the "forgotten many" and "great men." Despite having made a number of significant contributions to developmental psychology in Canada, the United States, and abroad, Blatz is little known to modern day developmental psychologists and completely neglected in developmental psychology histories. Even histories that describe in detail the work of the Laura Spelman Rockefeller grant recipients, fail to mention Blatz or the Institutes set up in Toronto and Montreal in this context (see for example, Cairns, 1983; Cravens, 1985; Sears, 1975). Despite being a Canadian, Blatz was well-known and well-received both in America and abroad. Thus, his neglect cannot be explained entirely by ethnocentricity on the part of American and European authors.

The small number of histories and assessments of Blatz's work and personality that do exist are offered by those who worked closely with him (see for example, Bernhardt, 1965; Bernhardt, Fletcher, Johnson, Millichamp, & Northway, 1951; Millichamp & Northway, 1977; Northway, 1973, 1975; Wright, 1964, 1974, 1983, 1984, 1985a, 1985b, 1993) or his associates (e.g., Raymond, 1991). These accounts are intended to celebrate the field of child study in Canada with Blatz as its leader. Their celebratory nature makes them unsuitable as critical historical documents. Since most histories of developmental psychology neglect Blatz and those that do mention him are written as tributes, there has been little critical scholarship regarding Blatz's position in the then emerging discipline of developmental psychology.

As will become clear, Blatz's career parallels rather well the coming of age of developmental psychology. The claim here is that developmental psychology itself went through a number of distinct stages and that Blatz's career can be fruitfully considered in the context of these changes. The main question is: In which ways does Blatz's psychology reflect the child psychology of the day and in which ways is it different? The present work then, is a critical biographical study of William Blatz in the context of the changing developmental psychology that he both influenced and was influenced by (Winestock, 1994).

In this chapter I will concentrate on the child rearing advice literature, which was one of Blatz's most significant contributions, covering only minimally other aspects of his career and of the discipline of developmental psychology. At the same time, I will include discussions of functional psychology, which Blatz was tutored in, and the mental hygiene perspective, which dominated Toronto psychology during Blatz's initiation into the discipline. These two influences were important factors in his work. Indeed,

Blatz's functional and mental hygiene principles largely account for his ultimate demise in the historical record since psychology in general and developmental psychology in particular discarded these perspectives.

William Emet Blatz was born in Hamilton, Ontario in 1895. He came from a close-knit family where educational values were highly prized. He learned how to debate in family games and his mother's neighbourhood ministering of the sick introduced him early to the vagaries of the ailing. He began his university training in medicine in 1916 at the University of Toronto and received his MB in 1921. During World War I he worked on the Hart House Re-education team which treated returned soldiers with chronic cases of shell shock. This project was under the direction of A. E. Bott and led to Blatz's interest in psychology. Here, he claimed, he found himself dealing with what he called "a phenomenon more elusive than any other—consciousness." His interest in motivation and explaining why some soldiers would work hard on their rehabilitation while others would give up, led him into considering the field of psychology for his career. He went to the University of Chicago to do his PhD in psychology under the supervision of Harvey Carr and graduated in 1924. Blatz's education at Chicago was to have a profound and pervasive effect on his later career.

Blatz was a prime candidate for the functional psychology associated with the University of Chicago. Blatz had already anticipated Dewey's progressive education ideas before even encountering them. In a letter to his niece advising her not to get disheartened by the fact that her foot was in a brace, he wrote:

> learn all you can of everything, and about everything, don't just learn what the teacher says. When you are knitting think of where the wool comes from, when did they first begin to knit, why use wool instead of cotton and so on and you will find that this system will lead you into many fascinating byways and all the time you will be adding to that store of knowledge which is going to make you able to sit back and laugh at all the rest. (Blatz, 1919)

Clearly, Blatz was well-suited for the functional psychology of the University of Chicago.

The University of Chicago had a unique place among American universities. Initially a Baptist institution founded in 1892 by the American Baptist Education Society, it would come to represent innovative and maverick scholarship. The University of Chicago had the advantage of an institutional atmosphere of newness. The spirit of freedom and experimentation led to revolutionary or nontraditional scholarship that could not be easily incorporated into the more established universities. In this atmosphere of innovation and freedom, eminent thinkers were able to break with traditional scholarship. This resulted in new ideas regarding human psychology developed by the members of the Chicago Philosophy

Department. The new ideas that emanated from the department concerning the philosophy of pragmatism and the psychology of functionalism were a coherent system. Their proponents were branded "the Chicago school" (Kiefer, 1988; Shore, 1987). Although many of the key figures that defined "the Chicago school" had left by the time of Blatz's graduate education, their legacy and influence were still keenly felt in the institution (Orlinsky, 1992; Rucker, 1969). For example, Rucker said of John Dewey, who had departed in 1904: "His former colleagues paid careful attention to all that he did, with the result that Chicago students could point to Dewey as their mentor even though they had never encountered him in person" (p. ix). The functionalism associated with the "Chicago school" would inform Blatz's theories considerably.

Initially this functionalism, based on the ideas of John Dewey (1896, 1897) and George Herbert Mead (1900, 1903, 1910, 1934), was characterized by an organism interacting *with* its environment. Later, when John B. Watson (1913, 1919) revised functionalism, it was characterized by an organism being acted upon by its environment. Blatz, like his supervisor Carr, vacillated between Dewey and Mead's more sociological functionalism and Watson's more behavioristic functionalism (Carr, 1925). Blatz would use the sociological functionalism of Dewey and Mead as an organizing principle for his views on child rearing and education. The child would always be an active and conscious participant in the learning process. However, Blatz would adopt the behavioristic functionalism of Watson as the method used to inculcate the child's choices into habitual responses in routine situations.

After graduating in 1924, Blatz was invited by Bott and Clarence Hincks, who were planning a research center based on mental hygiene principles related to child development, to become director of the St. George's School for Child Study in Toronto. This university affiliated school housed a nursery school and a parent education division. Later, as it expanded, it included a research division and graduate student training. The mental hygiene perspective, firmly established among the early psychologists at Toronto, would be the foundation for Blatz's work here.

The early psychologists at the University of Toronto adopted an approach to mental hygiene that was characterized as positive in its attempts at prevention rather than amelioration (Babarik, 1970; Pols, 1991; Richardson, 1989). Their emphasis was on a social definition of mental disorder, attention to the childhood period, prevention rather than cure, and normal development. The aim was to assure the conditions for the development of mental health and eliminate the factors interfering with such development. The point of entry for prevention was childhood and the education system since mental hygienists believed that adjustment problems had their roots in childhood. The premise was that society could be perfected through the socialization of children based on scientific principles. Happy, mentally healthy children, it was argued, would assure a rational and productive adult population.

Blatz began his work in child study in 1925 when the field was relatively new. It had only been in the previous quarter of the century in America that the field had gained respect and prominence. Several factors contributed to the emergence of this new identity.[1] First, the publications and ideas of Charles Darwin influenced developmentalists such as Wilhelm Preyer, George Romanes, and James Sully through to G. Stanley Hall, James Mark Baldwin, and Sigmund Freud. Hall and then Freud raised interest in early development within the popular culture in the late nineteenth and early twentieth centuries. Second, John B. Watson's *Psychology from the Standpoint of a Behaviorist*, published in 1919, legitimized the academic study of children by the use of experimental methods on the conditioning of emotions in children. Finally, Progressive social reformers made the child the *sine qua non* of their attempts to improve society. Originally a movement concerned with the prevention of delinquency and social problems, "child-saving" later became oriented toward research and investigation aimed at understanding the child. The reform mentality brought about the institutionalization and professionalization of developmental psychology through philanthropic foundations interested in child welfare and amelioration of social problems (Coffman, 1936; Cravens, 1985; Wandersee, 1991).

Originally established in 1918, the goal of the Laura Spelman Rockefeller Memorial (LSRM) was to advance the charitable work that Laura Spelman Rockefeller had undertaken to "further the welfare of women and children" (Fosdick, 1952, p. 136). However, in 1923 the foundation directors voted to change the goal to the "application of the social sciences for the purpose of reform" (p. 136). In the 4 years attendant on its newly-defined purpose, 1924 to 1928, the LSRM appropriated the unprecedented sum of over 20 million dollars for the social sciences. Indeed, the LSRM was the funding source for the St. George's school that Blatz was to direct. The LSRM directors invested heavily in research institutes because they assumed that the results of the research would be immediately practicable. Parent education programs would carry the latest scientific findings on how to raise children for a better society directly to mothers for instant home use (Schlossman, 1985).

At this time, developmentalists were establishing their professional identity and reputation by demonstrating their usefulness. This took the form of providing child rearing advice. In connection with Progressivist "child-savers," developmentalists were maintaining their expertise in the raising of a new generation of more perfect beings. Blatz's ideas conformed to the widely held view that infant impulses should be held in check through behavioral conditioning and strict habit training. Previously, in the advice literature, there had not been a great emphasis on rigid schedules of training for character building (Beales, 1985, 1991; Kiefer, 1988; Margolis, 1984; Sunley, 1955). Changes in social and economic forces in the 1800s led to a different conception of the family and the child which in turn led to a new prescriptive literature (Borstelmann, 1983, Brady, 1991; Cairns, 1983; Kessen, 1965; Schulz, 1985; Wishy, 1968).

At first this new advice which prescribed strict scheduling, ignoring crying, early toilet training, and not overstimulating the baby was in the interest of both the mother and the child. These practices were intended to reduce the work for mothers and ease their lives as well as benefit the child (Weiss, 1985). However, in the late 1920s the tone of the writing and the rationale for the procedures changed, although the advice remained primarily the same. There was little concern for maternal well-being. Mothers became secondary to child experts and were seen as an impediment to the scientific upbringing of children, or worse, as a potential threat (Cravens, 1985; Margolis, 1984; Vincent, 1951).

The advice literature of the 1920s and 1930s reflected many concomitant influences such as the rise of behaviorism, the social reform ideology, and the scientific orientation (Lomax, 1978; Margolis; 1984; Strong-Boag, 1982). Child rearing was a constant vigil, stressing regularity, punctuality, discipline, and cleanliness; characteristics important for the needs of business and industry. These were to be achieved by rigid scheduling of routine activities (Wolfenstein, 1953, 1955). Emotional, irrational mother-love would lead to weak, dependent children who would never make it in the competitive world of industrial capitalism. Despite the call for mothers to limit their affection and time with the child, they were still not supposed to leave the home (Oakley, 1986). Mothers were to spend all their time in the field of child rearing, but not any of their time loving the child. The mother was to read manuals of child care and stick to the rigid scheduling which was very time consuming, making a profession out of scientific child training.

The child rearing advice proposed to the post World War II generation was significantly different from the rigorous training of the 1920s and 1930s. The rationale of strict early training was undermined by the theories of Freud and Gesell (Lomax, 1978). Freud's psychoanalytic theory implied that strict discipline could induce detrimental personality characteristics in adult life. Gesell's maturational theory suggested that it would be useless to attempt to condition a baby until its nervous system had reached the requisite stage of differentiation or maturity. These ideas translated into prescriptions for permissive, but still vigilant care (see for example, Dr. Spock's *Common Sense Book on Baby and Child Care*, 1946).

Maintaining a proper balance of care and freedom required the mother's constant attention (Strickland & Ambrose, 1985; Weiss, 1985).

The attitude of permissive care persisted for decades. By 1963, the child rearing manual, *Child Care*, first published by the U.S. Department of Labor, Children's Bureau in 1914, advocated very few child rearing practices. Babies were resilient beings who knew what they needed, and the parent needed only to provide love and affection so that the baby would feel secure. One statement said:

> Getting enough to eat, and feeling safe and warm are about all a new baby needs. Food and love are about equally necessary, and when both are freely available, he can thrive.

This was hardly expert advice. Unlike the earlier advice, which in order to be expert had to be different from parents' natural tendencies, now just being natural was all that it took. The goal of child care was not to curb the child's natural tendencies and inclinations, but to give them free rein: "Since spontaneity and self-expression were now thought important to the developing child, the child would lead and the mother would follow." There was not much for authors of manuals to teach in this context, except to un-indoctrinate women who now believed maternal affection was detrimental and practiced rigid scheduling and discipline. Women just had to unlearn the old dicta and be advised to love their children, be permissive and open, and let the child dictate its developmental progress. But the onus was still on mothers to be there constantly for the benefit of their child's future development. The mother should allow the child to live for itself, but she should live for it. She should always be there engendering security and trust from which the child would be able to become independent. With the change in advice after World War II to the more natural tendencies of love and freedom, parents just needed to be convinced of why this was good and reacquainted with how to feed, toilet train, and care for the child in this way. It is probably not a coincidence that Blatz published five books on child rearing prior to 1944 and none after. Not only was he more of an adherent of the strict training doctrine, but there was little to teach here.

In the 3 books Blatz published in the first 10 years of his career, *Parents and the Pre-school child* in 1928 (with Helen Bott), *The Management of Young Children* in 1930 (with Helen Bott), and *Nursery Education: Theory and Practice* in 1935 (with Dorothy Millichamp and Margaret Fletcher), he prescribed strict scheduling, although his conceptual scheme was less reductionist and repressive than the other authors at this time.

In his books of this period, Blatz attempted to place the emphasis of child study on normal children in the context of mental hygiene and par-

ent education. Adopting the medical metaphor, the central tenet was prevention of mental disease. The main question was: "What principles can
be used to facilitate the normal adjustment process?" All behavioral difficulties were seen as a result of ineffective training for the intricate social
adjustments that the child had to make. The objective was to provide parents with the means of avoiding serious behavioral problems while, at the
same time, providing a child training plan for effecting an adjustment
should a problem arise. Serenity—a key word for Blatz—in the child's
activities and manner meant that the program was successful.

Blatz's theory was anchored on the conjoining of the individual and
the environment. For Blatz, like Dewey and Mead, the individual and the
situation could never be wholly differentiated. He maintained that when
environmental influences, animate or inanimate, act upon the child, the
child's reaction changes the environment in some way so that it is always a
new environment that next exerts an influence on the child. From a psychological point of view, the individual was a function of his feelings, his
clothes, his friends, and so forth. Blatz wrote:

> The related factors, howsoever conceived, are mutually dependent; wipe out
> the environment and the individual is likewise destroyed. The individual life
> has meaning and value mainly in terms of its social adjustments and cannot
> be fruitfully studied if this is ignored. The two terms, "the individual" and
> "the situation," must therefore be regarded as correlatives; joint factors in a
> relationship which we have chosen to describe as that of adjustment. (Blatz
> & Bott, 1928, p. 18)

The one major function of the parents in the adjustment process was
discipline. For Blatz, this meant:

> the reasonable regulation and supervision of the fundamental habits of a
> child throughout all stages of his development and a consistent plan for
> having the child observe those rules that are laid down. (Blatz & Bott, 1928,
> p. 28)

Part of the difficulty in promoting this idea was that the word discipline
was associated with restrictions, prohibitions, and penalties. Discipline
was seen as a means of restraining action rather than inciting it. For Blatz,
the goal of discipline was not in securing conformity to something laid
down, but rather stimulating the child's own activity; not with seeking
compliance, but rather with fostering desirable activity on the child's part.
Discipline was the principle of regulation or control within life. Attendant
with this control was the freedom to pursue other interests. Discipline was
not an end in itself, but rather a means toward freedom and creativity. If
the discipline failed to work, it should not be dealt with by the use of arbi-

trary and artificial methods. That is, using force in the form of corporal punishment would not solve the problem; rather, the discipline routine needed to be investigated and changed appropriately. Blatz's disdain for corporal punishment was one of his most well-known and controversial views.

Isolating the child was considered the only appropriate means of "punishment" because it showed the child that acting contrary to social customs would not be tolerated. The child could choose to conform if he wished to remain in the social community or accept removal if he did not want to conform. The decision was to be left in the hands of the child as was the amount of time spent in isolation. When the child realized the benefits of being in the social group, he would want to conform. This view of the relationship between society and the individual can be traced to the functionalism of Dewey and Mead.

Blatz's analysis of behavior was divided into three main categories, namely, appetites, emotions, and attitudes. For Blatz, the appetites were the characteristic ways the individual reacted in order to obtain from the environment satisfaction for his vital needs. Blatz discussed six basic appetites—hunger, thirst, sleep, elimination, change, and sex—which he considered to be the main appetitive processes to figure prominently in the adjustment activities of the young child, and which brought the child actively into contact, and often into conflict, with his physical and social environment.

Emotion was seen as an influence arising from the environmental situation and affecting the individual by altering the tempo of living to a marked degree, either upward or downward. The effect was to thwart the appetites, disrupt smooth functioning of behavior, and throw the whole adjustment process into a state of confusion. The two main emotions under study were fear and anger. Here Blatz avowedly adopted the work of Watson without reservation. Blatz wrote:

> Watson's work was so brilliantly conceived and so tellingly described in his *Psychology from the Standpoint of a Behaviourist* (sic), that his contentions have passed largely unchallenged in the ten years since his book was written. His work has not been to any considerable extent either modified or extended by further experimentation in the field of genetic psychology. It is therefore not easy to think or speak with equal clarity in terms other than those which he laid down as appropriate for the study of child behaviour. (Blatz & Bott, 1928, p. 220)

Attitudes were considered to be the adjustment made to the appetites and emotions by virtue of approach or withdrawal. Here Blatz adopted the concepts of self-assertion and self-negation as defined by McDougall (1960). Blatz believed that the proper management of the self-tendencies of the child during the preschool years offered the surest preparation for satisfactory personality adjustment during the whole life. As the infant grew and met more frustrations and less ministrations, he moved from self-assertion to self-negation. Here the importance of success and failure and the wise and unwise ways of control (the social approval and disapproval, the rewards and punishments by the parents) could scarcely be overestimated. One of Blatz's most controversial doctrines in this regard was his opposition to competition. Actions had to be intrinsically satisfying to be of value. Any rewards or evaluations, such as school grades, were detrimental to the learning process. This idea was more in line with Dewey's pedagogy than Watson's conditioning (cf. Dewey, 1902).

Blatz's fundamental premise was that as a member of a social community the child must be taught how to control his unbridled responses of appetite, emotion, and attitude so as to exist peacefully within that community. His approach to child training was best summarized in this question: "What are the laws of habit formation in accordance with which these crude original responses are modified into well-coordinated systems of response acceptable to the society in which the child lives?" The answer, with regard to the appetites, was that the method for regulating and directing these impulses or drives was conditioning, largely in the Pavlovian sense. Habits were learned forms of behavior built up by association until a satisfactory mode of response was organized in relation to a given situation (Blatz, 1936a.)

Regarding undesirable habits that the child picked up on his own, such as thumb-sucking or nail-biting, the course of action advocated was to avoid overreacting. In over-emphasizing the attempts to break the habit, the parent might call the child's attention to what was before largely an automatic process. More importantly, the parent should never produce feelings of shame or rebellion in the child. The proper approach was mild preventive measures and, where possible, adaptive positive substitutes. Patience was advocated as the most likely solution since these habits usually disappeared with maturity. Contrary to the restrictive measures for arresting undesirable habits advocated in the child rearing advice literature at this time, Blatz advocated a more tolerant approach. In this way, he anticipated the later permissive attitude of the advice, although only in the case of "bad habits."

In the case of controlling the appetites, strict habit training was required. Blatz prescribed specific methods for training each appetite. In common, however, was the need for consistency and calmness on the part of the parents. The parent's attitude was the single most important influence in the child's conditioning. Any emotional reaction to difficulties in training showed the child that he could manipulate the situation and control the care-giver. Unlike Blatz's views regarding bad habits, this notion of manipulation by the child conformed to the popular ideology of child rearing advice.

These books contained many indications of Blatz's general orientation. Clearly he was influenced by Watson's behaviorism, chiefly in the area of classical conditioning. There were many similarities between his publications and Watson's 1928 publication, *Psychological Care of Infant and Child*. Consistency, immediacy, and calmness all fell under the behavioristic umbrella. Yet the learning that Blatz desired was not from strict association, but rather from intentional understanding. Like Dewey, Blatz desired individual creativity and growth from within. The caregiver was there only to provide for and guide the child's emerging interests, not to determine or interfere with them. Watson, on the other hand, desired to engineer the learning.

Blatz also emphasized action which reflected both Watson's behaviorist functionalism and Dewey and Mead's sociological functionalism. Here, however, Blatz's ideas corresponded more with the latter perspective. Blatz saw the interaction of environment and child as a reciprocal cycle of effect. The child was not simply a passive recipient of environmental influence, but rather an active participant in social interaction. As well, Blatz's emphasis on individual motivation and purposive utility could be traced to the ideas of Dewey and Carr.

In the area of training children, Blatz was plainly influenced by the child study context. He adopted the engineering metaphors of management and efficiency. Not only did he title his second work *The Management of Young Children*, but the behavioristic conditioning promoted child *training* rather than child *rearing*. As well, Blatz adopted the behavioristic metaphor of science. The whole theory assumed that the child was involved in a scientific, experimental struggle with his environment and that the caregivers were required to take a scientific attitude to the success of their procedures and techniques.

These books were very well-received, with *Parents and the Pre-school Child* receiving an award from *Parent's Magazine*. As well, John Watson said of that book:

> It is so sanely and so clearly written. The material is very, very good and the attitude of the authors is beyond criticism.... Of all the books which have been coming out on children in the last few years, I think this is the best. (Watson, 1929)

However, the discipline of psychology was evolving a new structuralism combined with functionalism around the 1930s. In developmental psychology this translated to an emphasis on stages of development and cognition as in Arnold Gesell's and Jean Piaget's theories. However, Blatz's view of mental hygiene involved child training and parent education rather than the uncovering and understanding of innate unfolding stages. The purpose in parent education was not to have parents understand to advantage the developmental stage their child was going through, but to train the parent to manipulate their child's development toward the desired goal of mental health.

This orientation could be seen in the organization of the St. George's school. Informed by the mental hygiene strategy, the St. George's School for Child Study had two divisions: a nursery school, and a parent education department, both organized to study the adjustment of the normal child in an effort to prevent maladjustment and educate the population in this regard. Part of the success of the St. George's school was that it was organized around its practical utility to the community. More than simply attempting to discover scientific truths on the nature of child development, and in keeping with the LSRM mandate and the mental hygiene perspective, the staff at the school focused on the practical application and dissemination of this knowledge into society. Public lectures, parent education courses, and publications aimed at parents, were all part of this philosophy.

Since the normal child had not really been studied, the initial focus of those at the school was to obtain records of children's behaviors in a naturalistic setting.

Blatz employed local untrained women to work with children and consulted with them as equals in forming and implementing the program. This fostered a team spirit and inspired a great deal of loyalty and dedication. Teachers and parents were prompted to make observations on all behaviors so that these could be compiled to form a picture of the normal developing child. He enlisted the parents as preeminently knowledgeable as well as in need of more knowledge. William Kessen (1983a) labeled this strategy in the history of developmental psychology "Child Study," which he described as "a somewhat undisciplined but always enthusiastic interest in all the doings of children."

Blatz was also making a personal name for himself with his public and academic addresses. Speaking both in Canada and the United States, he became a controversial figure. Nursery school education in general, as well as his ideas on the unacceptability of corporal punishment, the undesirability of competition, the normality of sexual impulses, and the emotional detachment of parents, were radical and viewed suspiciously. He enjoyed provoking and, thereby, raising public consciousness. For example, one headline had Canon Woodcock proclaiming that Blatz was "a blot on modern society"[2] while a letter to the editor regarding talks given by Blatz about postwar nursery schools suggested that turning over babies to nursery schools was akin to a communist plot.

Although academia was turning away from practice and guidance toward psychological experimentation, Blatz was content to continue directing the St. George's school and promoting his ideas both publicly and academically. Despite veering away from mainstream developmental psychology, Blatz was to gain international fame in the next major epoch of his life. In 1935 Blatz received the unique opportunity to organize the 24-hour-a-day training and education of the Dionne quintuplets. Born in the northern Ontario town of Callander, Yvonne, Annette, Cecile, Emilie, and Marie Dionne[3] were the first surviving genetically identical quintuplets and as such caught the attention of the world. As educator of the sisters, Blatz was able to put his principles of child training into practice in a closed setting. Moreover, he was able to demonstrate to the world his theory of child training. Despite some contrary evidence in the archival material[4] and other publications,[5] in his *Collected Studies on the Dionne Quintuplets* (1937) and *The Five Sisters: A Study of Child Psychology* (1938), he suggested that the program was an unqualified success. In both of his publications resulting from this 3-year field study (from which he was abruptly and unceremoniously dismissed) Blatz attempted to idealize the sisters' development according to the benefits of his program. Any time there was delayed development, he attributed it to their premature birth, not to the limits of his training. Any time there was accelerated or exceptional development, he attributed it to his training program.

Blatz's neglect of important issues such as the guardianship controversy and the difficulties encountered in maintaining the training program suggest that he may not have been open to disconfirming or difficult evidence. One gets the impression that Blatz was not seeing the data impartially. His later publications failed to address questions regarding the difficulty of implementing and maintaining such a training program. As well, one might expect Blatz to have had a continued interest in the development of the sisters. Raymond (1991) claimed that:

> Blatz was deeply involved in his work with the children, but when it was terminated he showed no regret. There was no looking back. He never mentioned it again. Instead he cut his contacts completely and went on with other projects. (p. 142)

This was not quite accurate. Blatz did attempt to keep in contact with the sisters for research purposes and discussed their development in later work (cf. *Understanding the Young Child* (1944) and *Human Security* (1966)); however, citations in these works were used only as confirming evidence. Disconfirming or problematic evidence was either missed or not addressed. Blatz was considered by his colleagues to be a great intellectual and scientist, always open to new ideas and accepting criticism as an important challenge, yet the field study that he directed had very little impact on his later career. Regardless of the unique circumstances and his emotional attachment, Blatz was able to put the Dionne experience down to an interrupted experiment. He, unlike the rest of the world, never seemed interested in their later lives, perhaps because they appeared to be maladjusted. As far as he was concerned, he had collected some confirming evidence for his theory of child training and cited it when necessary. Neither his sensitivities nor his intellectual theory seemed to have been greatly disturbed by his experience with Yvonne, Annette, Cecile, Emilie, and Marie Dionne.

In terms of the history of developmental psychology, the Dionne episode represented an approach more in line with a strategy in the history of developmental psychology labeled "Child Science." Kessen (1983a) described this as "the hardheaded study of children, calling on classical research models and emphasizing its rigor and epistemological correctness."All the staff at the Dionne nursery were trained at the St. George's school prior to attending the sisters. They were tutored in the general principles of child training as outlined in Blatz's earlier works. The staff were also taught how to record different events of interest to developmental psychologists, such as vocalization patterns and play preferences, to supplement the data collected by the St. George's staff.

In 1938, St. George's School for Child Study became the Institute of Child Study. With this new status, and probably owing to the growing scientific orientation of child study, came a new emphasis on research. This research-oriented practice corresponded to the phase in the history of developmental psychology labeled as "Child Psychology" by Kessen (1983a). However, it did not correspond to the reductionist principles of learning theory that was prominent at the time.

The research projects were interrupted by World War II, but the newly formed Institute played a large role in the war effort. Early in the war, Blatz and some of his staff journeyed to England to organize the training of reservists for wartime day nurseries. In 1941, Blatz set up the Garrison Lane Nursery Training Centre in Birmingham, England. Here Blatz maintained that his theory of child training was proven successful because it also worked for underprivileged children ravaged by the war. Blatz's work and his public addresses abroad partly influenced the development of Infant Schools in Britain (Richardson, 1989; Weber, 1971). Later, at home, Blatz and members of his staff became involved in organizing and training staff for Canadian wartime day nurseries. The ideas implemented at the Institute were the source for the direction and standards of these nurseries and a committee of Institute staff determined the concomitant legislation (Stapleford, 1976). The Ontario Day Nurseries Act, drafted in 1946 and passed in the spring of 1947, specified that the time table for government sponsored nurseries was to conform to the standards of the Institute of Child Study of the University of Toronto (Millichamp & Northway, 1977; Richardson, 1989). A similar statement was included in every revision of the Act until 1968. Even the Ontario *Programme of Studies for Grades 1 to 6* published in 1968 contained a subtle version of the Blatzian formula for education. The primary precept included character training for social responsibility, service to all, and adaptability to change, with an explicit emphasis on cooperation and getting along with others (Richardson, 1989).

In the 1940s, Blatz published two more major works, namely *Hostages to Peace: Parents and the Children of Democracy* in 1940 and *Understanding the Young Child* in 1944. These would be the last two books he published in his lifetime. *Hostages to Peace* was written in the format of correspondence between Blatz and a childhood friend and questions and answers regarding child rearing were framed in terms of children and war. However, the discourse was largely a recapitulation of Blatz's earlier work and one wonders why it was written in this format. There was no indication that these were actual letters; they were not photocopies nor were they typeset in the style of correspondence. The letters were not dated and there were no signatures. Everything seemed too patent—not the least because his friend ended the correspondence, which she was enjoying so much, exactly at the end of Blatz's theory. While the published version had an unauthentic air, an examination of manuscript copies further suggests that these were not actual letters. For example, there were many editorial marks for deleting paragraphs and inserting attachments. If the format was not a contrivance then the letters were at least edited in part. Although not a rhetorical device unique to Blatz, I found the letter format false and manipulative.

Blatz's second book of this period, *Understanding the Young Child*, began as a project to disseminate his ideas on nursery school theory and practice through England during the war (Wright, 1984). As such, it reiterated much of the previous material concerning the framework of the training program; in addition, however, Blatz outlined in some detail the guiding and unifying principles of his security theory. This book was greeted with mixed reviews, ranging from extremely favorable, through commendable, cautiously positive, to downright negative. The advice literature of the 1940s was changing in perspective, and Blatz had attempted to do too much in this book. Not content to write yet another guidance manual (perhaps because his ideas had not really changed), he included abstract psychological principles and theories without the attendant evidence required by those who would be interested in these concepts. Child psychologists working in the period demanded strict methods of experimental enquiry for research that had moved away from practical guidance, so not only were Blatz's ideas somewhat outdated, his methods were not consistent with the emerging experimental psychology. Although following the discipline in terms of interest in education, mainstream developmental psychology was looking at the reductionist principles of learning while Blatz still maintained his more functionalist approach.

In the 1950s Blatz began working intensely on his theory of human security as the fundamental basis for human behaviour. He had already alluded to this topic and how it related to child training in earlier works, but now concentrated on its development until his death in 1964. The manuscript he was working on was posthumously published as a book in 1966, titled *Human Security: Some Reflections* and also appeared as a chapter titled, "The Theory of Human Security," in *Child Development: Selected Readings* in 1973. Security was the state of mind accompanying the willingness to accept the consequences of one's actions. The process was one of emerging from dependent security (where an agent takes responsibility for one's actions) into a state of insecurity (where one learns through persistence), until finally independent security (where one takes responsibility for one's own actions) is achieved.

In 1953 Blatz was awarded a major federal government grant to begin a 5-year project on the development of mental health. The goal was to investigate aspects of child development in order to discover those qualities which were conducive to mental health. The definition of a mentally healthy person was:

> he who is facing life appropriately at his own level and in terms of his peculiar qualities, and accepting the consequences of so doing.

Thus, mental health and security theory had become aligned in a broad research orientation. While this work resembled the praxis of the scientific "Developmental Psychology" dominant at the time (Kessen, 1983a), it did not fully correspond to the mainstream approach. The researchers at the Institute gathered data on the child's rate of development in whatever area interested them, then put this together with the security status of the child in an effort to see how each of these factors related to overall mental health. Moreover, these researchers employed small groups of subjects which gave rise to statistical difficulties and they proceeded very slowly, spreading testing over long periods in an effort to maintain the mental hygiene of their subjects and themselves. However, the research did involve developing tests of security or mental health. This type of research was more in line with the psychometric orientation that had come to dominate developmental psychology in particular, and psychology in general. As well, the theoretical orientation was what defined developmental psychology as apart from child study, child science and child psychology.

One of the most significant books to come out of the security research was *Measuring Security in Personal Adjustment* (1958), by Mary Ainsworth and her husband Len Ainsworth. Mary Ainsworth is perhaps the most eminent psychologist associated with the Institute. In the preface the Ainsworths acknowledged that their work was an extension of a research project directed by Blatz and guided by his theory of personality development and the concept of security. The Ainsworths' findings plus the Institute research suggested a number of new aspects of security theory. Blatz incorporated the ideas of his research staff, sometimes grudgingly and after strenuous debate, into a revised theory of human security (Millichamp & Northway, 1977).

Originally, the only satisfactory goal of development was to achieve independent security. However, the research showed that dependent security played an important role. Thus, dependent security was subdivided into mature and immature categories, and the search for or acceptance of mature dependent security was considered necessary and fruitful. Mature dependent security reflected reciprocal relationships where both parties were mutually supportive. The secure person no longer had to take the world on alone. In the theory's final stage, immature dependent security was also given heightened status. Immature dependent security in infancy and early childhood was seen as the base from which both independent security and mature dependent security grew (see Flint, 1959). It was believed that young children who were secure developed trust in both themselves and others and this facilitated the growth of self confidence and the ability to make decisions. A child confident in the secure base of those around him could venture off and try new things. In this way the child could grow to establish mature relationships where he not only gave help, but accepted it in mutually supportive ways. Although in no way a child rearing manual, the theory espoused in this book conformed to the philosophy of child rearing advice in the literature of the time.

Despite the conformity to the philosophy of child rearing advice and the adoption of a research orientation somewhat aligned with the positivistic notions of science at the time, security theory never became part of mainstream developmental psychology. Blatz's colleagues, such as Betty Flint, Mary Wright, Mary Northway, and Mary Ainsworth attributed its demise to a number of Blatz's idiosyncratic publication beliefs. Blatz had contempt for the stylistic practices of the mainstream journals and so most of his publications were in the Institute's in-house journal, *The Bulletin*, which served to limit the exposure to academia of his more theoretical work on security theory. Blatz was not one to make reference to other authors in his scholarly pieces. Ainsworth (1969) suggested that the lack of citations and integration of other sources was one of the causes of security theory's obscurity and that the in-house publications and devoted followers helped give the impression that "the whole security theory became a private language, and it just simply didn't communicate itself to anyone else who wasn't reared in the tradition."

While these idiosyncratic reasons may in part justify the limited appreciation for security theory, there were some experimental difficulties that may have contributed more fundamentally. For example, Ainsworth and Ainsworth (1958) claimed that while the tests for measuring security were ready for use for screening purposes, they could only be used in situations in which the group to be tested was large enough to provide its own norms. Moreover, because the tests required cooperation and frankness on the part of the subjects, the results could be compromised by anyone motivated to be or not be selected for whatever situation the screening was for. Concomitant with the subjective nature of the tests, validity was difficult to determine. The Ainsworths called for further revision of the battery of tests, but did not pursue this programme. The demand for statistical verification and objective tests had increased significantly within the discipline of scientific psychology: security theory did not satisfy these requirements, which likely served to obscure the potential of, and place for, it in academic psychology.

Clearly William Blatz had made several contributions to ideas on child rearing and preschool education. He had maintained radical views on punishment, rewards, competition, honesty, and sex. Blatz argued that strict obedience was counter to the goals of democracy. People, including children, were required to think critically about authority. Children should be given freedom of choice to learn through experience and accept consequences. One's mental health depended on one's ability to make decisions and cope with failures by turning them into learning experiences. Blatz also attacked mother love both in the early stages of the history of developmental psychology when that line was fashionable, and after when maturation theories suggested affectionate caring. Blatz argued that consistent, if boring, training would make the infant feel secure and from that point the infant could reach out beyond the parent for excitement and learning. Thus, he combined the strict habit training of the 1920s and 1930s with the security and attachment theories of the 1940s and 1950s.

Despite this impressive list, Blatz was sorely neglected in histories of developmental psychology. Yet his eminence cannot be denied. At the time of his death, the obituaries were respectful and full of praise for his innovations and iconoclastic personality. The resolution of the Senate of the University of Toronto contained these words:

> Dr. Blatz started on a forty-year career which was to bring him international recognition as lecturer, author, child-expert, parent-educator—and general all-round disturber of the intellectual peace. To suggest that Dr. Blatz was a controversial public figure is to be guilty of understatement.

Blatz's controversial nature was summed up by Max Braithwaite, a magazine journalist, who had written several articles on the school and Blatz. He said that Blatz was "probably the cause of as many letters to the editors as any other man in the country."

To be sure, Blatz's reputation was not confined to Canada. In fact, Braithwaite (1946) claimed that Blatz's fame was far greater in the United States than in his own country. Not only did Blatz lecture widely in the United States, but the press releases that mentioned his talks contained such characterizations as: "Dr. Blatz, one of the North American continents' most outstanding educators and child welfare experts." While he was often called "well-known," "eminent," or "an authority" in press clippings, one American newspaper went as far as to call him, "one of the greatest psychologists in America."

Nonetheless, Blatz's ideas and his work at the Institute did not conform to the scientism of the emerging developmental psychology. In the late 1960s the president's council of the University of Toronto suggested that while Blatz's emphasis upon education, counseling, and parent participation had kept the programme unique, it had also served to keep the Institute outside the mainstream of "scientific" research in human development. Blatz's continued commitment to questions of practice in child rearing could not satisfy the positivist rhetoric of objective and value-free research that came to define scientific developmental psychology. Educating parents and bringing them into the research environment as participants rather than subjects ran counter to the ideal of uncovering fundamental truths uncompromised by subjectivity and practical relevance to a particular group.

Blatz was both a product of and alien to the discipline of developmental psychology. Clearly, he was well-established in the field early in its development and seemed to develop along with it. Blatz employed nontrained observers in studies for determining child training practices for home and nursery school. This was in 1925 when he began directing the St. George's School for Child Study and might be said to be his child study period. With the opportunity in 1935 to organize the 24-hour-a-day training and education of the Dionne sisters, he entered his period of child science. Here he trained observers to watch for specific behaviors guided by specific research questions. His period of child psychology may be seen in the years 1938-1949. Here he was involved in studies of the nursery school system, although these educational investigations were not along the reductionist lines of the rest of the discipline. Last, he became a developmental psychologist around 1949 when he began a concerted effort to develop his security theory as an all-encompassing guiding principle organizing human behavior.

Despite the parallel developments, Blatz's ideas, while personally developing, began to run counter to the positivistic, scientific orientation of the discipline. The alienation of Blatz from the emerging trends of developmental psychology was partly due to the fact that Blatz's psychology always maintained its functionalist and mental hygiene roots. Both of these perspectives lost favour by the middle of the twentieth century. It would have been an enormous task for Blatz to have discarded these foundational perspectives of his life's work. Nor would it have been advisable. Blatz identified himself with the practical orientation and social responsibility mandated by these perspectives. He was suspicious of statistical manipulation, basic research without purpose, and the specialized practices, particularly publication rituals, of the new science. Even in his closest approximation to the new discipline, his security theory, he remained consistent with his functionalist, mental hygienist approach. Blatz's security theory rested on the assumption that one had the ability to act with respect to the knowledge of the consequences of one's actions and to consciously accept these consequences. The standards of judgment came from the course of experience that gave rise to the demand for them. The mentally healthy person was able to interact with his environment, both learning from it and changing it in the course of the interaction. In a 1959 interview with June Callwood, Blatz was asked: "What is the most critical time of a child's development?" Blatz replied promptly: "The present." She wrote that he savored his answer with evident satisfaction. He said: "That's rather good, I'm rather proud of that."[6] Despite the emerging scientism in the discipline, Blatz, like the functionalist educational principles he adopted, was child-centred rather than subject-centred.

Blatz contributed a great deal to theory and practice in developmental psychology in both Canada and the United States. His primarily functionalist and mental hygienist ideas may even reappear in the growing re-emergence of functionalism in psychology in general (Buxton, 1985; Heidbreder, 1973; Wagner & Owen, 1992) and developmental psychology in particular (Ferrara, 1992). If that should be the case, future histories may not neglect Blatz in the historical record. Blatz once said: "It is achieving, not achievement that matters. Life is fulfilling, not fulfillment —a complete life is never finished." This was true of his own life and development as a developmental psychologist. Perhaps it is true for a complete history.

NOTES

1. Histories of developmental psychology include, Anderson (1956), Bronfenbrenner (1963), Bronfenbrenner, Kessel, Kessen, & White, (1986), Cahan (1991), Cairns (1983), Dennis (1949), Dixon (1990), Dixon & Lerner (1992), Frank (1962), Hareven (1985), Kessen (1965, 1983b), Kuhn & Meacham (1983), Looft (1972), Morss (1990), Scarr (1986), Sears (1975), Senn (1975), Siegle & White (1982), Smuts (1985), and White (1986).
2. University of Toronto Archives, William Emet Blatz Clippings, Box 31, *Toronto Star*, May 16, 1934.
3. These five sisters were treated as a curiosity exhibit and as a single unit. The lack of privacy and individuality afforded to them by their birth caused them great unhappiness (Brough, 1963). In an effort to maintain their integrity, from here on they will be referred to by name or as the sisters rather than the "Dionne Quintuplets," the "Quints," or the "Quintuplets."
4. See, for example, reports from the staff at the Dionne nursery that discussed enormously difficult problems regarding the children early in the program such as refusing food, flinging their dinners around the room and running and sobbing. Thomas Fisher Rare Book Library, W. E. Blatz Coll., Box 36, Memoranda, May 1936 and November 1936.
5. See Barker (1951), Berton (1977), Hunt (1939), Nihmey & Foxman (1987).
6. Thomas Fisher Rare Book Library, W.E. Blatz Coll., Box 16, The Dr. William Blatzes by June Callwood, *Maclean's Magazine*, January 3, 1959, p. 32

REFERENCES

Ainsworth, M. D. S. (1969). Oral history. National Archives of Canada, Oral Histories, M. D. S. Ainsworth, RG I161, Volume 24, File: Ainsworth (Mary), (1969).

Ainsworth, M. D., & Ainsworth, L. H. (1958). *Measuring security in personal adjustment*. Toronto: University of Toronto Press.

Anderson, J. E. (1956). Child development: An historical perspective. *Child Development*, 27, 181–96.

Babarik, P. (1970). The buried Canadian roots of community psychology. *Journal of Community Psychology*, 7, 362–367.

Barker, L. (1951). *The truth about the Dionne quins*. Great Britain: Hutchinson & Co.

Beales, R. W., Jr. (1985). The child in seventeenth-century America. In J. M. Hawes & N. R. Hiner (Eds.), *American childhood: A research guide and historical guidebook* (pp. 15–56). Westport, CT: Greenwood Press.

Beales, R. W., Jr. (1991). The preindustrial family (1600–1815). In J. M. Hawes & E. I. Nybakken (Eds.), *American families: A research guide and historical handbook* (pp. 35–82). Westport, CT: Greenwood Press.

Bernhardt, K. S. (1965). Dr. William E. Blatz. *The Canadian Psychologist, 6a*, 1–3.

Bernhardt, K. S., Fletcher, M. I., Johnson, F. L., Millichamp, D. A., & Northway, M. L. (1951). *Twenty-five years of child study.* Toronto: University of Toronto Press.

Berton, P. (1977). *The Dionne years: A thirties melodrama.* Toronto: McClelland & Stewart.

Blatz, W. E. (1919). Letter to P. Carson. Thomas Fisher Rare Book Library, W. E. Blatz Coll., Box 1.

Blatz, W. E. (1936a). The mental hygiene of infancy: Regularity. Pamphlet No. 2, Canadian National Committee for Mental Hygiene. Thomas Fisher Rare Book Library, W.E. Blatz Coll., Box 8.

Blatz, W. E. (1936b). The mental hygiene of the pre-school child: Routine. Pamphlet No. 3, Canadian National Committee for Mental Hygiene. Thomas Fisher Rare Book Library, W. E. Blatz Coll., Box 8.

Blatz, W. E. (1938). *The five sisters: A study of child psychology.* Toronto: McClelland & Stewart.

Blatz, W. E. (1940). *Hostages to peace: Parents and the children of democracy.* New York: Morrow.

Blatz, W. E. (1944). *Understanding the young child.* Toronto: Clark, Irwin.

Blatz, W. E. (1966). *Human security: Some reflections.* Toronto: University of Toronto Press.

Blatz, W. E. (1973). The theory of human security. In L. M. Brockman, J. H. Whitely, & J. P. Zubek (Eds.), *Child development: Selected readings* (pp. 150–166). Toronto: McClelland & Stewart.

Blatz, W. E. & Bott, H. (1928). *Parents and the pre-school child.* New York: Morrow.

Blatz, W. E., & Bott, H. (1930). *The management of young children.* New York: Morrow.

Blatz, W. E., Chant, N., Charles, M. W., Fletcher, M. I., Ford, N. H., Harris, A. L., McArthur, J. W., Mason, M., & Millichamp, D. A. (1937). *Collected studies on the Dionne quintuplets.* Toronto: University of Toronto Press.

Blatz, W. E., Millichamp, D., & Fletcher, M. (1935). *Nursery education: Theory and practice.* New York: Morrow.

Borstelmann, L. J. (1983). Children before psychology: Ideas about children from antiquity to the late 1800s. In P. H. Mussen (Ed.), *Handbook of Child Psychology* (4th ed.Vol. 1, pp. 1–40). New York: Wiley.

Brady, M. D. (1991). The new model middle-class family (1815-1930). In J. M. Hawes & E. I. Nybakken (Eds.), *American families: A research guide and historical handbook* (pp. 83–123). Westport, CT: Greenwood Press.

Braithwaite, M. (1946, April). Liberty Profile: Dr. W. E. Blatz. *Liberty Magazine, 20,* 14–15.

Bronfenbrenner, U. (1963). Developmental theory in transition. In H. W. Stevenson (Ed.), *Child psychology* (pp. 517–542). Chicago: National Society for the Study of Education.

Bronfenbrenner, U., Kessel, F., Kessen, W., & White, S. (1986). Toward a critical social history of developmental psychology: A propaedeutic discussion. *American Psychologist, 41,* 1218–1230.

Brough, J. (1963). *We were five.* New York: Signet Books.

Butterfield, H. (1963). *The Whig interpretation of history.* London: G. Bell & Sons.

Buxton, C. E. (1985). American functionalism. In *Points of view in the modern history of psychology* (pp. 113–140). Florida, US: Academic Press.

Cahan, E. D. (1991). Science, practice, and gender roles in early American child psychology. In F. S. Kessel, M. H. Bornstein, & A. J. Sameroff (Eds.), *Contemporary constructions of the child: Essays in honor of William Kessen* (pp. 225–249). Mahwah, NJ: Erlbaum.

Cairns, R. B. (1983). The emergence of developmental psychology. In P. H. Mussen (Ed.), *Handbook of Child Psychology* (4th ed., Vol. 1, pp. 41–102). New York: Wiley.

Carr, H. (1925). *Psychology: A study of mental activity*. New York: Longmans, Green & Co.

Coffman, H. C. (1936). *American foundations: A study of their role in the child welfare movement*. New York: SAGE.

Cravens, H. (1985). Child-saving in the age of professionalism, 1915-1930. In J. M. Hawes & N. R. Hiner (Eds.), *American childhood: A research guide and historical guidebook* (pp. 415–88). Westport, CT: Greenwood Press.

Danziger, K. (1984). Towards a conceptual framework for a critical history of psychology. In H. Carpintero & J. M. Peiro (Eds.), *Psychology in its historical context: Essays in honour of Prof. Josef Brozek* (pp. 99–107). Valencia, Spain: Monografias de la Revista de Historica de la Psicologia.

Danziger, K. (1990). *Constructing the subject*. Cambridge, MA: Cambridge University Press.

Dennis, W. (1949). Historical beginnings of child psychology. *Psychological Bulletin, 46*, 224–235.

Dewey, J. (1896). The reflex arc concept in psychology. *Psychological Review, 3*, 357–370.

Dewey, J. (1897). My pedagogic creed. In R. D. Archambault (Ed.). *John Dewey on education: Selected writings* (pp. 427–39). New York: Random House, Inc

Dewey, J. (1902). The child and the curriculum. In P.W. Jackson (Ed.), *The school and society and the child and the curriculum* (pp. 179–209). Chicago: University of Chicago Press.

Dixon, R. A. (1990). History of research of human development. In R. M. Thomas (Ed.), *The Encyclopedia of Human Development and Education*. Toronto: Pergamon Press.

Dixon, R. A., & Lerner, R. M. (1992). A history of systems in developmental psychology. In M. H. Bornstein & M. E. Lamb (Eds.), *Developmental psychology: An advanced textbook* (3rd ed., pp. 3–58). Mahwah, NJ: Erlbaum.

Ferrara, R. A. (1992). Functionalism and the growth of developmental psychology. In D. A. Owens & M. Wagner (Eds.), *Progress in modern psychology: The legacy of American functionalism* (pp. 139–150). Westport, CT: Praeger.

Flint, B. M. (1959). *The security of infants*. Toronto: University of Toronto Press.

Fosdick, R. B. (1952). *The story of the Rockefeller Foundation*. New York: Harper Row.

Frank, L. K. (1962). The beginnings of child development and family life education in the twentieth century. *Merrill-Palmer Quarterly, 8*, 207–227.

Hareven, T. (1985). Historical changes in the family and the life course: Implications for child development. In A. B. Smuts & J. W. Hagen (Eds.), History and research in child development. *Monographs of the Society for Research in Child Development, 50*, 8–23.

Heidbreder, E. (1973). Functionalism. In M. Henle, J. Jaynes, & J. Sullivan (Eds.), *Historical conceptions of psychology* (pp. 276–285). New York: Springer.

Hunt, F. (1939). *The little doc.* New York: Simon & Schuster.

Kessen, W. (1965). *The child.* New York: Wiley

Kessen, W. (1983a). Preface. In P. H. Mussen (Ed.), *Handbook of child psychology 4th Edition* (Vol. 1, pp. viii–x). New York: Wiley.

Kessen, W. (1983b). The child and other cultural inventions. In F. S. Kessel & A. W. Siegel (Eds.), *The child and other cultural inventions* (pp. 26–39). New York: Praeger.

Kiefer, C. W. (1988). *The mantle of maturity: A history of ideas about character development.* New York: State University of New York Press.

Kuhn, D., & Meacham, J. A. (1983). Preface. In *On the development of developmental psychology* (pp. vii–xii). Switzerland: S. Karger.

Leahey, T. (1986). History without a past: Review of Kimble and Schlesinger (Eds.), "Topics in the history of psychology." *Contemporary Psychology, 31*, 648-649.

Lomax, E. M. R. (1978). *Science and patterns of child care.* San Francisco: W. H. Freeman.

Looft, W. R. (1972). The evolution of developmental psychology. *Human Development, 15*, 187–201.

Margolis, M. L. (1984). *Mothers and such: Views of American women and why they changed.* Berkeley, CA: University of California Press.

McDougall, W. (1960) *An introduction to social psychology.* New York: Methuen.

Mead, G. H. (1900). Suggestions toward a theory of the philosophical disciplines. *The Philosophical Review, 9*, 1-17. (Reprinted in Reck, A. J. (Ed.). (1964). *Selected writings: George Herbert Mead* (pp. 6-24). New York: The Bobbs-Merrill Company)

Mead, G. H. (1903). The definition of the psychical. *The Decennial Publications of the University of Chicago*, "First Series," *3*, 77-112. (Reprinted in Reck, A.J. (Ed.). (1964). *Selected writings: George Herbert Mead* (pp. 25–59). New York: The Bobbs-Merrill Company)

Mead, G. H. (1910). What social objects must psychology presuppose? *The Journal of Philosophy, Psychology, and Scientific Methods, 7*, 174-180. (Reprinted in Reck, A.J. (Ed.). (1964). *Selected writings: George Herbert Mead* (pp. 105–13). New York: The Bobbs-Merrill Company)

Mead, G. H. (1934). *Mind, self and society.* Chicago: University of Chicago Press.

Millichamp, D. A., & Northway, M. L. (1977). *Conversations at Caledon: Some reminiscences of the Blatz era.* Toronto: Brora Centre. Thomas Fisher Rare Book Library, M. L. Northway Coll., Box 44.

Morawski, J.G. (1982). Assessing psychology's moral heritage through our neglected utopias. *American Psychologist, 37*, 1082–1095.

Morss, J. R. (1990). *The biologising of childhood: Developmental psychology and the Darwinian myth.* United Kingdom: Erlbaum.

Nihmey, J., & Foxman, S. (1987). *Time of their lives: The Dionne tragedy.* Toronto: Seal Books.

Northway, M. L. (1973). Child study in Canada: A casual history. In L. M. Brock-man, J. H. Whitely, & J. P. Zubek (Eds.), *Child development: Selected readings* (pp. 11–46). Toronto: McClelland & Stewart.

Northway, M. L. (1975). *W. E. Blatz: His family and his farm.* Toronto: Brora Centre.

Oakley, A. (1986). Feminism and motherhood. In M. Richards & P. Light (Eds.), *Children of social worlds* (pp. 74–94). Cambridge, England: Polity Press.

Orlinsky, D. E. (1992). Not very simple, but overflowing: A historical perspective on general education at the University of Chicago. In J. J. MacAloon (Ed.), *General education in the social sciences: Centennial reflections on the College of the University of Chicago* (pp. 25–76). Chicago: The University of Chicago Press.

Pols, J. C. (1991). The school as laboratory: The development of psychology as a discipline in Toronto, 1915-1955. Unpublished masters thesis, York University.

Raymond, J. M. (1991). *The nursery world of Dr Blatz.* Toronto: University of Toronto Press.

Richardson, T. R. (1989). *The century of the child: The mental hygiene movement and social policy in the United States and Canada.* New York: State University of New York Press.

Rucker, D. (1969). *The Chicago pragmatists.* Minneapolis: University of Minnesota Press.

Scarr, S. (1986). Cultural lenses on mothers and children. In L. Friedrich-Cofer (Ed.), *Human nature and public policy: Scientific views of women, children, and families* (pp. 202-238). New York: Praeger.

Schlossman, S. (1985). Perils of popularization: The founding of *Parents' Magazine*. In A. B. Smuts & J. W. Hagen (Eds.), History and research in child development. *Monographs of the Society for Research in Child Development*, *50*, 65–77.

Schulz, C. B. (1985). Children and childhood in the eighteenth century. In J. M. Hawes & N. R. Hiner (Eds.), *American childhood: A research guide and historical guidebook* (pp. 57–109). Westport, CT: Greenwood Press.

Sears, R. R. (1975). Your ancients revisited: A history of child development. In E. M. Hetherington (Ed.), *Review of child development research* (pp. 1-73). Chicago: University of Chicago Press.

Senn, M.J.E. (1975). Insights on the child development movement in the United States. *Monographs of the Society for Research in Child Development*, *161*, 1–107.

Shore, M. (1987). *The science of social redemption: McGill, the Chicago School, and the origins of social research in Canada.* Toronto: University of Toronto Press.

Siegel, A. W., & White, S. H. (1982). The child study movement: Early growth and development of the symbolized child. In H. W. Reese (Ed.), *Advances in child development and behavior* (Vol. 17, pp. 223–825). New York: Academic Press.

Smith, R. (1988). Does the history of psychology have a subject? *History of the Human Sciences*, *1*, 147–177.

Smuts, A. B. (1985). The National Research Council Committee on Child Development and the founding of The Society for Research in Child Development, 1925–1933. In A. B. Smuts & J. W. Hagen (Eds.), History and research in child development. *Monographs of the Society for Research in Child Development*, *50*, 108–25.

Spock, B. (1946). *The common sense book of baby and child care*. Montreal: Pocket Books of Canada.

Stapleford, E. M. (1976). *History of the Day Nurseries Branch*. Toronto: Ministry of Community and Social Services.

Stocking, G. W., Jr. (1965). On the limits of "presentism" and "historicism" in the historiography of the behavioral sciences. *Journal of the History of the Behavioral Sciences, 1,* 211–217.

Strickland, C. E., & Ambrose, A. M. (1985). The baby boom, prosperity, and the changing worlds of children, 1945–1963. In J. M. Hawes & N. R. Hiner (Eds.), *American childhood: A research guide and historical guidebook* (pp. 533–585). Connecticut: Greenwood Press.

Strong-Boag, V. (1982). Intruders in the nursery: Childcare professionals reshape the years one to five, 1920-1940. In J. Parr (Ed.), *Childhood and family in Canadian History* (pp. 160-178). Toronto: McClelland & Stewart.

Sunley, R. (1955). Early nineteenth-century American literature on child rearing. In M. Mead & M. Wolfenstein (Eds.), *Childhood in contemporary culture* (pp. 150–167). Chicago: University of Chicago Press.

U.S Department of Labor, Children's Bureau. (1914). *Child Care*. Washington, DC: Author.

Vincent, C. E. (1951). Trends in infant care. *Child Development, 22,* 199-209.

Wagner, M., & Owens, D. A. (1992). Introduction: Modern psychology and early psychology. In *Progress in modern psychology: The legacy of American functionalism* (pp. 3–16). Wesport, CT: Praeger.

Wandersee, W. D. (1991). Families face the great depression (1930-1940). In J. M. Hawes & E. I. Nybakken (Eds.), *American families: A research guide and historical handbook* (pp. 125–56). Wesport, CT: Greenwood Press.

Watson, J. B. (1913). Psychology as the Behaviorist views it. *Psychological Review, 20,* 158–177.

Watson, J. B. (1919). *Psychology from the standpoint of a Behaviorist*. Philadelphia: Lippincott.

Watson, J. B. (1928). *Psychological care of infant and child*. New York: Norton.

Watson, J. B. (1929). Correspondence to William Morrow. March 1929, Scrapbook of book reviews. Thomas Fisher Rare Book Library, W.E. Blatz Coll., Box 15.

Weber, L. (1971). *The English infant school and informal education*. Princeton, NJ: Prentice-Hall.

Winestock, S. L. (1994). *William Emet Blatz: The development of a developmental psychologist*. Unpublished PhD Thesis, York University, North York, Ontario.

Weiss, N. P. (1985). Mother, the invention of necessity: Dr. Benjamin Spock's *Baby and Child Care*. In N. R. Hiner & J. M. Hawes (Eds.), *Growing up in America* (pp. 283–303). Chicago: University of Illinois Press.

White, S. H. (1986). Building human nature into social arrangements. In L. Friedrich-Cofer (Ed.), *Human nature and public policy: Scientific views of women, children, and families* (pp. 3–38). New York: Praeger.

Wishy, B. (1968). *The child and the republic*. Philadelphia: University of Pennsylvania Press.

Wolfenstein, M. (1953). Trends in infant care. *American Journal of Orthopsychiatry, 23,* 120–130.

Wolfenstein, M. (1955). Fun morality: An analysis of recent American child training literature. In M. Mead & M. Wolfenstein (Eds.), *Childhood in contemporary culture* (pp. 168–178). Chicago: University of Chicago Press.

Wright, M. J. (1964). William Emet Blatz (1895-1964). *O.P.A. Quarterly, 17,* 87-88.

Wright, M.J. (1974). Should we rediscover Blatz? *The Canadian Psychologist, 15,* 140-144.

Wright, M. J. (1983). The history of developmental psychology in Canada: Note 4. The saga of William Emet Blatz (1895–1964): Part I. Thomas Fisher Rare Book Library, W. E. Blatz Coll., Box 30.

Wright, M. J. (1984). The history of developmental psychology in Canada: Note 5. The saga of William Emet Blatz (1895-1964): Part II. Thomas Fisher Rare Book Library, W. E. Blatz Coll., Box 30.

Wright, M. J. (1985a). The history of developmental psychology in Canada: Note 6. The saga of William Emet Blatz (1895-1964): Part III. Thomas Fisher Rare Book Library, W. E. Blatz Coll., Box 30.

Wright, M. J. (1985b). The history of developmental psychology in Canada: Note 7. The saga of William Emet Blatz (1895-1964): Part IV. Thomas Fisher Rare Book Library, W. E. Blatz Coll., Box 30.

Wright, M. J. (1993). William Emet Blatz (1895–1964): *A Canadian Pioneer.* Paper presented at the annual convention of the American Psychological Association, Toronto.

Young, R. M. (1966). Scholarship and the history of the behavioral sciences. *History of Science, 5,* 1-51.

CHAPTER 6

CULTURAL PSYCHOLOGY AND ATTRIBUTIONAL CONCEPTIONS

Implications for Security Theory

Peter J. Gamlin

To understand Blatz and his frame of reference with respect to learning, it is necessary to understand two things. First, learning (Blatz would say "real" learning) is always conscious and adaptive (Wright, 1985). Man, he said, is a conscious striving being. "As long as he is alive he will be asking something every moment of his life" (Blatz, 1966, p. 21). In the functionalist tradition, Blatz viewed learning and development in terms of adaptation. Learning, for Blatz, always begins with a challenge, and this notion introduces the second and related aspect of the Blatzian framework. The individual is always conscious of the challenges presented through life experiences and can always *make choices between taking one course of action or another.* "The essence of consciousness was for Blatz *selection* ... the making of predictions about the possible outcomes of these choices. Selection was set in motion by motivation: the ebb and flow of the physiological appe-

The Secure Child: Timeless Lessons in Parenting and Childhood Education, pp. 97–114
Copyright © 2010 by Information Age Publishing

tites (hunger, thirst, elimination, rest, change, and sex).... Motivation was, he insisted, always conscious" (Wright, 1985, p. 13). Blatz did not believe in unconscious wishes. Indeed he said *"with us the emotions are the most highly conscious aspects of our lives"* (Blatz, 1951, p. 3). Since Blatz believed that the individual is conscious of his or her motivations and emotions, he gave particular emphasis to the role of personal decision-making based on accurate assessments of a situation. The keystone in the Blatzian framework is the individual's ability to make accurate predictions as to the possible outcome of his or her choices.

It is instructive to note the similarity between Blatz and Fritz Heider (1958) on this point. For Heider and attribution theory, it is important to make realistic attributions or explanations as to the antecedents and consequences of causes that "the person on the street" uses to explain events in life. For Heider, individuals are motivated to arrive at a realistic understanding of the causes that have led to different events in their personal domain. On this account, the individual's "latent goal is that of effective management of himself and the environment" (Kelley, 1971, p. 22). We can see in the Blatzian/Heiderian views a consensus that the individual is capable of learning from or interacting with the environment in a consciously determined manner. "Blatz stressed the active role of the learner as a change agent, emphasizing the person's perception of a situation as a primary determinant of action" (Wright, 1985, p. 13). There is one significant difference between Blatzian and Heiderian accounts. Attribution theory describes social learning, emphasizing external contingencies and global internal states; the Blatzian view is cognitive—developmental. "Blatz accounted for all behavioural change and development in terms of the growth of knowledge and understanding—and the resultant modifications which occurred in the way the child regarded a situation" (Wright, 1985, p. 13). The notion of *qualitative* change underscores Blatz's conception of the growth of knowledge and understanding. Although Blatz (unlike Piaget) did not describe "stages" of development, qualitative change is explicated in Blatzian theory in the relationship between learning and personality development.

LEARNING AND PERSONALITY DEVELOPMENT

In Blatz's account of personality development, three distinct and qualitatively different kinds of "security" relationships with caretakers are described. The end-state of security development for Blatz was "in large measure, the peace of mind which grew out of a person's faith in his or her ability to cope with consequences. It was this faith, he said, that rendered an individual capable of making decisions and accepting the insecurity that decision-making always entails" (Wright, 1985, p. 13). For Blatz, the first important step toward this goal was achieved when infants develop an immature secure dependence on their caretakers. Children require a predictable environment where they feel safe and protected. Secure children are most likely to be courageous and adventurous since they can always count on, and return to, these early dependent relationships. Consequently they are most able to embrace the insecurity implicit in exploring the unfamiliar. From this experiential backdrop emerges *independent security*. Children develop the skills and knowledge that enable them to be responsibly autonomous, able to accept the consequences of their actions. Responsibility is a fundamental concept in Blatz's account of personality development. In his writings *mature dependent security* is stressed. Blatz saw immature dependent security as being gradually supplanted by mature dependent security. Originally Blatz conceived an independent personality construct, but research began to show that mature dependent security complimented independent security behavior. "In mature dependent relations, the individuals had trust, faith, and confidence each other, did not shirk responsibility but shared it, and supported one another in a reciprocal fashion" (Wright, 1985, p. 13). By the 1950s, the results of security research revealed that in young adults independent security and mature dependent security were correlated, suggesting that they had a common origin (Ainsworth & Ainsworth, 1958). The underlying assumption which would weld independent and dependent security was that there were areas where complete independence was not possible and responsibility must be shared. If it was not shared, then insecurity might result in an unproductive return to an immature dependent state or the adoption of deputy agents to replace the parents as decision makers. Sharing responsibility in a mature dependent security relationship prevents this kind of regression and consequent rationalization of behavior. Dependent and independent security can be viewed as two sides of a coin. They develop in balance together. One is able to maintain a caring, responsible relationship with others that will endure over time, while remaining independent in important respects. For this reason, Blatz and his colleagues

> concluded that young children who are secure develop trust in both themselves and others and this facilitates the growth, not only of self confidence but of confidence in others, a willingness to accept help as well as give it and the ability to relate to peers in mutually supportive ways. (Wright, 1985, p. 14)

Security theory can be used to identify *qualitatively* different learning strategy outcomes. Central to the Blatzian view of learning is the interaction between person and situation that dictates what is experienced and subsequently understood.

According to Blatz, it is the child who must initiate the action if "real" learning is to occur. "The *appetite of change* demands satisfaction in the form of new perceptual or ideational imaginative content of consciousness" (Blatz, 1944, p. 100). The child seeks novelty and variety, and attention stems from the appetite for change. Blatz's overall goal was to help children "learn how to learn," to set the stage for children to become discoverers (curious exploratory), constructive (planful and purposeful), creative, (flexible, innovative problem solvers) and considered (reflective). This objective was achieved through the development of personality and appropriate *opportunities* for learning to occur.

From the foregoing analysis, we have seen that Blatz was convinced that there was a relationship between feelings of security, the assumption of responsibility, and the way we learn. Blatz asserted:

> Security may be defined as the state of consciousness which accompanies willingness to accept the consequences of one's own decisions and actions. Only thus can an individual feel comfortably adjusted to his environment. This concept of security is dynamic, for man's adjustment can never become static. Any attempt on the part of the individual to maintain the status quo is ineffective, because life is a continuous process and man's security is based on the future, not on the present nor on the past. It is unfortunate that in our language there is no term to distinguish security as here described from the common meaning of security which implies safety. Safety is the antithesis of this type of security. An individual seeks to be secure and must continue his search, for as soon as he stops he becomes insecure. (Blatz, 1944, p. 165)

For Blatz, the willingness to accept the consequences of one's own decisions and actions can be achieved only when individuals move from dependency on others, to more autonomous personal decision-making and action. This kind of autonomy will open the possibility for what Blatz called "independent security":

> Independent security can be attained only in one way—by the acquisition of a skill through learning. Whenever an individual is presented with a situation for which he is inadequately prepared, or whenever he is striving for something and finds that his preparation is inadequate, he must make one of two choices—he must either retreat or attack. This situation is emotionally charged, but there is more than the emotional content in such situations. The individual must, if he is to attack, emerge from the state of dependent security and accept the state of insecurity. This attack, of course, will result in learning. The degree of skill which he acquires will depend upon his persistence. But once having learned, he will meet this situation in

the future with assurance, because now he possesses a behaviour pattern which makes it possible for him to adapt himself satisfactorily. Furthermore, he has become familiar with the consequences of his advance and is willing to face them. (Blatz, 1944, p. 167)

Blatz continues:

> The individual, through his efforts, learns that satisfaction results from overcoming the apprehension and anxiety experienced when insecure, and that he may reach a state of independent security through learning. He develops a habit of accepting *insecurity* as the only way towards independent security. Having once experienced independent security, he learns that he may continue this state only if he continues to learn more and more, because learning itself exposes the need for further learning. (Blatz, 1944, p. 167)

Blatz observed that most individuals are not willing to make the effort toward becoming independently secure. In large part this is so because, especially in early childhood, there are few occasions where independent action leads to consequences that must be faced and "owned" by the child. The child must frequently say "I did this, and this is what happened. Do I want this to happen?" The child must experience the consequences of actions:

> Responsibility may be defined as the habit of choosing, and accepting the consequences of the choice of behaviour. Whenever a child is considered to have developed or acquired sufficient experiences in anticipating the consequences of his acts, he should be expected to accept these consequences. If this behaviour shows that he *cannot* do so, then the opportunity for choice should be deliberately withdrawn. If, on the other hand, his behaviour is interpreted as an *unwillingness* to accept the consequences, then responsibility should not be withdrawn. (Blatz, 1944, pp. 187-188)

For example, occasions for eating can become learning experiences. Very young children, as Blatz observes, cannot be expected to decide *when* to eat or *what* to eat. "These responsibilities rest with the parent, and cannot be delegated to the child." Children, however, may choose *whether* or not they will eat on any particular occasion—but then they must live with the consequences. Furthermore, as children develop and acquire more autonomy and feelings of independent security, the when and what of eating must be open to personal decision-making and consequent responsibility for those decisions.

For parents watching the child "testing the limits" in this kind of situation, the temptation is to step in either "to lay down the law" or to "help." However, when parents attempt to shorten the process, they are taking away the child's opportunity to experience the consequences of actions. By intervening they take away any responsibility the child might have acquired for those actions. The parents become what Blatz called *deputy agents*. The child becomes dependent on these agents, and the only security the child knows is dependent security. The deputy agent accepts the consequences of the child's actions rather than the child.

Because accepting consequences is such a difficult exercise, children may adopt deputy agents rather than making an effort toward independent security through learning. This is

> the commonest technique used by the individual for avoiding the immediate effort necessary to achieve independent security. If he uses a deputy agent only as a temporary expedient which he recognizes as such, no harm arises; but if he persists in using it to solve the same problem again and again, then it becomes a mentally unhealthy device. (Blatz, 1944, p. 170)

The use of deputy agents to reduce insecurity has a potential negative consequence for the entire life span. Nevertheless, Blatz believed that a certain degree of *immature* dependent security and reliance on deputy agents was a necessary precursor to independent security and the acceptance of personal responsibility. Healthy development is impossible when the child is in a complete state of insecurity. Immature dependent security is the first step away from insecurity, and in that sense it paves the way for independent security. It is important to remember that for Blatz independent security is always accompanied by anxiety, because the individual never knows *exactly* what consequence to expect or whether the preparation is adequate. The child develops "a habit of accepting *insecurity* as the only way toward independent security." To deal with this kind of insecurity, the individual must have already experienced feelings of security, even though they may have been tied to the actions of deputy agents. Without an adequate foundation of dependent security, the individual would never be able to take the risks associated with taking independent and responsible action. But once the risk has been taken and the individual begins to learn,

> he will meet this situation in the future with assurance, because now he possesses a behaviour pattern which makes it possible for him to adapt himself satisfactorily. Furthermore, he has become familiar with the consequences of his advances and is willing to face them. (Blatz, 1944, p. 193)

The child needs to experience consistency and the gradual relaxation of deputy agent expectations. The child is given the opportunity to make independent choices and to accept the consequences of these choices. Parental behavior is particularly important because the child must be reassured that this kind of autonomy is appropriate and valued. As mature dependent development begins to supplant immature dependent behavior, the individual achieves a reciprocal relationship with others and a state of independent security, learning to handle the consequence of taking risks. Additionally, the individual understands "that he may continue in this state only if he continues to learn more and more, because learning itself exposes the need for further learning."

BLATZIAN MENTAL HEALTH CONSTRUCTS AND LEARNING

The Blatzian framework describes how children become self-reliant in meeting societal demands. The individual with this self confidence exudes an attitude of "yes I can," "I'll try again," and "let me at it," and mentally healthy individuals continue to adapt successfully throughout their life-span. These individuals are independent enough to tolerate the anxieties of new learning. Individuals are able to embrace *insecurity* as the only route to new learning. While these individuals may experience vulnerability in the learning process, they also become stronger in the knowledge that it was successful. Healthy individuals seem to be able to imagine and to construct a *vision* of what is possible for them as well as to take responsibility for moving toward it (see Gamlin & Fleming, 1985, chapter 7). Healthy individuals do not attempt to realize their vision independently. They are able to relate to others in an intimacy that in the language of Eric Berne, is "game free." They do not "throw expectancies at one another" (Fritz Perls). This is what Blatz described as mature dependent behavior. Healthy individuals experience interpersonal relations in the same way they learn "what is possible." These individuals are open to others and make themselves vulnerable to criticism. They become stronger in the realization that any response they receive, critical or not, is a response to a "cards on the table," authentic and intimate "me." A negative response is at least a response to the authentic "me" and not a response to the "me" that may have been thrown up (like a mask) to appease another person's expectations.

Healthy individuals offer no excuses for the self that is totally exposed in an intimate relationship. This is because these individuals are learning continuously about the self as they continue to learn other things. In this context, healthy individuals focus on what is possible (a personal best self) and not on the frozen snapshot of another person's perceptions.

Blatz emphasized the importance of development in the acquisition of these health skills. Children must experience both immature and mature dependency states before they are able to accept responsibility for their actions and before they are able to experience the autonomy associated with being independently secure. As children become more independent and more able to achieve reciprocal relationships with others, they are more able to tolerate the feelings of insecurity that are a necessary consequence of exploring the unfamiliar. These individuals are learning to trust in the future, to understand the expression "the universe unfolds as it should," not in the fatalistic sense but rather in the sense of trusting in themselves to work towards their *vision* of what is possible.

SUMMARY

The Blatzian view of learning is intimately related to personality development. Central to this development is the individual's increasing awareness (consciousness) of behavioral alternatives and their implications (consequences) for ensuring that a harmonious (reciprocal) relationship is sustained in the interaction (balance) of mature dependency and independent security states.

Qualitatively different learning strategies emerge as a function of personality development. The strategy that produces the most learning motivation is a product of both mature dependency and independent security states. The creative, curious, planful problem solver is one who has the most motivation to learn. This individual is responsibly self-reliant, explores with an open mind, makes the most of any opportunity to learn, yet is responsive to societal demands. Above all, this individual "consciously" interacts with his or her environment with full understanding of the causes and effects. These individuals are therefore able to bring about changes adaptive not only for themselves but for society as a whole.

A last point with respect to the Blatzian framework relates to cognitive development. I want to stress that the motivation to learn is always situation dependent. For example, when I refer to a person as immaturely dependent or securely independent, I am making a relative, not an absolute statement. My observations of that individual must necessarily include only a limited number of situations and are based on that individual's *modal response pattern* (see Lerner, 1976, p. 136; Lerner, 1986, pp. 221-225). In other words, there may be situations when an independently secure learner will behave in an immaturely dependent manner and vice versa. Nevertheless, modal response patterns have a good predictive validity, enabling one to identify individuals who have different motivational states and different learning styles. Consequently, learning outcomes are different for these individuals as well.

The practical implications of this view are that one assumes there is a "better" motivational state or a "better" cluster of mental health variables. As a practitioner, one wants to provide the opportunity for individuals to modify their action to move closer to a "better," more adaptive, repertoire of behaviors. One does not simply "write an individual off" as having maladaptive response patterns.

Although a hierarchy of development types is implicit, there are no sharp edges bordering each type. Performance reflects a "modal response pattern." In the Blatzian framework, it is possible to have a dynamic exchange or dialectic between types. It is precisely by helping individuals understand the nature of their immature dependencies that "movement" towards mature dependent and independent security states is possible. In Vygotskian terms, one would observe the movement of an individual's modal response patterns in a "zone of proximal development."

Dweck and Elliott (1983) raise an important issue—namely, the relationship between motivation and intelligence; indeed the more profound problem is how to characterize "intelligence." At this point, I should reiterate one of Forsterling's (1986) comments: that

> it is "realistic" to take stock of one's ability level, recognize one's limitations, and "give-up," at least with respect to working toward a particular goal ... lack-of-ability attributions are, under certain circumstances, quite realistic and could therefore lead to "desirable" consequences.... It generally appears to be quite functional for individuals to know when they have failed because of limited abilities. The knowledge of their limitations could help the individuals to avoid dangerous situations they would not be able to cope with and, as a consequence, could be helpful for survival. In addition, the individual's realization that he or she has failed to attain an important goal because of low ability could motivate the individual to seek the help of others and as a consequence, attain the goal after all. (p. 278)

Clearly, there are situations where giving up, getting angry, and so on may be appropriate. "Realistic" appraisals may, *on the surface*, appear to be maladaptive, but this is not necessarily the case. We must have a substantial understanding of how the *child* perceives or experiences the situation (see de Charms, 1983). From a Blatzian perspective, every new situation is threatening since every new situation produces a certain degree of anxiety. For Blatz, children experience situations differently as a function of their security. They are able to embrace the insecurity that accompanies learning something new or they have difficulty with this. "Intelligent" behavior on this account is only possible when optimum levels of security are present. Maladaptive motivational patterns emerge when the child relies upon deputy agents in *immature* dependency relationships. Adaptive motivational patterns emerge in an atmosphere of *mature* dependency relationships that foster independent security. Interestingly, both the personality profiles and the learning strategies associated with these profiles are congruent with the views proposed by Dweck and Elliott (1983) and

Dweck (1986)—intelligence is malleable (the incremental theory). One is tempted to speculate upon the relationship between the child's feelings of security and the emergence of these different theories of "intelligence." Discussions about the modifiability of motivational patterns must take into account both cognitive developmental and social cognition variables. "Intelligent" appraisals of situations must surely involve variables like feelings of security, which in turn must influence the kinds of goals individuals set for themselves, including their explanations for success and failure. Behavior may appear to be maladaptive yet may turn out to be "realistic" when these variables are taken into account. Nevertheless, "realistic" behavior may not turn out to be particularly "intelligent." Put another way, these "realistic" behaviors may not be "best" for the individual. I concur with Dweck and Elliott's view that every individual is potentially able to acquire more adaptive motivational patterns. I would add that they also are able to modify their dependency on others and their feelings of security.

Setting or situation is particularly important in that early attempts to modify one's behavior must find support in the immediate environment. The setting must be one where individuals can examine the kinds of relationships they have with others, particularly the degree to which they are able to act independently. As well, they must be able to think about their ability and what that means for their own learning and expectations for personal accomplishment. Modal response patterns are just that—modal. Motivational patterns can be modified but opportunities must be available for this to occur.

Motivational patterns are modifiable as a function of how one accounts for success and failure, the kinds of beliefs one has about one's intelligence, and the particular setting where learning occurs. Attributions, goals, and experience/perception relate to motivational variables. The common thread running through each of the frameworks discussed is that when children learn, they seek change. They are change agents. Furthermore, children are conscious and intentional as they go about the learning process. They usually have clear ideas about what they want to achieve (see Gamlin, 1978). There is usually a functional, adaptive consequence to strategic learning: children develop realistic attributions to account for success and failure and they are able to set realistic goals which they monitor against their current view of their own "personal best" behavior. And with this dynamic, children become personally responsible for their learning and are able to *value* the goals that others set for them.

The down-side of this analysis is that some children resist acquiring the strong version of this motivational pattern. A possible reason may be found in the children's early experience. These children may not have experienced an environment that was sufficiently challenging to require initiative. The importance of parental involvement to establish the parameters is obvious. The good news is that even "resistant" children have been able to modify their motivational patterns when the setting has been favorable.

Blatz anticipated many of these conceptions. In particular, his stress on the child as change agent and his insistence that children must learn how to depend on themselves in predictable environments to develop learning goals are either implied or explicitly stated in his theoretical perspectives. Blatz also provided a compelling discussion about how children become reciprocally responsible as a consequence of motivational pattern and learning style. Blatzian conceptions about learning how to learn have significant implications for the role of consciousness in learning. Understanding how consciousness and learning are related clarifies questions concerning whether intelligence can be modified.

CONSCIOUSNESS AND LEARNING

I have suggested (along with Dweck & Elliott, 1983) that motivation and "intelligence" are inextricable. I have also made a distinction between "realistic" explanations of causal events and more "intelligent" ones. I have suggested that more "intelligent" attributions are achievable by modifying one's beliefs about learning by becoming more strategic or more conscious of alternatives and more responsive to learning situations. For example, individuals who believe they have lower ability (when in fact they do) can learn to tackle challenging situations—perhaps with the help of others—which will modify what they believe individuals with lower ability can do. They come to understand that they are capable of "acting smarter," and they come to a new understanding of their own "personal best." This position is consonant with the "incremental" theory of intelligence proposed by Dweck and Elliott (1983) which has the goal of learning (for the sake of learning) as a primary objective. It is also consonant with Blatz's description of the independently secure learner. Every individual, regardless of perceived/experienced ability level, is able to learn how to "act smarter" or become more conscious of his or her learning. Implicit in Blatz's suggestions for optimal child/adult interactions in learning is the requirement that the child must be coached to become more responsible and intentional in his or her learning (see Wright, 1985). In order to better understand how "greater" consciousness-intentionality is a prerequisite to "acting smarter," it is necessary to consider how the Vygotskian perspective on consciousness and learning is compatible with Blatzian conceptions.

VYGOTSKY

I have found the Vygotskian framework to be particularly useful in respect to *modifiability* of "intelligence" notions, because Vygotsky discussed how individuals were capable of *greater* consciousness and "acting smarter." To introduce his reader to an understanding of "modifiability," Vygotsky (1978) asks us to consider 2 children who are both 10 years old chronologically but only 8 years old in terms of mental development. He suggests that these children are able to deal with tasks "up to the degree of difficulty that has been standardized for the 8 year old level." But he goes on to question whether these children have the same *potential* to learn. Suppose that we help these children understand the nature of the problems that they could not solve. Suppose with instruction one of these children can go on to solve problems at the 12-year old level while the other can only succeed at the 9-year old level. For Vygotsky, this result means that they are not mentally the same age. Vygotsky goes on to make this often quoted assertion:

> This difference between twelve and eight, or between nine and eight, is what we call the zone of proximal development. It is the distance between the actual developmental level as determined by independent problem solving and the level of potential development as determined through problem solving under adult guidance or in collaboration with more capable peers. (pp. 85-86)

Vygotsky was adamant that the phenomenon of consciousness could not be understood or explained by consciousness. This would be tautological. One can not say, for example, that "I have come to higher ground or greater consciousness because being conscious enables me to do so." This would be tantamount to saying, as one youngster put it,—"Well, we are not cows" (see Davydov & Radzikhovskii, 1985; Zinchenko, 1985; Wertsch & Stone, 1985; and Kozulin, 1986 on this point).

For Vygotsky, "activity" was the explanatory concept for consciousness (see Wertsch, 1981; and especially Kozulin, 1986 for an historical-theoretical analysis of the concept of activity in Soviet psychology). Activity was the generator of consciousness: building consciousness *from the outside* through the relations with others. This is why Vygotsky's "Zone of Proximal Development" is so important. The kinds of activities that occur in transactions with others are exactly those activities that lead children on in their development and produce greater consciousness, helping these individuals to greater intellectual control.

I began by suggesting that consciousness and learning are related and that achieving "greater consciousness" is essential to "getting smarter." I proceeded to discuss "consciousness" from a Vygotskian perspective because one of the key considerations in the "Zone" is the modifiability of consciousness which is essentially modifying "intelligence." The semiotic activities of the child, particularly as they relate to the exteriorization of private ideas for others, are essential for progress. The motivational patterns of the child are important here because they impact upon strategic, intentional learning which begins with transactions between a knowledgeable other and the child around the given and the new. Indeed, the interaction in itself will influence the child's beliefs about what it takes to learn something new. Vygotsky was of a similar view:

> Thought is not begotten by thought; it is engendered by motivation, i.e., by our desires and needs, our interests and emotions. Behind every thought there is an affective-volitional tendency, which holds the answer to the last "why" in the analysis of thinking.... To understand another's speech, it is not sufficient to understand his words—we must understand his thought. But even that is not enough—we must know its motivation. No psychological analysis of an utterance is complete until that plane is reached. (Vygotsky, 1934/1986, pp. 252-253)

We gain some additional insight into motivational considerations as we reconsider the Blatzian perspective on consciousness and learning.

BLATZ ON CONSCIOUSNESS AND LEARNING

Blatz was convinced that "man ... is a striving animal, continuously seeking a *goal*" (Blatz, 1966, p. 330). He believed that "There must be an overriding goal that consolidates human endeavour and gives it coherent meaning.... Fortunately there is a phenomenon which describes such an overriding goal.... This is the sequential nature of moments of consciousness" (p. 30). The sequential nature of consciousness was important for Blatz because it enables us to anticipate the next moment, which is a kind of "projection into the future.... This projection into the future provided a background for early enlargement of perception, a broadening of experience, *the basis of learning*" (p. 30, emphasis added). For Blatz, the ability to anticipate what will come to pass makes it possible for individuals to decide what will happen next. "The phenomenon of selection is the most significant aspect of security theory, since selection is the basis for making decisions" (p. 27). In Blatz's view, the individual is able to *consciously* select and/or anticipate his or her next actions and the individual is ultimately *responsible* for these actions. "The most important aspect of consciousness is that it is the basis for the reaction of the individual to his environment"

(p. 25). It is precisely the potential for accepting the consequences of one's behavior that is the keystone in Blatzian theory.

Blatz tended to reify consciousness. In so doing, he committed the tautological error described by Vygotsky, using as explanatory principle the very phenomenon that was the subject of his investigations. Given the nature of Blatzian theory, he seems to have chosen this position.

Clearly, Blatz concretized consciousness. For him it was not necessary to define consciousness, "to define what is immediately known. If you are conscious, that is it" (Blatz, 1966, p. 17). This is a position quite similar to that of Fritz Heider and forms the basis for the development of attributional conceptions. Unfortunately for Blatz, it meant the quasi-alienation of his cognitive-developmental theory from consciousness. I suspect that this is why he is able to say in his last volume "the chapter on consciousness forms the basis of the subsequent argument. However, it can be skipped without interfering too much with an understanding of the theory" (p. 13). But clearly Blatz would want his theory to underscore his conviction that the phenomenon of consciousness "is the most fabulous of all the universe may boast" (p. 17). In other words, Blatz seemed not to realize that the subject of his investigations was indeed the phenomenon of consciousness, and hence he failed to notice the tautology.

Blatz correctly saw the implications of his theory for the development of mental health, which seemed to be the development of functionally adaptive responses to ever-changing real world experiences. This is why attitudes about learning were such an integral part of his theory. Personal responsibility in its mature dependency form was a *necessary* consequence of healthy development. He failed to see the implications of his theory for cognitive development. I do not think he fully appreciated the extent to which his theory could describe how individuals get to "higher ground." Had Blatz asked himself how it was that individuals acquire *knowledge* about their world and how individuals seem to have the potential for *qualitatively* different interpretations of their experience and knowledge, he might have come to a fuller appreciation of his theory. And, of course, had he had recourse to the Vygotskian perspective, or had access to contemporary criticisms of this perspective, he might have realized that for each of his personality-learning constructs—the immature-dependent, mature-dependent, mature-independent learner—he was essentially suggesting that "consciousness" could have different functions. As I pointed out, in Blatz's view, individuals have qualitatively different kinds of attitudes about learning associated with each of their learning constructs. To put it succinctly, these different attitudes imply striving for different goals, making different selections/decisions, as well as deriving qualitatively different kinds of attributional conceptions to explain one's behavior. Consequently we can say that the various kinds of activities in these different learning styles imply consciousness(es) with different functions. But because Blatz reified consciousness, he was never able to exploit this aspect of his theory.

Here I can only sketch some possible directions that might prove useful for extending Blatzian theory. Ideally one would begin to develop underlying units of analysis (see Zinchenko, 1985) for Blatz's central concept: the ability to anticipate the future, to make accurate predictions as to possible outcomes for particular selections/decisions. I would suggest that some aspects of Blatz's "projection-to-the-future" notion is carried in Vygotsky's "Zone" construct. The implication for future development is integral to both conceptions. Implicit in the notion of future development is that individuals will progress "to higher ground," greater consciousness, and more control (intentional behavior). For both Vygotsky and Blatz, individuals are able to make use of the "scaffolding" introduced by knowledgeable others as they engage in an "inner dialogue" between the given and the new. Both Vygotsky and Blatz believed that behavior must be practiced and spontaneous before what Vygotsky called "good learning" could occur. "Good learning" is equivalent to "real learning" in the Blatzian sense since it always occurs further along the "Zone" and is oriented as a "projection to the future."

I believe the Blatzian perspective offers a good deal of potential for providing a different understanding of Vygotsky's "inner dialogue." Blatz emphasized the emotional status of the child, including the development of motivational patterns that impact upon the child's attitudes about learning and consequently learning activities. For example, the independently secure learner has learned to embrace the *insecurity* that always accompanies new learning:

> Any attempt on the part of the individual to maintain the status quo is ineffective, because life is a continuous process and man's security is based *on the future*, not on the present nor on the past. (Blatz, 1944, p. 165, emphasis added)

The individual, through his efforts, learns that satisfaction results from overcoming the apprehension and anxiety experienced when insecure and that a state of independent security may be achieved through learning. He develops a habit of *accepting insecurity* as the only way toward independent security. Having once experienced independent security, he learns that he may continue in this state only if he continues to learn more and more, because *learning itself exposes the need for further learning* (Blatz, 1944, p. 167, emphasis added).

We see in the Blatzian perspective an opportunity to understand the inner affective states of the individual as he or she engages in an "inner dialogue" about learning. Consequently we are better able to understand the nature of the kinds of "affective" impediments or facilitators that will accompany any conversation between novice and knowledgeable other around the given and the new. These comments are at best suggestive. However, I remain optimistic that further work in this area will yield results that will have significant implications for the more qualitative aspects of the given-new dialogue and more generally for the "scaffolding" metaphor as it is applied in "zone of proximal development."

CONCLUSION

I have established an alignment across several subdisciplines in psychology because this particular alignment demonstrates how important Blatz's theory has been for our understanding of the child. Blatz's contribution was his theory about the relationship between personality development and learning style. I believe that Blatzian theory contributes some much needed "depth," rooted in development, to Heiderian attributional conceptions, explaining the basis for one's successes and failures and the beliefs about one's "intelligence" and learning style.

Although attributional theory may be somewhat naive with respect to developmental notions, I have attempted to show that this perspective is particularly robust in explaining how situations have the potential for influencing attributional conceptions, beliefs, and learning goals. In particular, I have focused on attributional theory to show that "intelligence" can only be understood in relation to motivational patterns influenced by situation. Consequently one comes to an understanding that "intelligence" is *modifiable* as a function of motivational patterns, patterns that become established and modified in response to "setting" characteristics.

One is left with many nagging questions. Foremost among them concerns how Blatz's independently secure learners are "realistically" influenced by situation—occasionally stopped in their tracks as it were. Presumably, even these individuals experience the "going getting tough." Presumably that's when the "tough get going." And I think that is the answer. Not only are secure learners conscious of setting constraints but they take control by acting intentionally to find the most adaptive behavior possible *given the circumstances*. In my view, the most "intelligent" behavior is always exhibited by individuals who are the most conscious of problem and extenuating circumstances. And as I have attempted to show, consciousness is modifiable through learning. As Blatz (1944) put it: "he learns that he may continue in this state [independently secure] only if he continues to learn more and more, because learning itself exposes the need for further learning" (p. 167). I believe that this was Blatz's most profound message because it is saying that there must be conscious, intentional selection of a new activity before there will be any evidence of "real learning." Blatz did not go on to emphasize that *greater* consciousness and control was achievable through learning but he did say something similar. For Blatz, it was by learning how to learn that individuals could achieve the *greatest adaptation*, thereby engaging their ever changing environments successfully.

Although Blatz may not have seen the full implication of his theory for the phenomena of consciousness, he was nevertheless suggesting that "intelligence/consciousness," was *modifiable*. I have found the Vygotskian perspective to be particularly helpful in respect to "modifiability" notions. Vygotsky's insistence that consciousness be understood by applying a unit of analysis other than consciousness itself has helped me understand that Blatz's typology of learners essentially describes different kinds of learning "activities" which, in turn, yield qualitatively different kinds of mental activities, giving rise to different types of consciousness and consciousness functions. Furthermore, we see in Vygotsky's "zone of proximal development" opportunity for the emergence of greater consciousness or the attainment of "higher ground." I believe that with some extension of Blatzian theory, a somewhat comparable view can be derived, especially since Blatz insisted that every individual had the potential to become securely independent in mature dependency relationships. Central to this notion is the role played by significant others in learning environments that provide opportunities for individuals to learn, "exposing the need for further learning."

REFERENCES

Ainsworth, M. D. S., & Ainsworth, L. H. (1958). *Measuring security in personal adjustment*. Toronto: University of Toronto Press.

Blatz, W. E. (1944). *Understanding the young child*. Toronto: Clarke, Irwin & Co.

Blatz, W. E. (1951). Freud and the Institute. *The Institute of Child Study, 48*, 1-3.

Blatz, W. E. (1966). *Human security: Some reflections*. Toronto: University of Toronto Press.

Davydov, V. V., & Radzikhovskii, L. A. (1985). Intellectual origins of Vygotsky's semiotic analysis. In J. V. Wertsch (Ed.), *Culture, communication and cognition: Vygotskian perspectives* (pp. 335-365). New York: Cambridge University Press.

de Charms, R. (1983). Intrinsic motivation, peer tutoring and cooperative learning. In J. M. Levine & M. C. Wang (Eds.), *Teacher and student perceptions: Implications for learning* (pp. 391-398). Hillsdale, NJ: Erlbaum.

Dweck, C. S. (1986). Motivational processes affecting learning. *American Psychologist, 41*(10), 1040-1048.

Dweck, C. S., & Elliott, E. S. (1983). Achievement motivation. In P. Mussen & E. M. Hetherington (Eds.), *Handbook of child psychology* (pp. 643-692). New York: Wiley.

Forsterling, F. (1986). Attributional conceptions in clinical psychology. *American psychologist, 41*(3), 275-285.

Gamlin, P. J. (1978, April), *Writing as intention.* Paper presented at the meeting of the American Educational Research Association, Toronto. ERIC Document ED 162 299.

Gamlin, P. J., & Fleming D. R. (1985). *Responding to individual needs: A guide for teachers.* Toronto: Hogrefe.

Heider, F. (1958). *The psychology of interpersonal relations.* New York: Wiley.

Kelley, H. H. (1971). *Attributions in social interaction.* Morristown, NJ: General Learning Press.

Kozulin, A. (1986). The concept of activity in Soviet psychology. *American Psychologist, 41*(3), 264-274.

Lerner, R. M. (1976). *Concepts and theories of human development.* Don Mills, ON: Addison-Wesley.

Lerner, R. M. (1986). *Concepts and theories of human development* (2nd ed.). New York: Random House.

Vygotsky, L. (1978). *Mind in society: The development of higher psychological processes.* Cambridge, MA: Harvard University Press.

Vygostsky, L. (1986). *Thought and language* (A. Kozulin, Trans.). Cambridge, MA: MIT Press. (Original work published 1934).

Wertsch, J. V. (1981). *The concept of activity in Soviet psychology.* Armonk, NY: Sharpe.

Wertsch, J. V., & Stone, C. A. (1985). The concept of internalization in Vygotsky's account of the genesis of higher mental functions. In. J. V. Wertsch (Ed.), *Culture, communication and cognition: Vygotskian perspectives* (pp. 162-182). New York: Cambridge University Press.

Wright, M. J. (1985). The saga of William Emet Blatz (1895-1964): Part III. *Canadian Psychological Association Section on Developmental Psychology* NEWSLETTER, *4*(2), 8-15.

Zinchenko, V. P. (1985). Vygotsky's ideas about units for the analysis of mind. In J. V. Wersch (Ed.), *Culture, communication and cognition: Vygotskian perspectives* (pp. 94-118). New York: Cambridge University Press.

CHAPTER 7

THE EXPANDING WORLD OF THE CHILD

W. E. Blatz, E. A. Bott, and H. Bott

The following essays were discovered with the project files of the first major Canadian Longitudinal Child Study—the Canadian Mental Hygiene Committee Public School Project 1925—begun at the Institute of Child Study, University of Toronto. Found in an old brown envelope likely unopened since 1934, these writings speak with striking wisdom and understanding to a seemingly kinder, gentler, age than present; one filled with the confidence that, through knowledge, we could anticipate and experience a better spiritual and psychological life by the application of knowledge. The essays were written at the conclusion of World War I, reflecting confidence that a unified world, expressed in the League of Nations, could contain man's aggressive national drive and maintain peace—freeing the mind and spirit and ultimately leading toward an improved global civilization for all. Now thoughts could be turned inward, to dwell on ways to make the life of each individual happier and more creative. Dedication to a collective state could be replaced by an investigation of the psyche and the phenomenon of man's unique adaptability to his world. Unhampered by the complexities of a multicultural society, the authors confidently addressed a largely homogenous audience whose values and goals were a reflection of Toronto in the 1920s. Some ideas were radical for the era in which they were written, but are evidence of highly intelligent humanists whose insights about children's development and behavior in many ways remain unsurpassed today. Management strategies recommended to parents and teachers were based on observations of young children and dealt with universal concerns. Many truths researched by Blatz and his associates have now been absorbed into our culture, and the assumptions underlying their recommendations have proven amazingly well founded. The essays are offered here as a chance to examine the reasonings and share some insights of those who first explored the newly developing field of child psychology.

—Richard Volpe, 2009

CHILDHOOD

What are the distinctive features of development in the period that lies between early childhood and the beginning of puberty—the period roughly coincident with the child's life in the public school? To ask this question may suggest an artificial division between the preschool and school periods as if different principles were operative. Actually the school period calls for consolidation of the methods employed in the training of the preschool child. If learning is to supply the keynote for child training, then there must be amplification and modulation but no denial of a fundamental process. At the same time, the very fact that the child goes to school involves the introduction of new influences from without to meet his developing capacities. We shall look therefore, first at how the familiar values of the preschool period are consolidated in the school age child, and secondly at the new influences by which society at large seeks to modify the growing up process.

What are the objectives of training in the preschool period? We have discussed these in detail elsewhere but they may be recapitulated in very simple terms: we want children to be disciplined in their personal lives, creatively active in their use of materials, and friendly, or socially adjusted in relation to people. And these three aspects of behavior must function in nice relation to one another so that there may be balance, harmony, integration of the developing personality.

By discipline we understand not only the external control exercised by adults, but fundamentally the regulation by the individual of his own impulses and desires, which also should be the objective of any discipline by others. Discipline operates primarily on the fundamental drives, desires, motives of the individual. It functions through a process of learning by which our crude original appetites, emotions, and attitudes are molded into forms usable by us and acceptable to the society in which we live. Parents in the beginning set the pattern of what children are to be and how they develop in that direction. They regulate eating, sleeping and other bodily habits, subject to the responses that the child is capable of making. They likewise determine the emotional set of the child's life and by their handling of early situations they largely decide whether the fundamental attitude of the individual is to be one of acceptance towards novel experiences or one of doubt, distrust, and withdrawal.

Parents determine likewise *how* learning shall proceed, whether the learning process shall depend mainly on motives in the child, that is on his biological needs for food, for activity, etc., or whether it shall be governed mainly from without, by incentives of reward and punishment, of social approval and disapproval. The balance between inner and outer forces in determining the direction of learning is a delicate one, often disregarded in the process of training.

Authorities differ as to the degree of importance which is to be assigned to early experience in the later growth of the individual. The psycho-analytical school considers the shocks of early childhood determining forces in the direction of character; schools of thought which emphasize learning, on the other hand, have a more hopeful and forward-looking philosophy of change, of the possibility, at any stage of the life cycle, of a basic redirection.

A still more fundamental question, however, is that of the final authority in the life of the individual. It is easy to see that with the young child the parent assumes that role, later the teacher embodies a new form of adult authority. As he approaches adulthood the state takes more and more cognizance of the individual and his behavior. Developing concurrently with these external controls which are in the last analysis compulsive, is great variety of voluntary commitments, clubs, gangs, societies to which the developing child and youth chooses to owe an allegiance, whose authority he wills to accept and obey. Finally, there is the matter of how far the individual is capable or willing to assume responsibility for the direction of his own life; how far he can emancipate himself from external controls, social or maternal, through the building up of an inner discipline of thought, feeling and action. And in achieving this self-discipline he must face the issues of making it self-centred or an harmonious adjustment to his fellow beings and the values he sees in the universe at large.

It is vital to think clearly on this issue. Every system of training either in the home, the school or the state is working either to perpetuate its authority or to make that authority unnecessary. The parent seeks either to mold her child's life or to train him to make his own decisions and accept their consequences. The teacher is either a source of knowledge or a guide to experiences which the child will learn to appropriate for himself. In the state, even in countries with a democratic tradition, the swing at the moment is away from individual initiative and responsibility in favor of centralized control in the interest of "strong" government. It is hardly necessary to point out how important are the implications of the philosophy adopted in the home for the wider spheres of school and society; nor how incompatible the conception of personal responsibility is with a regimented school or an absolute state.

If the training of the preschool period has given the child an experience of an ordered way of life based on acceptance first of a rational control and later of individual responsibility, it should also give him an initial experience of the creative use of things. Early play experience is fundamental for this purpose. It is important to reorient our thinking about the uses of play. In every normal young child is a tremendous urge to be active—this is the raw impulse which may be turned to constructive purpose if the right materials are supplied on which it may work. It is unnecessary here to recite how, by supplying variety of constructive play materials we may guide the child into activities which are satisfying to him and acceptable to the people with whom he lives. It is important to recognize that such play is not a trivial activity, a way of keeping the child contented and of least trouble to adults; it is the first step in an essential part of the process of education—learning to enjoy and use the world in which we are placed. The question must be asked as to what formal education does to this omnivorous interest of the child. Does it nurture it by studying it and supplying opportunities for its development or does it stifle it by forcing development into fixed molds that are barren of meaning to the growing child?

As in discipline the keynote of development lay in individual responsibility, so in creative activity *interest* is the dominant word. Interest involves a recognition of and respect for individual differences, a willingness to find out what the child likes to do, and to feed that liking with suitable opportunity. Thus an educational procedure is not predetermined but is pliant to the needs of each particular child. This principle of individuation is more commonly accepted in the home than in the school. Any mother will assert that her children are all different, that they have varied needs which must be met in distinct ways. Because she sees each child as an individual she will modify her treatment to meet his needs. The teacher on the other hand is the exponent of a system which thinks not so much in terms of individual needs but of a pattern of society or of curriculum matter to which the child is to be fitted. Individual tastes, interests, capacities are secondary considerations to be met at all only after these universal requirements have been satisfied. Thus the emphasis in the scholastic thinking is inevitably on curriculum—on what subjects must be taught rather than on what does this child need. Spelling and arithmetic, for example, are regarded as of first importance because they are presumably needful in the world in which we live. The fact that few children find them inherently interesting is not deemed important. On the other hand *activities* which fascinate young children such as making things, dramatizing situations, rhythmic games and dances, are accepted only as frills—to be added if there is time after the serious work of education has been taken care of.

If the principle accepted in the enlightened home, that interest of the individual child as a basic factor is to be seriously reckoned with in education, we must have a complete change in thought—a turning away from the needs of society to the needs of the individual. It may be said that at the present time the needs of social organization are so problematic that we may treat them with less respect than has been our wont. The spectacle of thousands of young people trained for a society which has no vocations to offer them makes one wonder if to train these same young people to be creatively active in ways which they can enjoy would not be a better policy, even from the narrow point of view of vocational fitness.

The question arises, do we know what things children really like to do? Can we be sure that activity growing out of the child's immediate interest may be trusted to carry him forward into some form of integrated and effective life instead of being merely dissipated in random experimentation? The answer to this question lies with various types of educational experiment which have taken the child's interests as their point of departure. These will be referred to as we proceed.

The third thing which the home asks for the child is experience in related living, that is, the ability to get on with other people. This is supplied in limited measure in the home, but a wider context is needed. People learn to live together best when they are working together upon a common task, and it might seem that the school provides the ideal setting for such learning. But one may question whether a schoolroom which puts a premium on individual achievement, on competition, which penalizes help given and received and regards communication between children as a serious offence, is supplying the ideal situation for the development of friendly relations. There is no short cut to social adjustment—it must be learned as any other form of behavior is learned, by experience in living. The home, and especially the nursery school, have played their part in setting the stage for and in guiding such social experience. The school faces the responsibility of augmenting that experience through further opportunities for the child to live with adults and with other children of his own age and stage of development. It may be desirable also for the school to supply opportunities for children of different ages to work together on a common project. This makes possible the integration of experiences at different levels of achievement.

Such in skeleton form, is the heritage which the enlightened home offers to the school. The home in no sense abrogates its authority, but asks of the school cooperation towards the same goals of child training. If the child is to be a balanced, integrated personality, home and school must function together for the same goals to be achieved by the same methods. This objective will be discussed in the next chapter. It remains now to look at those emergent values in the child's experience which call for special handling and which make the school a necessary addition to the training already begun in the home.

What are the distinctive needs of the child of five or six years which the home is unable to meet adequately? When we look at the child as a developing organism we see that his prepotent *bodily needs*—sleep, hunger, etc. —have been met by a system of training in routine habits; that his *motor development* has called out a response in opportunity for activity which is creative and socially acceptable; that *language* is the condition of developing social intercourse. *Intellectual curiosity* is the new capacity which calls for an organized answer in terms of the school situation. The growing child becomes increasingly curious about the world in which he lives. He begins to be able to react not only to the immediate situation but to what has happened before and what may occur in the future. He can project himself into places other than the one in which he is at the moment. He has a developing experience of time and space through their intersection in himself. In other words, he is able to remember and to imagine. This ability to transcend his immediate experiences opens the door wide and is the golden opportunity for home and school to provide the new activities by which the child may appropriate other cultures and other epochs. It is the moment when racial and social experience can be assimilated if presented in suitable form to the child. The great opportunity of the school is to whet the child's desire to know more of life. This involves giving him opportunity to participate in living through the situations which are presented to him. He is, it is true, beginning to get some power in handling ideas, in recognizing and using concepts; but the ability to generalize and to think in terms of absent objects should not be too greatly strained. Concrete realities are still the daily bread of the child's life and he needs help in realizing the past in time and distance in space by embodying this in dramatic tangible forms in the present. Because the home lacks both the training and the equipment to do this satisfactorily, modern society has delegated this responsibility to the school.

We have already touched on the child's need for wider social experience and we shall return to that point again when we consider the distinctive contribution which the school has to make in supplying social experience. It should be noted here, however, that when the child enters school he becomes a citizen of two worlds, between which he swings like a pendulum. His entry into the home was without his knowing, but in going to school he is fully conscious of the passage to a new world. A second great institution of organized living has emerged to govern his experience.

Such, in vista, is the expanding world of the child. In the home the development of trends is already well established; the school provides the emergence of a new social order whose definitive function is to open to the child broader experiences in space and time and human relationships. The ramifications and interrelations of these two major experiences of school and home will occupy the remainder of this course. We shall look first at the contrasts between the two regimes of school and home and the problems of adjustment that these may involve for the child. Next we shall consider in some detail the school situation, as regards the child's needs and how those needs are met. This will involve looking at the child's interest in the world around him, in events past and present, in himself as a person and in ideas, relationships, conceptual thinking. It will mean considering the mechanisms of the learning process, first in relation to attention, or concentration, and secondly in the development of the imagination. Turning to the home situation we will try to envisage the growth in the child of standards of behavior, of a sense of responsibility in relation to materials and people, of friendships and quarrels and of sharing in the life of the family. Lastly, we shall look again at the question of team play between home and school, and the responsibility of these two to create in the child an integrated personality.

CONTRASTING DISCIPLINES OF HOME AND SCHOOL

Going to school may be regarded as a major crisis in the life of a child. In so doing he passes abruptly from the world where he is thoroughly at home with the customs, people and surroundings, to one where strangers are in control, where the rules of the game seem different and where even the physical environment is eloquent of a new range of activities and code of behavior. Most significant of all these changes is the disturbance of the child's hitherto unquestioned acceptance of his own significance. In the little cosmos of the home many activities have revolved around the child's needs and interests; even in a large family he has held his own unique place. But in the school he experiences a new kind of social organization less intimate, less adjusted to his individual needs, more objective in character than the home. He is no more, and no less important than all the other children in the heterogeneous assemblage of the classroom. The universe no longer centres in him, and this Copernican revolution may leave him for a time lost, without place or direction or fixed point of reference—adrift in a strange new universe.

This swing away from the almost inevitable egocentricity of the young child to accepting one's place in a complex social setting is a salutary phase of the process of growing up. The child who for one reason or another is shielded from making this change over is almost sure to show marks of retarded development of personality. But too often the burden of making this difficult adjustment rests with the child rather than with the people responsible for creating the situation with which he must learn to cope. A case recently occurred of a child of five who, after a few days at school became reluctant to continue, begging her parents to let her stay at home, refusing to go without their escort or to stay in the classroom without the teacher. On one occasion when she was there without supervision she ran out screaming in manifest terror. On going home she took to bed and insisted that she would stay there indefinitely rather than go back to school. The parents were deeply perturbed over the child's behavior, but felt helpless because there was no child psychologist within reach. Their immediate recourse was to spanking. Yet surely this was a case where the situation and not the child should be attacked. Parents and teachers should get together to investigate the causes of her disturbance and then to regulate conditions so that the child might learn to tolerate and accept them.

The need for such mediation of environmental demands to the child's capacity is clearly seen in an extreme case of this sort. Most children, however, conceal their qualms in a new situation and make a passable adjustment. But the process could be made easier and more effective if there was understanding on the part of parents and teachers of the issues involved. Mothers are often sentimental over relinquishing their exclusive control of a child; teachers accept the new child's homesickness, timidity or bumptiousness as all in the day's work. But how far do teachers and parents combine to study the component factors of the complex situation to which the child must adjust? What ways have they invented of making home and school congruous elements in the child's experience? The issue is more than a passing one, for the kind of adjustment which the child makes in this new situation may be prophetic of his adjustment to novelty throughout life. It would be interesting to know how many adults are hampered by fears of strange places, strange people and unfamiliar situations, or how far these are legacies of untoward early happenings. If one objective in child training is to develop flexibility, to produce individuals who welcome rather than dread new experiences, and who have cultivated attitudes adequate for handling the unexpected, then going to school may well be seized on as a learning situation of universal importance. Adjustments to new places, new people, new habits and new ideas may thus be studied and directed in the interest of the future as well as of the present well-being of the child.

How may the child be most happily introduced to a new school situation? Where there are older children in the family the transition from home to school occurs most naturally with their aid. They are nearer both to the situation and to the child than are parents. Children often visit school on special occasions with older brothers or sisters; they usually make the first venture under the aegis of the more experienced child, who is an experienced guide to a new world. But a *rapprochement* between parents and teachers is desirable in any case. It is ideal if the teacher can visit the home before the child enters school. A picture of the physical surroundings in which the child lives is often one clue to understanding the child. Incidentally, the country school, where the teacher shares in the community life, affords opportunity for just this intimate knowledge. It used to be the custom in rural districts for the teacher to go home overnight with the children of the various families to pay a visit. The rigors of the spare bedroom in winter were more than compensated for by this picture of the child's environment. The depersonalizing of many relationships is one of the losses of urban life.

The parent, on the other hand, may go to the school, not to part in tears from her offspring at the gate, but to meet the teacher, see the schoolroom, and, if need be, tide the child over the first strangeness. Some children, of course, feel that this involves "babying," and much prefer to start off "on their own." The thoughtful parent will be sensitive to the wishes of the child and will give or withhold reassurance according to his feelings rather than her own. Usually children are very keen, at least when they are established in school, to have their parents visit to meet the teacher, see their activities and be able to envisage the conditions under which they live and work.

Whatever the medium, whether through visiting teacher, parent-teacher associations, visits in home or school, knowledge and cooperation of parents and teacher would seem to be the first condition of an intelligent plan for the *whole* life of the child. This is a little developed field for social invention but before we can hope to integrate the work of parents and teachers it is necessary to chart those areas of the child's experience which call for their combined efforts at regulation and interpretation.

It is the points of *difference* which are likely to give rise to conflict in the child. One must know how far the differences in home and school procedure reflect real divergence of function, or how far they are due to lack of conformity in purpose in school and home. How far does the life of the school provide significant new influences to sustain the growth of the child's personality, thereby reinforcing and supplementing the work of the home? How far, on the other hand, do home and school espouse different concepts of social behavior and employ different, even conflicting methods to accomplish their purposes? An examination of the various aspects of the disciplines of home and school may throw light on these questions. By discipline we mean the regulative, organizing forces brought to bear on the child's life by the planning of those adults who control the situation. Discipline may be discussed in terms of the persons in authority, of routinized and free activities, and lastly of the types of motivation employed.

NEW AUTHORITIES

When he enters the schoolroom the child exchanges one adult authority for another. Teachers are sometimes described as parent surrogates, but this blurs the real distinction in their function. It is difficult to overestimate the value for the child of encountering a persistent adult influence other than that of his parents. We all generalize from too limited experience, and the young child inevitably construes the adult world in terms of his home environment. He needs the corrective of a point of view different from that in which he has been reared. While there are times when a child craves the reinforcement which only the bonds of family affection can give there are other times when he welcomes the more objective treatment of the outsider who has no personal state in his concerns. Though there is thus value in the fact that these two authorities are essentially different, it is well to recognize the strain that may be put on the child in making a dual adjustment if the authorities are not in harmony. The same child may exhibit marked personality differences in home and in school because he is adjusting alternately to quite different demands. At school he may be industrious, quiet, contented; at home restless, boisterous, unmanageable. The integration of his personality will be well-nigh impossible so long as he is compelled to oscillate between two conflicting authorities. Ultimately each individual must accept the responsibility of weighing competing authorities and choosing between them, but such a choice implies a degree of maturity and experience not possessed by the young child. Harmonizing the standards and purposes of the parents and the teachers where possible would seem a first step towards securing a good adjustment for the child. This implies, as we have said before, that parents and teachers must come to know one another before they can hope to share purposes.

ROUTINIZED AND FREE ACTIVITIES

The child who comes from a well-regulated home has already been indoctrinated with the idea of order in relation to his daily routine of eating, sleeping, toilet and play. With school life his experiences are at once more routinized and more free. The schoolroom presents a situation which is in many ways highly stereotyped. There is less adjustment to special needs than in the routine of the home. Thus, punctuality becomes a rigorous requirement of all children; the child enters and leaves the school by certain doors, and in a designated fashion. In the classroom he sits in a fixed seat, has classes in a set order, and learns a code of behavior almost as rigid as the proverbial goose-step. It is amusing in a group of adults to note the vestiges of old habit in response to a situation which suggests the teacher-pupil relationship. Certain individuals may stand up to answer, use certain formal responses, or even snap their fingers or hold up their hands when the urge to expression is overpowering! It will be said, of course, that the schools of today are different, and undoubtedly the progressive schools have set in motion forces which are tending to free children from rigid uniformity and allow greater adaptation to individual need. But this whole question of routine in home and school, its purpose and value will bear much thinking about by both parents and teachers.

If life in the classroom is more mechanized in the average school than in the average home, this restraint is compensated for by the greater freedom of companionship on the playground. Prior to entering school the child is usually dependent on the companionship of siblings or of the small neighborhood group. A much wider range of varied associates now confronts him. He is faced with the challenge of finding and maintaining his place in a large group, of making friends and allies, of defending himself and his possessions in the classroom, on the playground and in the unusual freedom of the streets. He is no longer under his mother's watchful eye. Teachers will interfere in extreme cases, but in the main children are allowed to manage their own affairs with one another. The code of the group enters as a competing influence with that of adult authority. Children develop their own standards of loyalty, honour, obligation. These standards are often little understood either by child or adult. Interpretation and relation to the larger context of the child's life may aid in the process of emancipation of which independent group activity forms so large a part.

MOTIVATION

What are the means used to motivate children in school as compared with home situations? Motivation may be considered as material, that is, rewards and punishments, as social, approval or disapproval, or as natural, the child's success or failure in his enterprises. Is there disparity in the uses of these different types of motivation due to inherent differences in the two situations as well as to different stages of enlightenment among parents and teachers?

The use of material incentives or deterrents is probably diminishing in good schools as it is in good homes. Punishment is fast becoming an anachronism. Rewards are not so generally dispensed with. The gold-star parent coexists with the gold-star teacher. Probably neither has been challenged to investigate what she really accomplishes with her rewards, whether the improvement that she notes is due to the reward or to some unrecognized factor of the situation, and whether the good results could not be got by a type of motivation intrinsic to the learning situation itself.

Approval and disapproval are methods which have only limited applicability. We all like to be commended when we have done well; but we do not admire the person who works for the praise he hopes to receive. Similarly the parent who overworks these motives is developing dependence or a disagreeable assertiveness in the child. The teacher who seeks to attach children to her by personal bonds is losing the unique value of her position, that is, its objectivity. Social approval and disapproval are by-products of a social situation rather than acceptable means of regular social control. There is, however, one aspect of social approval and disapproval which becomes extremely important with the school age child, and that is the judgment of his peers. This is a form of motivation which is not deliberately employed but is a natural outcome of a free social situation. As such it is undoubtedly powerful, though it still calls for the adult interpretation which we bespoke in regard to the general social situation. For the child to learn to stand out against social judgments marks a higher form of development than does mere conformity.

What are the incentives which one can endorse without qualification? The natural incentive of satisfaction in accomplishment is the most powerful as well as the most legitimate form of motivation. In the home it is relatively easy to adjust the scale of performance so that each member of the family has the satisfaction of success in certain chosen undertakings. In a school organized on a competitive basis success is possible only for the children at the top—the great majority never experience this stimulus. This, as Burnham has pointed out admirably in his texts on mental hygiene, is a great indictment of the prevailing school system. No less deleterious than the fact that few children can succeed under a competitive system is the further result that cooperation is discouraged—children are definitely penalized for helping one another. Again the progressive schools are to the fore, substituting cooperation for competition; but now we are told that such schools are creating maladjusted personalities by making children unfit for a competitive society. The logic of the situation seems to be, not to retract in the schoolroom, but to extend our strictures to the present-type of social organization.

What is the underlying basis of successful accomplishment? It lies in finding activities which interest the child, stimulating him to the use of all his faculties so that he identifies himself with their pursuit. The home can do this to a rather limited extent; its function is rather to direct, interpret, and integrate the child's outside activities than to provide the main setting for carrying them out. The school is *par excellence* the field for the activity of the growing boy and girl. Activities must have a wide range of variety to satisfy all kinds of children; they must be physical as well as mental, so that skill may be united with understanding; they must be changing so that the child's attention is sustained; and they must gain reality through having a significant relation to the larger purposes of outside life. When these conditions are met the problem of discipline will have solved itself. Learning is the most satisfying of all pursuits, provided by learning we mean mastering of those activities which have a significant relation to real life. If home and school focus on the conditions which are favorable to such learning their efforts will swing into a natural harmony.

EXPLORING THE WORLD

Increasing mastery of his own body means for the child increasing acquaintance with the world in which he lives. All parents are familiar with the early phases of the exploratory impulse, when the child just learning to walk is tireless in running, in climbing, in touching, tasting, handling all objects that he can reach. With school age this curiosity has modulated into less distracting forms; the child has become somewhat more selective, and has also extended the range of his investigations.

The forms that the child's curiosity now assumes will depend largely on the ways in which the early behavior has been handled by his parents. If he has been given a steady supply of interesting materials, which he has learned to use and enjoy; if he has been taken on visits to zoos, gardens, museums, libraries, and such places, then his appetite will have been whetted for further adventure. If on the other hand, his tentative explorations have met with "don'ts" and removals, his interest in the world and in things will take more furtive forms—he may hide objects and run away from home when opportunity offers.

Adults need to remind themselves how large a part excursions play in the life of the growing child. It is almost universal for parents to complain of children's failure to come directly home from school. This is usually because the child is seeking emancipation from too great dependence on the parents' supervision—because he wants the thrill that comes from choosing his own way and seeing something of the world for himself. While it is right that children should accept certain rules about reporting when they come in from school, parents in turn should recognize the need for some independence on the child's part in regulating his movements to and fro. The child, for example, who is always taken to school and called for, loses the development that comes from choosing his own way. Parents have, of course, to balance the possible danger of letting the child go places by himself against the dangers of a too great dependence on adult initiative and direction.

Besides being taken places, children need freedom to roam the countryside, to go down town, to go to shops, to churches, to concerts, by themselves. It is unfortunate that motor traffic has made bicycling so hazardous for the bicycle is the ideal vehicle for the growing boy or girl for his wanderings. Hiking in parties or in groups of two or three is a good substitute. The interest which children show in flowers, in animals, in all the phenomena of wild life when taken into the woods is an indication that some deep-seated need is supplied in this manner.

Besides his explorations of the natural world, the growing boy or girl needs to be exposed to the projects of our cultural history. In a city where a series of symphony concerts are given for children, music becomes a reality in experience. In museums, art galleries, historic buildings he sees the record of other forms of life. Similarly plays kindle a new interest. More significant than those occasions in which the child is in the spectator role are those when he himself participates and through drama, the dance and music relives the experiences of his forbears. In such ways as these the child acquires fresh, immediate acquaintance with the world of time and space in which he lives.

Without the suggestion implied in the creative works of others the child's activities remain vague and meaningless. Margaret Mead tells how the children in New Guinea, although furnished with paper and crayons, made only meaningless scratches, because they had no pictorial representations to serve as guides to their invention. So the raw materials for representative art are never enough; we must supply patterns for their use. This is best done indirectly, through seeing other people do things. Creative activity in adults is the most powerful stimulus to a like process in children.

While immediate experience is the starting point of our knowledge of the world, no life can be complete which is limited to the present. It is our job to release the child into the spatially remote and into the past and the future. In other words, the child learns when first-hand experience is used as the means of interpreting second-hand experience. How then are the experiences of others mediated?

To be meaningful to the child, second-hand experience should be concrete. That is, it should be expressed first in tangible objects and in places. One may talk for a year of Tudor England and convey less than will be realized from a visit to an Elizabethan room in a museum. An old house, an historic church has its own aura; the child *feels* the realness of the past. Objects come in time to have a representative meaning so that, as the geologist can reconstruct a prehistoric animal from one bone, so the child learns from certain objects to rebuild a civilization. The comb of a Roman lady may recreate Pompeii, the pots and pans of Ancient Ur may conjure up Father Abraham. So great is the suggestive power that lies in an object that interpreted in this fashion by those skilled in the art, our museums become the keys to vanished cultures. Children are avid for such knowledge. It is their elders who tire in such places, their imaginations having been dulled or never developed, not the children.

From representative objects children may progress to representative events, that is to plays, stories etc., which recreate dramatically situations from the past. They may do this through themselves working out historical scenes which they plan, design and enact; they may do it through puppets; or less realistically through reading. While the latter method is less vivid it has the advantage of being more free than are more literal representations. Probably nothing is more characteristic of the school-age period than the development of the child's ability to participate emotionally in other lives. Hence his ready response, for example, to the emotional attitudes of the teacher and the latter's responsibility for making this an educational asset. The range of such participation exceeds human experience; he lives in the lives of animals with an intense sympathy. The exploits of his heroes are as real to him as the doings of his next door neighbors.

Again, the child apprehends the non-present through sensory means—such as pictures and movies. In this connection one might note also the value of the spoken word to paint pictures. No teacher ever outlives the need to be pictorial, and much instruction fails of its mark whenever we couch it in abstract terms rather than in the vivid imagery of daily life.

Not less significant for the child than familiarity with the past is the challenge of the future. Invention represents man's desire to project himself forward into a changing world. The interest of the growing child in mechanical invention, in means of transportation such as streamlined trains and motor cars, in aeroplanes, in radio, television and such like is the normal expression of this forward reaching impulse. How important it is to encourage this can hardly be measured. Yet parents and teachers may find the activities involved in such projection inconvenient, or may label as "queer" the child whose mind seeks persistently after new objects or new ways of doing things.

We have tried briefly to suggest some of the ways in which this growing curiosity about the world in which we live may be met. To do this adequately requires the cooperative efforts of home and school. If this analysis of the child's interests is correct then geography and history, broadly interpreted should be basic subjects of the public school curriculum. This would involve acquaintance with animals as a very important part of geography; it would include knowledge of peoples and races as well as of places, i.e., human geography. History would be visualized also as the pageant of the past made to live again in the child's experience. The ability to read and to construct would be cultivated as means of discovery and of expressing these wider areas of experience. The ages and stages at which this can be effectively done with children is likewise a matter for discovery on the part of educationalists.

The school is equipped for organized effort in respect of these interests, that is, for helping children in projects through which they relive the past and project the future. The home has a subsidiary though no less important function. We have spoken of the importance which travel can have for children. A home with quite moderate resources can make such opportunities available for children. For example, here are two families in neighboring cities. The fathers are professional men with limited salaries in both cases. In one instance the children have grown up within an overnight journey from the Rocky Mountains without ever having seen them. In the other case the family bundles each summer into an old car—overflowing indeed into the trailer. In such fashion they have visited the Pacific Coast, the Rockies, and even the Peace River district. It is unwarranted, of course, to say which has chosen more wisely without knowing all the circumstances governing the choices. But the educational implications of the latter plan are easy to recognize.

Again, the home has the responsibility of enriching the child's experience if the school proves inadequate. At the present time the enlightened home must supply as luxuries many of those elements in education which in coming days will be accepted as commonplaces of consumption. Opportunities to construct, to dramatize, to express in terms of music and rhythm must today be sought largely outside our public schools. Yet the significance of such experiences is just that they enable the child to participate in racial experience and thereby to unloose his own creative power so that experience may be carried forward in a deepening stream.

A third responsibility, obligatory alike for home and school is to coordinate for the child the various elements of such cultural experiences. We are all familiar with the unfortunate victim of his mother's urge for culture who takes Music on Mondays, Rhythms on Tuesdays, Art on Wednesdays, French on Thursdays—on through a week of horrors. Let us be honest with ourselves—there can be no education by proxy. If parents desire such things why not satisfy their desires directly instead of trying to do it vicariously through their children? When the child is the victim he does the work and the parent gets the satisfaction.

If the child's genuine interests are the key to his development we will not force him into situations which are alien to those interests. We will give him the opportunity to choose what he really wants to do after he has had some opportunity to weigh the values of such a choice. It was suggested to a child of 8 that she do some work at a local art center. After thinking it over she left a note on her mother's desk which read: "I have decided to go down to the art gallery but I want you to take me and let me look around first. *I will not be pushed.*" This is a wholesome resistance to adult pressure. After the child has made his choice it is of course incumbent on the parent to see that he abides by it, at least long enough really to know what it involves. This is only the familiar principle of accepting responsibility for our decisions. It then rests with the particular activity to justify itself by demonstrating its relevancy to the child's interests and needs. If this is done successfully the push becomes a pull and the problem then is to keep the child away.

Activities which adequately express cultural needs will coordinate many interests. Thus a dramatic reproduction of an historical event will involve using the library, visits to museums, design and construction of costumes and scenery, composition of the commentary or dialogue which accompanies the action, practice in speaking, acting, dancing etc. Such a project coordinates a great variety of interests and develops many latent abilities. The growing tendency of schools to centre their teaching in such projects is the answer, first to the child's interests and secondly to the adult's responsibility for coordinating and unifying the elements within the child's experience.

PERSONAL AND SPECULATIVE CURIOSITY

Parallel with the extraverted interests which we discussed in the preceding chapter is the introverted tendency of the child to look in on himself and to enquire about the mechanisms of his own personality. Coupled with such personal interest is curiosity about other people, about their relationships and about social customs. Both extraverted and introverted tendencies lead to a further realm of speculative interest where the child exercises a growing capacity for generalization, playing with the ideas of time and of space, of cause and effect, and at the outermost rim of the circle with the idea of God.

Personal interests focus around the child's own body and its functions. They may relate to sex development. School undoubtedly widens the child's knowledge, and probably his experience of sex. It is of importance that parents and teachers think sanely in relation to such experiences. It is perhaps suggestive of our adult way of thinking that attempts at sex experimentation are described in our classification as obscenities. The relative infrequency of such forms of behavior may mean either that they are rare or that they are seldom found out. Attitudes of exaggerated disgust or horror at sex experimentation in young children are indications of inadequate training or a repressed interest in sex in parents or teachers. Till we face frankly the place of sex in our own lives we are unable to deal adequately with its manifestations in others. Curiosity about sex in children is a perfectly understandable impulse and should not cause shock in adults. It causes feelings of exaggerated guilt and shame in children only if they have been conditioned to feel this by adults or by other children.

How may children's normal interest in sex be handled constructively? First on the basis of adequate early sex training. If this has been neglected it must be supplied by parents or teachers. Parents should recognize, however, that early training is not enough, but that it needs to be supplemented with knowledge related to the child's development. Thus, well before the onset of puberty boys and girls should be given simple, adequate information about seminal emissions and about menstruation. Such instruction should anticipate not only the occurrence itself but should make clear its biological significance and should set these functions in relation to growing up and adult and family responsibility. It matters tremendously whether a girl is taught to regard menstruation as a "curse" or as anticipation of a creative function. The implications of such an attitude are much more far reaching than the area of sex; they extend to her whole projection of herself as a fully developed, constructive personality.

If parents and teachers can get clearly before them the picture of the child as growing up into meaningful and socially related ways of living they will have the key for dealing, not only with specific education, but with difficulties such as masturbation or experimentation with other children. They will view these latter forms, not as evil in themselves, but as blind alleys in experience, leading away from the main path of growth. They will also see sex in relation to the other appetites, important in relationship to them and in its social implications but not as exercising a unique or determining influence unless it is wrongly handled.

It is probably wise not to postpone too late the giving of adequate information about pubertal change. The child needs to know what to expect. He needs to be told by people correctly informed rather than by other children. He needs time to adjust his thinking before the phenomenon occurs. A natural, informal occasion should be taken when it offers. If, as the child grows older he becomes reticent and shies off discussing sex with his parents this need not cause concern, provided the topic has been wisely handled earlier. Such reticence is a natural and desirable aspect of maturity, a relegating of a bodily function to its proper place once it has been understood and accepted.

Older brothers and sisters may have a significant part to play in sex training. Once the first child has been taught what is necessary, younger children especially of the same sex absorb information from him or her. Then it is only necessary for the parents to be enough in touch with the situation to be sure that the channels of communication are open between them and their child should need arise. Probably older children learn from one another much of their fundamental attitudes to sex. What they do not learn in this way they acquire informally from their parents' implicit attitudes. These in themselves are the most powerful single conditioning factor in the whole situation.

If children have not received adequate early sex training, who should supply it? Probably we are unnecessarily timid about stepping in. Where the need exists and an adult is aware of it and of her ability to meet that need it may be right to do so, placating the parent if necessary, but thinking of the child's development as the first consideration.

It must not be thought that sex is a preoccupation of the growing boy or girl. Other personal interests are equally prominent. The hygiene of the daily routine becomes of interest, especially with those children who are looking to sport and athletics as a means of expression. Diet, exercise, sleep, all become important in relation to such a goal. It is valuable at this stage that the child should be motivated to think positively about health. Courses in hygiene should be more than informative. The child needs help in thinking through a regime suited to his particular capacities and needs. This is the next step in transferring from the parent to the child responsibility for the child's routine. Instead of a letting down of the strict rules of early childhood the child needs a positive conception of a disciplined life. He should learn to think of his body as the vital centre of his life, so that its care and use becomes his first concern as the foundation of the efficiency and enjoyment of his whole nature. If this could be done consistently with children we would not have a generation of adults who alternately indulge and overwork themselves physically. We should have instead people physically alert, powerful and receptive who had learned to live at a steady pace, with reserves adequate for emergency strains. To accomplish such results home and school will have to combine their efforts, operating under the guidance of scientific physical hygiene.

It is a natural transition from the child's interest in himself to an interest in other people. Curiosity about relationships is frequently expressed especially about family relationships, about marriage, and its social implications. From his early naive dependence on his parents as the source of his security the child is feeling his way to his own place in a wider social context. From acquaintance, conversation, the newspapers he is gathering impressions of how people live; of what forms of behavior are tolerated, or condoned, or approved in the society in which he is being reared. He early becomes aware of discordant notes, if not within his own home, then in wider society. He learns that there are certain things that one does not speak of, and others that one does not do.

The manner in which adults interpret social relations to children is of the greatest importance. To realize the child's inexperience while crediting his fundamental intelligence calls for insight, restraint and sympathy. A little girl asked at the dinner table: "Sylvia's father is dead and her mother is going to marry again. Is that committing adultery?" Thus, without preparation the meaning of a primary relationship, of social judgments as to when it was being violated and when respected, had to be explained.

The sordid side of life is constantly presented in newspapers. Films and movie magazines early familiarize children with ideas of unfaithfulness in marriage and of divorce as the acceptable way out. To attempt to keep children from such knowledge is futile, nor should they be brought up in ignorance of the prevalent customs of the society of today. Nowhere is clear thinking more necessary than in relation to the question of fundamental loyalties in social relations. The parent who in his own life accepts full responsibility for his own choices, and who is bringing up his children on the same principle has a regulative principle to apply in assessing such questions. Then there is no blanket ruling on all cases, but a governing principle applied to the inner life of the individual.

The child is interested in the life cycle, in the sequence of birth, growth, age, death. He begins to think of these, not as isolated events but as parts of a whole. Curious phantasies are frequent in young children, such as that adults grow small in old age. The revenge motive is frequently manifested here—the small child will be large and powerful and the big adult will have shrunk and will fall within his power. It is usually during this period that the child first encounters the fact of death. A good adjustment here may have far-reaching results in later life. Young children who have been frightened at funerals, or by stories about death may carry the scars of fear into adult life. Fear of death is one of the most paralyzing forms of fear. Learning to accept death as a natural and inevitable part of the life sequence is an essential part of a balanced view of life.

Death is, however, an incidental motive; the thinking of the active, healthy child is positively oriented to life. He is looking forward to what is to be and to the part he is to play in the world. Thus occupations intrigue the growing child. He anticipates in imagination the choices of adult life. His early choices are usually made through identification with some person that he admires. Thus the boy is going to be a railway engineer or an aviator; the girl a teacher or a mother. As experience widens the child thinks in terms of his prepotent interest of the moment, he is successively a farmer, a naturalist, an explorer, an author or artist. Reading, which opens the door to a wider world is often the basis of these choices. Another phase represents social identification when the son accepts his father's profession or business or the daughter the family tradition of a social or educational career. In all these tentative choices the governing factor is probably a personal one, that is, the child chooses, not an occupation so much as a person. This tendency is still marked even with high school children who react to teachers rather than to subjects.

A too early channelling of the child's interest is probably to be avoided. The opportunity for a wide variety of experience is the best foundation for intelligent later choice. For parents to attempt to make such a choice for a child is, of course, indefensible. To encourage the set of a premature choice based on an accidental or transient interest is almost as culpable. It is an old fallacy that there is one best thing in terms of inherited special ability, which a child should do. Rather he has certain capacities which may find expression in various ways; and interest rather than inherent ability is the significant factor. An educative program which exposes the child to a rich variety of interesting occupations, which demonstrates the ability of adults to find satisfactions in such occupations, and which postpones a final choice till it occurs as the natural and inevitable consequence of the inner direction and decisions of the life of the developing individual is the best kind of nurture for the vocational interest.

While personal terms are most natural to the young child, there develops concurrently an interest in ideas, in words, in concepts. We probably fail to do justice to the capacity of the young child to generalize. Piaget has argued that children employ processes of reasoning generically different from those of adults. But it seems more likely that children employ the same logical processes as adults but that their lack of experience explains the often bizarre effects of childish thought.

Children are able to appreciate the distance that the mind travels through the association of ideas. They accept the relation of cause and effect although they may be inexperienced in applying tests for such a relationship. The concepts of endless time and space may early be apprehended, indeed, the concept of infinity is probably as terrifying as that of death.

How these speculative questions are met is important. What do we do when a child asks the meaning of a word? Do we tell him not to bother us, do we define the word for him, do we show him how to find it in a dictionary and discuss its meaning with him? The early use of dictionaries, encyclopedias, books of reference builds up into a habit of seeking adequate dependable sources of information instead of depending on guesses or haphazard sources. Neither homes nor schools at the present time seem to be training children in habits of precise statement. The "or something" qualifications of many young people indicate the need for help in defining meanings with greater accuracy.

Similarly, with questions of causation adults may turn the questions aside, may answer them inadequately or may take the trouble to give or help the child to find a scientific answer as far as he is able to understand it. For example, the question, What makes the rain? or where does the rain come from? may be evaded, answered in terms of God sending the rain, or met with a statement of the sequence of natural phenomena adapted to the child's comprehension. The results of these alternate procedures may be far-reaching. Curiosity turned aside in time is dulled; the child learns not to ask. To explain a series of known relationships by any general formula is to invite laziness or to try to substitute a trick for the painstaking understanding of a process. To answer the question in terms of an analysis of a sequence of happenings is to encourage an attitude of enquiry of orderly thinking—in other words, the scientific habit of mind.

Does this mean that God has no place in the child's experience? What is to be our attitude to the idea of God either as we employ it as an explanatory principle or as the child absorbs it from others and questions us about its meaning? The answer to this will have to be in terms of the parents own conception and experience of God. There are two main historical ways of approach to God which are as representative today as in other times. We may have a concept of God; or an experience of God; that is our approach may be philosophic and biological or it may be concrete and practical. For example, on the former basis one may interpret God as the principle of order that makes matter into the cosmos and that unifies human experience and gives it meaning. Acceptance and identification with such a power of order and unity carries one beyond the realm of thinking about into the area of will and action. This is distinctively the sphere of emotion, and those forms of human experience which are aesthetic or practical in character have their place here. As over against the weighing of evidence or the suspension of judgment which characterizes the scientific or philosophical attitude we have the impulse of feeling and will which seeks to make itself one with the object it contemplates. Art, distinctive religious rites, action in obedience to the divine will are all forms of such identification. These two ways of approach are, of course, not divorced from one another; theology builds on the data of experience, and experience is constantly refined and interpreted by critical thinking.

It is, however, important to have these two approaches in mind when we have to answer children's questions about God. Does a child want knowledge about or experience of God? Both have their place. The history of religion is an answer to the first part of the question, and to reinforce this should be some acquaintance with the great religious literatures. An experience of God, on the other hand is mediated to the child through living with people who themselves have such an experience. The inner consciousness of God as a unifying power in experience, the demonstration of the results of such power in the ordered lives of parents or teachers are bases of genuine acquaintance for the child.

The family is probably the best analogy of the relation of the individual to God; it is in terms of his experience of his parents that the child will learn to think of God. The quality of that relationship is more significant than the verbal framework put upon it. The parent is God's surrogate in the child's life. If he represents security, wisdom, sanity, guidance to the child it should be relatively easy for the child to pass as he grows older from the concrete and limited to the general and unrestricted.

THE SCHOOL AGED CHILD

Learning to Concentrate

Perhaps no question is asked more frequently in reference to the school age than, "How may I teach my child to concentrate?" The implications of this question might provoke counter questions. *Why* is it asked so frequently? Does it refer to all parts of the child's experience or only to his work in school?

In order to answer these questions, let us look first at the development of the attention process as we see it in young children in the nursery school. If we observe a child who is new to the nursery school situation we will usually find him wandering about rather aimlessly, watching the people and things around him. In this phase the child shows little discrimination in the parts of his environment to which he reacts, any change seems to call out a response, but it is usually momentary, and he drifts on to the next phase. He makes no effort to attend, his regard shifts rapidly from one thing to another, and he responds without resistance to any slight change in the situation. This may be described as the non-voluntary phase of the attention process.

The beginning of a differentiated response may be seen in the momentary reaction to some sudden stimulus such as a loud noise on the street, a scuffle between two other children. The response to such sudden interruptions is sometimes referred to as involuntary as distinct from non-voluntary attention. It is occasional, brief, compulsive in character.

This is, however, only the beginning of the story. Look at the same child a year later. He marches to one spot on the playground, selects without hesitation the material that he wishes to play with, and plays, often without interruption, over a considerable period. His interest is no longer diffused over the whole playground; it is concentrated on the particular task which he has in hand whether that be building with blocks, riding on a tricycle or making a garden. He is still subject to interruption, but it is harder for any outward happening to break through to what he is doing. It is only occasionally that he lapses back to the original form of undifferentiated response to the whole situation. We say that he has learned to attend voluntarily, that is, his interest is *selective, sustained* and *satisfying*.

One interesting aspect of this process which is often overlooked is that with a developing power to attend goes a corresponding inattention. Whenever we attend to one thing this means that of necessity we disregard other parts of our present experience. Such discrimination is not absolute, a child may be building a tower, let us say, but at the same time he may be aware of another child on a swing nearby; the child-on-the-swing motif may be quite subordinate, or it may rise to prominence and become a competing interest with his block building. The difference is one of degree. There are certain parts of his environment with which the child identifies himself for the time being, while there are others which he temporarily disregards. The central parts we speak of as being in the focus, the others as on the fringe of attention. Such terms are relative. In extreme cases there may be complete dissociation of one part of experience from another. These are seen in abnormal states such as amnesia or in the phenomenon of divided personality. At the other extreme is the person who develops little selectivity but reacts to each momentary stimulus, in other words is extremely distractible, at the mercy of every slight change in the environment. In between we have a wide range of individual difference in the capacity to attend with its accompanying ability to ignore. These are correlative states both of which must be taken into account in any program of training.

Attention is largely a matter of learning. At the extremes mental inability or disability may operate, but with the great majority of people learning is more potent than original mental equipment in determining the power to attend. This is seen in the fact that normal young children all show increasing attentive adjustment in a nursery school situation; this adjustment being measured in terms of increasing time in any chosen activity and in fewer shifts in activity with development. If we *learn* to attend it is therefore important for us to understand the conditions favorable to such learning.

We said previously that the marks of voluntary attention are that it is selective and sustained and satisfying. An examination of these three qualities may furnish clues for learning to attend. Why, first of all, do we attend to some things more than to others? It is easy to see why certain stimuli elicit the involuntary type of attention—bright lights, loud sounds, movement, any sudden, unexpected change in the environment captures immediate interest; but this interest is usually momentary, and is more significant for self-preservation than for the development of the capacity for attentive adjustment. It is difficult at the present time to say whether a mental "set" in interest and activity is determined by special abilities or by accident and training. Does one become a pianist, for example, because of a special ability, or because one's parents were determined to have a musical child, or, because one liked music and identified oneself with it?

Does a runner develop his ability because he has unusually long and strong legs, or because he determined to out-distance another boy during childhood? Many motives may underlie selection—physiological capacity, opportunity, compensation for some defect, identification with some admired person. No one of these alone is sufficient to explain why one child selects one activity and not another. Yet certain sets are already marked in early childhood. One boy will build persistently with blocks, disregarding other possible activities. He may show a skill in design far in advance of the other children in his group.

Another child copies an occupational set from an older child whom he follows like a shadow. For still another the fact that he cannot perform a certain act is the strongest incentive for its mastery. Another shows no special interest but seems to satisfy himself equally in a number of alternative activities. As so many possibilities seem to be operative in the selection of interests it would seem that the important thing is to provide children with a wide range of occupations among which they can freely move and make their own selection. Parents are sometimes apprehensive that if children have too wide a range of choice they will become distractible through the conflict of competing interests. Actually the child who, as in a nursery school situation, or in a progressive school is presented with a variety of choices and *left free* to make his own selection, develops that very power to choose which is so much desired. Formal education, on the other hand, largely removes this opportunity for choice by presenting the child with a rigidly determined program of interests to which he must conform. Deprived of the free choice of the activity which best meets his need, the child loses the power to be selective—in other words to attend. The school thus defeats its purpose by a too early channelling of the child's interests into ways that may not be congenial, ways which are arbitrarily imposed instead of being freely chosen by the child.

When choice of an activity is denied the child will strive to satisfy his impulse for selection in indirect ways. Thus in a formal school situation where certain activities are prescribed and others forbidden, the child resorts to all sorts of furtive forms of behavior in order to maintain this right to select his interests. Thus he whispers, passes notes, reads books on the sly, performs a whole series of acts which are labeled inattention. Actually, of course, these acts are surreptitious interests; they are the things to which the child really attends. His behavior acquires the label inattention only if we accept the schoolroom task as the centre of interest. If the child does not accept this he attends elsewhere. The problem is, therefore, not that he is unable to concentrate but that he does not want to concentrate on the things which adults prescribe for him. This, of course, applies equally in the home situation where our choices often uncongenial to him, are forced on the child.

Because the ordinary school curriculum offers a limited range of choice of activities often unrelated to the child's real interests the belief has become firmly established that school work is a dull task. *Effort* has been emphasized out of all proportion in relation to work. There is a place for effort in the process of "warming up" to an activity, and of keeping going after the initial novelty has worn off, but effort should never be accepted as the keynote of adequate work. Interest is the right alternative. Instead of thinking in terms of the pressure which the individual puts on himself, or which we put on him for the accomplishment of a given task, we should think rather of the incentive of interesting activity which can be held out before him. Yet children and teachers alike are caught in the vicious circle of self-effort, the teachers straining to make the children work; the children if they are conscientious, driving themselves to tasks which they dislike, all in the belief that there is some merit in doing distasteful things.

What would happen if, instead of this compulsive emphasis, children were exposed to a variety of occupations and interests which they could really enjoy and allowed to follow those which most appealed to them? Would this mean, as some people fear, that children would lose the capacity to overcome obstacles, that they would become spineless, distractible, pleasure-seeking? Actually the very reverse should happen if the emphasis on selectivity is sound. The child who chooses his own task picks out from the environment that part which corresponds with some need within himself. Thus one child will develop in relation to construction and mechanical invention, another in music, another in physical abilities. The child's choice will represent a fusion between the direction and impulse of his own life and the opportunity afforded by the environment. Because he has freely chosen an activity he will tend to find pleasure in it and therefore his attention will be sustained in its pursuit.

Anyone who observes the activities of young children in relation to tasks which are freely chosen is struck at times by their capacity for sustained attention, a capacity directly proportionate to their interest in the activity. When a child is keenly interested in something that he is doing he will work to the point of fatigue without recognizing the symptoms. Indeed, adults have to protect children against over-concentration with its accompaniments in irritation and emotional upsets, when the child's interest is focussed intensely on the thing that he wants to do. The young child in the nursery school shows a development in the capacity for sustained interest during the years that he spends there. In the beginning many interests compete for his attention, and he divides himself among them. As he grows older there should be a unification of interests so that certain related interests fuse together. The emotional counterpart of this fusion of interests is what is called "sentiment" a relatively stable emotional set towards a group of congruous ideas or activities. The more the child's interests are consolidated the more sustained his attentive adjustment becomes.

Sustained attention demands, not an unchanging object, but change either in the object we look at or in the sequence of ideas. Thought to maintain its unity must be carried forward in a stream of related images and thoughts. Children find such a relation in activity. Their play is held together by the impulse to translate into immediate action the ideas that come to them. In pictures and stories they demand a like mobility if their interest is to be sustained. Yet our educational procedure deliberately checks this immediate outpouring of idea into action with resultant loss of effectiveness in the child. There are, it is true, times when action should be arrested, when inhibition creates a reserve of power in experience, but an education which puts undue emphasis in restraint, on sitting still, on not speaking out of turn, on ideational rather than motor expression is making attentive adjustment increasingly difficult for the children who experience it. We shall come later to some of the leakages in the process of attention. The consolidation of a growing interest is a forward moving process and is determined largely by this progression and growth in the object or experience to which we are attending.

The satisfying quality of the things to which we attend depends on their adequacy to meet our emotional needs. Indeed the emotional set underlying the attentive process is probably where we should begin if we wish to understand difficulties in children. Unless he suffers from some obvious mental disability a child is able to attend, and does attend to some things, but usually not to the things we wish. Therefore to find out *why* he does this is the first problem. Why does my eleven-year-old daughter love animal stories and hate arithmetic? Why is your 10-year-old son able to concentrate on building bird-houses but unable to learn to spell? Is he really unable, or is he unwilling? The child identifies himself with some interests and repudiates others; he will not really attend to anything from which he cannot derive satisfaction. What is to be done about it?

There is no trick for learning concentration, despite the schools that claim to teach it. The gist of the matter lies in the saying that "where the treasure is, there the heart will be also." But there are certain things that parents and teachers can do, and should do to help the child to a satisfactory adjustment between his needs, which are fundamentally for novelty, for change, for enrichment of his experience, and the parts of the environment which can satisfy those needs.

First, adults need to ask themselves whether they are providing a sufficiently varied, stimulating, interesting environment for the child to choose from! Is he being exposed to activities which can meet his needs and lead on into developing experiences in the future? For example, parents are often concerned about their children's preoccupations with movies, or with comic strips, or daredevil stories. These may be passing phases, and probably should not be taken seriously. Their most serious feature is that they call out no active response from the child. His participating is of the passive, onlooker type and leads nowhere, unless into an imitative activity which is usually undesirable. The child, however, who acts in a play instead of watching one, identifies himself with the person and the period he is representing; and there is literally no bound to the development of that interest. The obligation to provide creative activities, that is, activities which elicit the child's full response and lead on into other significant efforts, rests with the adult. Fundamentally this is the privilege of the school as only the school is adequately equipped to do it. The home has the obligation to pass judgment on the adequacy or inadequacy of the school in this task; and then to create public opinion to change the school, or to supplement what the school is able to do by enriched experience outside, coordinating such opportunities in relation to the child's needs.

Second, adults have a responsibility in guiding the child's efforts in relation to his chosen interest. Children may freely choose to build a boat, let us say, and then find the task beyond their powers. The adult must be at hand so that together the child and he may get the plan for the thing that is to be done, and then together think through the way in which to do it. This means, not that the teacher directs and the child performs, a procedure which kills the child's interest and stultifies growth in the adult; but that *together* they solve a problem. This means growth for the teacher as well as for the child. Indeed this may be carried a stage further back, and we may say that together they *find* their task through together looking for the thing which the child really wants and needs to do.

Such a type of learning requires freedom alike for the adult and the child to discover what the child's interests really are; it involves guidance in which the adult is always behind the child, with the child's interest as the direction and the adult's experience as the sustaining power in any activity. Only adults who are themselves capable of being deeply interested in activities and processes can create and sustain such interests in children.

It is timely at this point to look at the processes of attentive adjustment as they are experienced by an adult instead of viewing them objectively in their early stages in children. By understanding how we learn to attend we may be better able to cultivate the power to concentrate in children.

First, we may recognize in ourselves the type of involuntary attention that we have been describing in children. This is less often accompanied by motor behavior; it is usually a train of ideas which follow one another in effortless sequence with no effort on our part at arrest or control. We describe such states as reverie or day-dreaming. The ease of association, the freedom from any effort on our part is their distinctive quality. They usually are determined partly by casual suggestions from the environment, partly by wishes, hopes, fears which rise to the surface when our thinking is not focussed on other things. When the pressure of an immediate task is removed we usually think in this way; we lapse into it when we are very tired; it is probably the stuff of which our dreams are made. Its ease may rest our minds, but it has no drive, is unrelated to action, so that the day-dreaming tendency is usually suspect. The relaxation is excellent, but if day-dreaming becomes habitual there is no pressure to generate action.

Non-voluntary attention is important, because we need to learn how to deal with distractions. When we attempt to concentrate on one train of thought we are apt to be conscious of interruptions, doors banging, conversations heard around us, the radio and the telephone, people passing near our window. We may even cultivate such interruptions in order to put off the task which confronts us. We accept all sorts of minor tasks, sharpen our pencils, write up our accounts, tidy our desks, to put off the exacting job which awaits, or, again, we may work with our eyes on the clock; or be interrupted in our thoughts by recalling something that we have to do. It is doubtful if it is wise to try to eliminate all distractions. We may seek a quiet room and still be disturbed by irrelevant thoughts. A practical suggestion is to keep a note-book at hand on which to note down any remembered duty which lies outside the task at hand. This frees the mind to return to the central theme.

Less important than the elimination of distraction is the focussing of our thoughts on the subject in hand. Certain aids are useful in this process, such as making notes if we are reading a book, stopping at the end of a paragraph or chapter to put the gist of it in our own words, making notes in relation to a given project as they occur in our thinking. In the early stages of any attentive adjustment it may be necessary to hold ourselves to the task in hand till it really grips us. This warming up process should not be difficult or prolonged if the task is one which we have really accepted. If the task is really distasteful we must decide whether it should be refused as not being consonant with our nature and desires, or whether it must be accepted as part of a larger whole with which we identify ourselves. To absorb drudgery and give it value in relation to a significant whole is necessary both in practical life and in thinking.

A further step lies in recognizing how long we can attend efficiently, and in alternating periods of rest and activity. The subject of fatigue is a delicate and important one. Is our feeling of ennui due to real physical exhaustion or is it merely disinclination for the given task masking itself as disability. We touch again on the emotional implications of the attentive process. If there is real emotional identification with a task we will carry on beyond the point of physical weariness; if emotionally we reject the task we will tire easily and attempt by every possible evasion to escape its performance.

There seems in the course of any attentive adjustment to an accepted task to be a definite progression of activity. First is a stage, akin to that of involuntary attention when a miscellaneous assortment of ideas present themselves in relation to the theme in hand. These should be caught on the wing, so to speak, recorded, and subjected to further scrutiny. As this process of contemplation goes on certain difficulties present themselves and certain suggestions are automatically eliminated as being irrelevant to the problem in hand. Finally there emerges a coordinated picture, or plan for the desired task, a design which seems to shape itself independently of effort on our part—almost as if we lent our mind to the process. Such a design is simpler than the original suggestions because many of these have been eliminated and the rest have been knit into a unity. This unified plan or design or configuration then awaits the test of action. It has about it a quality which may be described as "effortless thought."

How may adults learn this process? Simply by doing it. We learn to attend by being attentive, by merging ourselves in the object of our desire or regard till our minds are molded by the thing on which we concentrate. The vital point then is our selection of interests. What are those things which bring ultimate satisfaction? The patterns of attentive adjustment which we develop as adults will be transmitted to the children with whom we live by a kind of social heredity.

Development of the Imagination

Much that has been said in preceding chapters, particularly in chapter 3 implies imaginative capacity in the child's experience; it remains to look more closely at the processes to which we apply this term in order to see the values of such experience in the life alike of the child and the adult. We talk freely of the imagination but actually we need to remind ourselves that what we are talking of is not an entity distinct from other types of experience. We talk of past, present and future, but these are abstractions of our thinking; in experience all three merge and interpenetrate one another. Perception, memory and imagination are other ways of expressing the same indivisible unity of experience. Memory differs from perception insofar as it always has a past reference in time; imagination in that instead of the "given" quality of an actual experience, combinations are envisaged which have had no counterparts in actual perceptual experience. Thus, if I *remember* my friend it will be as I saw him last week, let us say. The fact that my memory may be incorrect does not affect the past reference of the experience. If I perceive my friend he is present to my senses. If I *imagine* my friend the experience may be projected into past, present or future, but the distinctive thing is that I am not constrained by perceptions past or present as in the other two forms; I may see him without a hat, or with a new hat, or with a beard, or in prison, or become a multi-millionaire. I may even imagine a friend whom I have never known. This power to add and subtract from experience is what we mean by imagination.

When we grasp this point our thinking about the genetic picture of imaginative development is at once placed in focus. Instead of being an independent, innate power, self-existent in the child, imagination depends on experience. We may combine freely, but we are limited in the last analysis to situations of which we have some measure of experience for those combinations. For this reason, the young child is restricted in the possible combinations which he achieves by the range of his actual experience. And because that range is of necessity so much greater than that of adult life, his imagination functions with much smaller scope. The limitations on adult imagination are of a different character as we will see later.

Young children are, for this reason, extremely *realistic* in their imagination. Observation of free play in preschool children certainly bears out this statement as so large a part of their play is concerned with trains, motor cars, "house," animals etc.—all the familiar counterparts of their experience. As they grow older cops and robbers, kidnapping, Indians, etc. reflect, sometimes in undesirable forms, the ideas current in their reading and in the hearsay world in which they live. It is the unusual child who lives in a fairy world. When this happens it is because *adults* have fed the child on fairy lore. The response of children to the Santa Claus myth is a case in point. For the child, experience is novel enough to engage his attention, and his play is usually more closely allied to memory than to imagination proper, in the sense that it is concerned with the reproduction of past experience more than with an attempt to project new forms.

It is easy to see what conditions are favorable to imaginative development of children. With every new experience we put the raw material of fresh imaginative combinations in his hands. Perception, memory and imagination are thus components of a causal series.

If experience supplies the elements of imaginative life, can we discover anything of what determines the combinations? This question discloses an important difference between adults and children, a difference which has led to the mistaken idea that children have more imagination than adults. Children are more free in combining elements in experience because they have not been educated as adults have to a sense of congruity among these elements. They combine freely what they know because they are less inhibited by customary associations than adults are. More limited in the materials at their disposal they are freer in their use, largely because they do not know any better.

Adults, on the other hand, with resources increasing each year, become more and more constrained in their use of these materials because they have become enmeshed in customary forms of thought and action. Our homes, our meals, our amusements, our educational practices are over-whelming witness to the dead-weight of convention and tradition in determining combinations of experience. Whenever a new force arises in art, in music, in literature, in cookery, in religion, it is because some man dares to try combinations which everyone else thought incompatible. The artist is simply the *enfant terrible* let loose in a world of molds and accepted procedures. The value of courageous new combinations for the enriching of our experience of values can hardly be exaggerated.

The results in practical life are equally stimulating. Here again, the child supplies the pattern. With him impulse always flowers immediately into action unless it is restricted by some environmental force. Invention in adults has equally practical results. New combinations in thinking seek expression in new material or social combinations. Child, artist and inventor are akin in their urge to translate their imaginative thought forms into new modes of action.

Such being the raw materials of the imaginative life, what principles determine their combinations? As in attention, it would seem that the governing forces are emotional rather than intellectual. As in attention we saw an hierarchy of organization from undirected reverie to the most intense forms of concentrated thinking, so imagination displays a similar progression. Perhaps it is more accurate to say that the same phenomena, viewed from one angle are described in terms of attentive adjustment, from another as imagination.

Probably wish-fulfillment describes the simplest forms of imaginative thinking. The child begins to envisage some toy that he greatly longs to possess; it is unnecessary to labour the distinction between productive and reproductive construction as the line drawn is arbitrary, or, he may desire to escape from an unpleasant situation; he then imagines himself as run-ning away. This longing often spills over into action; other illicit desires are usually suppressed at least in their first stages. The child may long to kill the parent who thwarts him; he may even be driven to threaten, "I'll kill you;" patricide is, however, uncommon.

The power motive is another common source of phantasy in children. Joseph, the tail-ender dreams of his brothers bowing down to him; the poor boy dreams of fame and fortune. The child who is suppressed by adults imagines himself telling them just what he thinks; or he may look forward to the time when he will be full-grown and they will be old and at his mercy. One of the most interesting examples of the power motive is the internal dialogue in which we get the better of someone with whom we have a difference. This is one of the commonest mechanisms for resolving a conflict; it is ineffective because the debate never seems to settle itself to our satisfaction but goes round in a vicious circle till it is broken by some new influence from outside.

Fear, anxiety, worry, may determine a strain of imagination. Children may live over some experience with so many embroideries that it grows out of all recognition to its original counterpart. Worry usually takes the form of the projection of some suspicious event which has an unpleasant emotional tone, such as the death of a parent, the loss of a pet, failure in an examination.

Another form of imaginative projection is that of imaginary companions; usually the resource of the only child or the child who is overlooked in a social group. The lonely child seeks compensation in this way. It is not without reason that the time between bedtime and sleep is the time when such imaginary games are invented.

It would be interesting to know how much of the imaginative life of children is a projection into adult situations. The tendency for adults to project themselves back into childhood is undoubtedly strong. Probably the constituency of readers who enjoy the works of Robert Louis Stevenson, Lewis Carroll, A. A. Milne, is made up much more largely of other adults than of children.

In these differing types, whether the underlying motive be fear, escape, revenge, mastery, wishful thinking, the determining factor is the *personal bias* of the individual; his need to reinforce his own experience by some form of imaginative compensation. There is, however, another use of the imagination, determined by objective rather than subjective needs, by the *situation* rather than by the emotional set of the individual. It is in this region of experience that imagination reaches its highest forms. The personal factor is, of course, never eliminated, but sublimated in the more generalized aspects of experience.

Mechanical invention is one type of the objective imagination. The psychology of invention has been studied introspectively; it may be that observations on the constructive activities of young children furnish further clues as to the development of this ability. At present one can only make guesses in respect to this, but it seems probable that a variety of materials which lend themselves to a number of uses, plus the indirect stimulus derived from watching other people use materials constructively, from seeing objects which demonstrate mechanical skill, from reading and studying designs, are the conditions which most favor the growth of constructive ability. To these one must add the psychological requirement of freedom to try out combinations at will without direct control from adults. A too early patterning of the child's combinations is the great crime of formal education and is at all costs to be avoided. Indirect suggestion in the form of a rich environment is the desideratum.

Processes of aesthetic invention are probably more nearly allied to mechanical than we commonly assume. In the experience of young children any division is arbitrary; the child draws, paints, builds, models indiscriminately. Arts and crafts are traditionally associated; and only the extreme specialization of modern experience differentiates art and science. Mechanical skill underlies the arts, and scientific work when it realizes itself in precision and perfection of form takes on an aesthetic quality. Leonardo da Vinci stands as the prototype of the fusion of these two motifs in one personality. In him mechanical invention, engineering, architecture, sculpture, painting, were the many facets of a single attitude; that of questioning contemplation of the facts of physical and human nature.

In reasoning and problem-solving imagination has an important role. Here the individual must envisage alternatives and make his choice between them. The precision with which such alternative courses can be projected is an important factor in reaching a correct conclusion. This kind of play at imaginative consequences is the best training children can have in the exacting art of making decisions. Schoolroom situations could be utilized much more freely than they are at present for giving just this kind of training.

A last sphere for the exercise of creative imagination is in the realm of social life. Creative thinking usually means thinking about people, seeing their possibilities, envisaging them in new situations, projecting them into experiences for which they can be prepared only by our picture of their potential life as realized in action. Parents and teachers should be experts in this art of living vicariously in the imagination. They should firmly form the habit of seeing each child not as he is but as he may become. If faith in the realization of his abilities can be conveyed to the child that is the earnest of its actually happening.

This use of imagination is important in relation to criticism. There is always the danger that adults accept a certain "mental set" towards a child, categorizing him as dull, or bright, or troublesome, or diligent, good or bad. Having pigeon holed him they forget to take him out and revise the estimate from time to time, and the original label has an unpleasant way of sticking. In time the child assimilates it and believes himself to be what his elders say he is. We need to recognize that every human relation is dynamic and changing; the possibility of forming fresh combinations, which we posited as the essential characteristic of imaginative thought is nowhere more to be honoured than in the sphere of human relationships.

Criticism, to be effective, involves identification through imagination with the person we criticize. This is a reversal of the customary tendency to set off the person or object that we criticize, dissociating ourself from it. This procedure has a spurious appearance of accuracy; but actually it is only when we understand a book or a picture of an act by placing ourselves as nearly as possible in the place of the person who created it that we can see its meaning. And only imminent criticism, which takes account of meaning can really touch the person whom we criticize. This would demand from the critic a sympathetic identification with the person whose behavior is under scrutiny; it would require understanding the *why* of every form of behavior and dealing with that and with its overt expression. The application of this principle to the behavior of children would revolutionize methods of discipline.

In these phases of objective imagination, whether physical, aesthetic, intellectual or social, certain steps may be recognized. These have been plotted by writers on the subject but they are repeated for the benefit of those adults who are concerned with guiding the imaginative processes of children. There is first of all the stage of *preparation* or the assembling of ideas. In this phase the freest possible association of ideas is to be encouraged so that as many combinations as possible may be collected regardless of their relevancy.

The second stage, that of *incubation*, gives time for ideas to incubate. A period of time may often elapse during which the mind is not actively preoccupied with the assembled ideas. But even in this latency period something is happening even though we may not be aware of what it is. The place of passiveness in our thinking has perhaps not been sufficiently recognized. Wordsworth was the classic exponent of the contemplative mind in poetry:

Think you mid all the might sum
Of things forever speaking
That nothing of itself will come
That we must still be seeking.

And again he speaks of "feeding these minds of ours in a wise passiveness." This phase of our thinking is ignored at the expense of depth and relatedness in our thinking. Yet it is just here that the creative act is manifest; it always has the appearance of coming into our experience from some outside source. This distinction is arbitrary and has no value for the interpretation of experience; the essential thing is that new thoughts, ideas, forms of expression do emerge, and that to hold the mind quiet, especially after a period of somewhat intense concentration is the circumstance which is most favorable for their appearance.

When they come they have a distinctive configuration, a convincing quality that has led investigators to use the term *illumination* to describe this third phase of the inventive process. In this phase the rejection of many of the original suggestions is as important as the retention of others. The *relatedness* of the accepted ideas into some design, plan of action, or new organic thought-form is absolutely distinctive and is the source of our concept of a creative, unifying power available in our experience. Voluntarily to submit ourselves to the operation of such power is to make purpose, direction and order available in the terms of human life.

The fourth and final stage is described as verification; it involves testing the given plan in action. This final stage can never be omitted if the creative process is to reach its full expression, as it authenticates or discredits the design. Ability to take this last step and validate imagination in action differentiates the creator from the dreamer.

It is extremely important that children learn how to experience this creative process. This involves for them, first a variety of interesting suggestions, mostly through available concrete materials, secondly, freedom to allow their own ideas to incubate, thirdly, the challenge to bring their latent ideas to a crisis and lastly, the test of their ideas in some tangible project. Drawing, composition, designing simple constructions—in fact almost any school project which is not a mere reproduction of the ideas of others can be carried through in terms of this process.

To carry it through, however, implies a kind of humility, a willingness to contemplate and learn, to accept the new, which is the essence of the scientific and also of the religious spirit. It involves also the discipline of translating vision into action, of testing any hypothesis by the strict logic of experience. Children can learn this more readily than adults whose minds are apt to be set in stiff molds of conventional opinion. They can learn it only from adults who have themselves learned to use their minds for the projection of possibilities, so that they actually create in their thinking the new forms of our social and intellectual life.

Truth and Falsehood

We have been concerned up to this point with the emergent aspects of the child's development; it remains in the second half of this book to look at some of the practical aspects of these genetic stages, more particularly as they involve specific problems which parents often encounter in training school-age children. One question most frequently raised is that of truth and falsehood.

If by truth we mean the degree to which a statement describes accurately an actual happening, we understand from the previous chapter how hard it is for a young child to reproduce faithfully the conditions of a given experience. To do so involves not only accurate observation, but a sense of the relative importance among the ingredients of a situation. This is rare even with adults as experiments in the reproduction of an incident and comments on the psychology of legal evidence show. In such cases there is no desire to deceive but merely inability to reproduce events accurately and in right relation. Young children, untrained in criticism and without a framework of meaning in which to place events are even more susceptible to exaggeration and distortion than are adults. They also distinguish less exactly between perceptual and imaginary elements in their experience, vivid imaginings having often the complexion of actual happening. Thus they often confuse fact and fancy.

A playful motive may lead to lies or exaggerations. The desire to hold the centre of the stage is in no sense confined to children but as adults we become somewhat more subtle in assuming the star role in a drama. In dealing with phantasy and exaggeration it is well to understand the motive which underlies it. The power of imaginative projection is so valuable that we do well not to throw out the baby with the bath in the interests of literal accuracy.

Dependent on our habits of attention is the distinction between accurate and vague statements. Few children are trained to state exactly what they have seen much less to have a repertoire of nice description to convey their findings. The "or something" attitude indicates a failure of training to emphasize the value of accurate observation and precise statement.

Wishful thinking underlies many of our deviations from strict truth. The emotional slant here is significant as it indicates a turning away from the reality principle. This carries into every area of life until as adults we may become almost incapable of accepting a truth which does not jibe with our predilections. We become defensive in the area of our affections and even in scientific work impartial judgment may be destroyed by the temptation to wishful thinking. Scrupulous as contrasted with distorted interpretations are the result of a long training which emphasizes the subordination of personal desires.

It is suggested therefore, that truth-telling is an attitude derived from our imaginative interpretations, our training in thought habits, and especially our emotional patterns of behavior. The complex sources of truth-telling should be kept in mind in dealing with deviations.

Honesty has always been regarded as a significant aspect in the development of personality. In relation to the personal life of the individual it means his willingness to know himself; to acknowledge his real motives, to face his failures and assess his successes. Few people are skilled in this art of self-evaluation. Children are fed so often on badly balanced diets of extravagant praise and emphatic blame that we cannot wonder if they are unable to place themselves precisely in the scheme of things. If they were taught to face the facts of their own performance with less emotion and more intelligent understanding of the learning process we might confidently expect more effective adaptation in adult life. Until honesty in this sense is accepted as the core of our personal life and until we have a new generation of children reared on this principle, we may accept it that nothing less than a profound emotional upheaval can break through old molds of thought and enable adults to face squarely the facts of their own natures.

In the use of materials honesty is equally important. It lies at the foundation of all sound workmanship; the instinct for perfect materials and for skill and perfection in their use is the craftsman's heritage. It may be lost sight of in the mass production of today; but confidence in the nature of the product is basic to buying and selling. How far advertising is dominated by motives of honesty, and how far merely by rivalry, competition and the desire to market goods is an open question; but no one will doubt that honesty in production and in salesmanship is in the long run the basis of sound business. The instinct of sound workmanship should be part of the early experience of children. At home they should learn to do each task thoroughly and competently. At school exact, careful work is the expression of this impulse. It is only to be hoped that the requirements of adult society do not give the lie to this early training.

It is in social life that we commonly recognize the implications of truth and falsehood. Much of our social intercourse is a tacit recognition of the fact that to be honest is too painful for ourselves and for those we meet. Manner, form, politeness, conventionality, sentimentality in social intercourse are all ways in which we glaze over our inability to speak the truth and the unwillingness of our friends to hear it. We have, of course, the occasional blunt person who prides himself on always saying what he thinks; and this is usually a cloak for rudeness.

Yet one can envisage a different attitude whereby we learn, in the terms of the apostle's injunction to "speak the truth in love;" when instead of a formal politeness we get a genuine expression of real regard and willingness to be available; when instead of unquestioning acceptance of form and tradition we are flexible enough to adapt forms to present social needs; when instead of giving our friends the counterfeit of a conventional agreement we give them the real coin of our genuine convictions. Actually people are hungry for reality in social life and will respond to it when it is dictated by genuine concern for them and not merely by the desire not to offend or to seek approval. When honesty becomes the ground of our intercourse social relations become significant; it is only when we are genuine that our lives have meaning socially. This requires people who are friendly and fearless. The combination of these two qualities in children will be produced as the result of our recognition of their value and our willingness to accept the discipline of producing such attitudes in ourselves.

Our next step therefore is to look at the matter of the child's training to see how it may produce the type of personality which we have been describing. We may ask first of all why truthfulness should be a problem. *Why* do parents emphasize the importance of honesty; should it not be accepted unquestioningly as a self-evident need of the good life? One answer is that parents and teachers who are preoccupied with this question rarely strike the positive note; they are more preoccupied as a rule with falsehood than with the truth; they are more concerned to prevent children from telling lies than to train them to seek truth and ensue it. The reason for this negative emphasis may lie in a conflict in their own lives—a disparity between a formal allegiance to truth-speaking and an underlying sense of something to conceal. In such cases the root of the problem is in the parent rather than in the child. He must be helped to achieve a fundamental sincerity in his own life in order to reproduce a like attitude in children.

The second case in which truthfulness becomes a problem is when fear is used to determine the child's behavior and he lies to escape punishment. Here the adult must be helped to see that the child's untruthfulness is a symptom of bad discipline and that, far from being a cause for punishment, it is the adult's repressive methods which must be attacked rather than the child's lies.

The emphasis, therefore, in dealing with untruthfulness in children should always be on the adult, and only indirectly on the child. And treatment should always be on the level of causes, not of symptoms. Adults need to be familiar with the variety of motives which produce in children what we denominate as lies. Children may be untruthful because of *ignorance* and *inexperience*, a real inability to report occurrences accurately or to describe correctly the meaning of a given happening, or lies may be due to *phantasy* and *exaggeration,* an unwillingness to constrain imagination to the strict literalness of actual happening. Again we may have lies of *imitation*; lies of custom and tradition, of loyalty, all the so-called polite lies and expedients of social life of all within this category. A fourth class are lies due to *faulty training,* and here fear is the chief cause. The intent to deceive is almost always traceable to fear. Lastly are the pathological lies, where the subject seems to derive satisfaction from lying regardless of any purpose served. Such lying is akin to kleptomania in the area of material things. The treatment of such abnormal states lies with the psychiatrist and outside the purview of this discussion.

Lying is essentially a social offence, and a scrutiny of this list of causes may suggest that habits of untruthfulness are usually the result of bad training and example by adults. Children are fundamentally honest—they have no reason to conceal until we teach them to do so. Their power of statement is often inadequate, they have difficulty in getting a just sense of proportion in a narrative but these faults of inexperience are readily corrected. They involve no intent to deceive. Imaginative play is harmless so long as it is recognized as play and not allowed to impinge on the child's conceptions of reality.

Social lies are serious because they train the child to accept two standards, one for ourselves and another for the world. They break the unity and sincerity of his response to life and set up conflicts between the parts of his experience. So in lies of loyalty, the child is never free to give an undivided loyalty but is pulled in two directions at the same time. Only a higher loyalty to some conception of truth and of honour can resolve this conflict. It need not be forced upon the child if the adult's life is adjusted to one principle, that of integrity in all social relations. Difficult as this may seem in our present social organization, it might be an interesting experiment to rear a generation of children on standards of truthfulness in order to observe the effects on family, business, social and international life.

Lies which have their root in fear are definitely the responsibility of parents and teachers who should have the confidence of children in a friendly relationship which makes fear impossible. If the child knows that the adult is identified with him so deeply that what he does may grieve but will never estrange, then he is strengthened to tell the truth whatever the consequences may be. Those consequences will not be arbitrary ones, but will grow out of the situation, and will be accepted by the child, not imposed by the adult.

From this it will be seen that training should have the positive emphasis, not of preventing or punishing falsehood but of cultivating a love for truth. This involves for adults and children that first of all we learn to face ourselves, to accept responsibility for our mistakes instead of projecting the blame on someone else. The little child should learn that it is his clumsiness, not the floor that is responsible for his bump; the older child that it is his careless work and not the examiner that is to blame for his failure. Parents must be willing to recognize faults of training which have estranged their children, and teachers the lack of stimulating teaching which causes a bored class. To accept responsibility where it is ours is the essence of self-knowledge and self-discipline.

Secondly, we must train ourselves, and train our children to discriminate, to analyze a situation and see what the real issue is towards which they should react; to appreciate social rules and decide when to accept and when to disregard them. A critical re-evaluation of customs and habits would do much to establish social life on a more realistic basis.

Again, honesty must be recognized as the basis of sound social relation-ships. This does not call for a verbal insistence on it, or for a cavilling spirit of literal interpretation; it does involve a quality of directness, sin-cerity, simplicity, and integrity in us which will be reproduced unwittingly in our children. Such an attitude is as essential to scientific thought as it is to social relations.

Confidence, implying mutual trust is the secret of a good relationship between parents and children. If we deceive children we destroy that naive trust and it is never recaptured. The dentist who lures the child with false promises that the drill will not hurt may fool him once, but never again. It is never good strategy to deceive a child.

Lastly, freedom for ourselves and for our children rests on having noth-ing to conceal. Fear paralyzes and only a catharsis which relieves the mind of the poison of a concealed something can really set the person—child or adult—free. In order that children may escape the poison of concealment it is well to bring them up in an attitude of openness. It is better to be vul-nerable than to be defensive.

The Use of Money

To discuss the use of money is really to determine our scale of values in the use of material things as money represents essentially control over materials and services. Certain underlying motives will determine our use of money. If life is regulated by the power principle money will be valued as an expression of the *power* to command the services of others and to reinforce our personalities by the collection of things. The possessive motive is a tributary of the power or mastery trend. If, on the other hand, the pleasure principle dominates our thinking we will value money as a means of *enjoyment*. As the capitalist is the custodian of the power princi-ple, so the spendthrift is of the pleasure *motif*. Another type values money as *security*; protection against old age, illness, dependence. Here the underlying motive is essentially fear. Still another attitude is that of *respon-sibility* which sees in the possession of money a trust to administer it in the best possible way, whatever that may be. These are essentially adult atti-tudes, but it is with these that we must begin. Children will absorb a phi-losophy of money from the circumstances in which they live and the ways in which they see money used. Such a philosophy will be nebulous and unformulated in most cases because so few parents have thought through the question of money clearly. To help parents to do this is the first step towards any plan for the training of children in the use of money. It involves leaving the child free to make the *choice*, *without pressure* to sway the decision. Lastly, it means no intervention consequences. If we release a child from the results of his choice the learning value of the experience is destroyed. Thus a child who had stayed away from school to spend a week-end in the country, thereby neglecting her homework, asked her mother to write a note to the teacher explaining that she has been away and unable to do the homework. The mother refused, on the grounds that the child could have done the homework had she chosen to do so.

Our attitudes to money are largely a reflection of the times in which we live. In good times power and enjoyment are probably the dominant values; in depression, security and responsibility become the dominant notes. Yet this may not be wholly true; if security seems to be disappearing in an economic or political debacle, then enjoyment may be the dominant note. We become spendthrifts because we feel that it is futile to try to save. A characteristic note of the present day is the sense of insecurity, the feeling that to mortgage the present for the future is useless when at a stroke the savings of years may be wiped out. This is probably the characteristic note of an unstable age when old values have dissolved and new ones have not yet emerged. Life may be stabilized on either a poverty or a plenty basis; at the present time we are not wholeheartedly identified with either of these and it is correspondingly hard to find our bearings. It may be worthwhile to glance briefly at both before we concentrate on our own dilemma.

Life in the early days on this continent was organized on a poverty basis, that is, there was not a sufficiency of this world's goods to satisfy the needs of everyone. In such a state a premium is set on thrift; to forego present enjoyment for the sake of the future represents the most adequate adjustment to the situation. Accumulating, hoarding, may be the extreme forms of this regime, but actually the wealth of the country has been built on a foundation of discipline which involved willingness to forego present pleasures for the sake of some future good. There is a kind of irony in this attitude which is a tonic ingredient in character. To meet obligations squarely as soon as they arise is one of its characteristics.

When the development of natural resources made possible by such an economy results in plenty, then new values are emphasized. The basic need then is not production but distribution; not securing enough for everyone but seeing that everyone has some share in the abundance of goods which can be produced. Emphasis then shifts from saving to spending; as power to produce is increased new needs are developed and a whole range of luxuries developed to take up the slack in the consumer's power. Whereas in the earlier economy it was incumbent on all who would to work, in an economy of plenty a leisure class develops and society is faced with the problem of educating for a satisfying use of leisure.

At the present time we are experiencing an age of plenty without having yet developed an economy or a morale adequate to its demands. That is, material resources are available to a greater extent than ever in the history of the world, and those resources could be multiplied almost indefinitely by the application of known scientific methods. The mechanics of distribution, however, have proved inadequate to the needs of the situation and industry is paralyzed because the resources we have are not being made available to those who need them. In such a crisis the first impulse is to fall back on the principles of the earlier economy in which most of us were reared, to emphasize saving and hoarding and thrift as the basic needs. Yet as soon as this note is sounded economists tell us that this is only to aggravate our present difficulties. The average, unenlightened person is completely bewildered—caught in the vortex where two opposing currents meet. How is he to regulate his material needs?

It may be a mistake to look at the present time to the formulation of a national economy in answer to this problem. It may be more important for individuals to think through their own convictions in relation to a personal economy in order that these may serve as suggestions for an emergent national economy in answer to our present difficulties. Certain questions may be suggested to govern such thinking.

First, what are the *sources* of my material supply? Are these personal or social? Whether I depend on inherited capital, my own enterprise, a salary for services rendered, the earnings of some other member of my family, or on relief, can I claim that what I have is directly and solely the product of my own exertions; or commensurate in amount with the degree of service rendered? Only one principle seems to be accepted here, that is the assumption that the state, all of us, in other words, are responsible that no one is allowed to starve. Beyond this there is no consensus of opinion as to a just proportion between individual effort and an adequate societal repayment. It is impossible to maintain a *quid pro quo*. There is no nice balance between service and reward. Both have to be adjusted in relation to some absolute value. This means that whatever our line of activity we do it to the limit of our powers without regard for recompense. We measure in terms of realizing our capacity, not in terms of commensurate payment. This principle is commonly recognized in the home when we expect children to do their share of work, and when we give them an allowance adjusted to their needs but not determined by the services they render. Similarly, in adult life, whether the income we have to administer is large or small becomes a secondary consideration. The important thing is a sense of stewardship in the administration of that income.

The second question is therefore, what is my responsibility in using such material resources as society has placed within my power? To ask this question is to bring our thinking into the realm of values. What objects or ends are to determine my use of money? What things are worth spending money for? One answer to this question might be that using is always more significant than having; that money should contribute to vital processes—scientific research, discovery, art and literature, rather than to the amassing of things. Seen on a simple scale, it is the difference between giving a child raw materials which he can employ in a variety of constructive uses, and giving him manufactured toys so fragile that he keeps them for display. It is the difference between the well-thumbed volume and the *deluxe* edition which never leaves the library shelf. Another principle might be that human beings are more important than things, and that an economy which ignores this value is bound to be false. In practice this distinction breaks down because material things are representative of human values. If I spend money for diamonds it means that I am employing certain workers in the Transval, other people concerned in shipping, others involved in the merchandizing of goods to work for me. If, on the other hand, I give my money to feed the poor, or to educate my child, those purposes are translated into material things—food for the hungry, books and fees for the student. Fundamentally, therefore, this reduces to the fundamental functional concept of use versus accumulation.

This brings up the third question, that of *security*. In the past our thinking has been in terms of security through accumulation; it may be more important now to think of security in use. The Gospels have never been taken seriously as a guide to economics, yet it may be worthwhile to reflect on this contrast as it is expressed in the parable of the talents. We all know people who have been so intent on hoarding for a rainy day that they have never begun to live; the alternative is not the spendthrift but the person who extracts from each present opportunity its full value, trusting that for each new day new means will be provided. The development of capacity that this implies is the best guarantee for the future.

When we think about the ways in which these general principles may be applied in practical situations, the first question becomes one of a *family economy*. What constitutes a good rationale of production, distribution, and consumption within the family group? How are questions of security, proportional allotments, earning, allowances and so on to be arrived at? This question each family must answer for itself, the important thing is that it should be answered by the family, not merely by one or even both parents. This involves taking children into our confidence as soon as they are old enough to have any understanding of the value of money. It means a frank statement of what the family resources are as the first step towards family budgeting. Secondly, certain values must be agreed upon, such as the proportion of income that should be spent for food, for clothing, for shelter, for operating expenses and for education and personal development. No arbitrary standards can here be set up. Ideal budgets may be prepared but each family must determine for itself where the emphasis is to fall; whether a house in a good district is more important than having money released for travel; whether clothes are to take precedence over books and theatres. When the question of value is brought into the area of concrete experience it is evident that the choices made express our fundamental conceptions about life. Children unwittingly absorb their standards from us; it may, however, be important to discuss frankly in the family circle the why and how of such preferences.

The basic principle of distribution is expressed in the way the family income is shared among the different members. The importance of giving children allowances is often recognized without recognizing that it is equally important that the allowance should be set in the context of the family resources. When children know the available sources of income they are willing to be reasonable in accepting a fair distribution of that income in relation to their needs.

It is important also that a family should think through together those questions of earning and spending which have been suggested in the early part of this chapter. This would involve an acceptance of the resources available as given, but as independent actually of the service rendered. It would mean that, given such available resources, the family should develop a philosophy of spending. Such a rationale might involve recognition of the need of some reserve fund on which to draw in case of emergencies. It might emphasize spending as determined by permanent rather than by transitory interests. It should provide some sense of freedom for individual discretion and judgment, some leeway of choice for all the members of the family group.

It is now possible to look at the detail of the child's training in the use of money. It is axiomatic that a child should have an allowance as soon as he has any understanding of what money is and means. With a young child the allowance may be very small in amount, no more than a few cents each week. These may be adjusted to his age—as many cents as he is years old, until he is old enough to go to school and has regular instead of merely incidental use for his money. Then the allowance should be regulated by the additional factors of the family resources and the child's needs.

The allowance should in all cases be at the child's disposal instead of being parcelled out in advance so that he is deprived of all freedom in spending. It is the sense of responsibility engendered by freedom which is the fundamental reason for giving an allowance. The child must be free to learn by his mistakes, and must be allowed to take the consequence of his mistakes.

This involves for parents being disciplined in keeping to fixed allowance once these have been adjusted to the child's needs. Nowhere is it easier to be indulgent; yet this is simply to nullify the advantages of the whole scheme. Faithfulness in prompt payment, in analyzing with children their expenditures, in holding them down to live within their incomes is the best possible training for a responsible attitude to material things in the future. It should inculcate neither lavish expenditure nor parsimony but a sense of stewardship in the use of what is given us, whether that be much or little.

Wherever possible, responsibility for spending should be given to children. On entering high school children may take over the buying of school books, of lunches, of their clothes. Money should remain over and above this for other purposes such as charity, amusements, books etc. The parents may function as consultants but it is better that boys and girls in their teens should be responsible for their own wardrobes than that they should have everything provided for them, even into college years, thus remaining babes in the use of money. A simple system of accounting will help them to keep track of the elusive income and to proportion it wisely. When it is possible they should be allowed to travel, taking responsibility for buying tickets, paying for meals, engaging rooms. Subordinate responsibilities for family spending such as buying food or supplies, handling the detailed expenditures of a journey and so on may well be delegated to children. Overworked parents do not capitalize the resources they have at hand in the interest and capacity of a growing family. Such team work frees the elders for the things that only they can do, gives children a steadying sense of responsibility and trains them to recognize and demand value in return for what they give.

The question of earning by children calls for brief comment. Children should not be paid for services rendered to the family which they contribute as members of the family group. If a given child is assigned to black the shoes or wash the dishes he should do this as his part of the work of the household without expectation of pay. Similarly, outside the family, he should be willing to render occasional service without bonus. The habit of tipping children for the odd friendly office is an odious one. On the other hand, where children render regular service as the equivalent of hired work outside the family, they should be paid at a regular rate in relation to their competence to perform the work in hand. Sweated labor or the exploitation of a child's willingness or inability to refuse is as indefensible here as in the larger field of labor. A fair wage should be the return for service adequately performed.

How far the child's earnings are his own and how far he is required to contribute to the family funds is a question of the needs of the situation. If the child keeps his earnings he should be free to use them as he wills. If they are required for the family budget he should have a voice in the apportionment of the total income. If a child desires to make his contribution to some family project his impulse should be respected even if the amount given is insignificant. A family were buying a farm, and the boys aged five and seven each offered five dollars, which represented savings over a considerable period. These contributions were gravely accepted with genuine respect for the motive underlying the gift.

Quarrels and Shyness in Children

When we turn from the sphere of material things to social relations there are two main types of behavior which stand in sharp contrast with one another. The first may be described as the process of identification, whereby the individual seeks to merge his life and experience with that of another. Friendship is the exemplification of this motive. Its motor counterpart is the attitude of approach while on the emotional level love and sympathy are its components. The desire to understand is a fundamental element. All processes leading to a better adjustment within the individual life or between one individual and others are derivable from this trend of identification, the fitting of the parts into a congruous whole, or the functioning of members in an organic unity.

In contrast with this are the mechanisms of dissociation, by which, instead of identifying we separate ourselves from people or situations. All unfriendly attitudes fall within this category. Quarrelling represents an extreme form of dissociation. The emotions which govern it are anger, fear and jealousy. Supporting these is the tendency to self-assertion or mastery, the urge to dominate people or circumstances.

Another form of dissociation consists, not in attack but in withdrawal from a situation. This tendency is less often recognized and less seriously regarded than the disposition to quarrel. The shy, reclusive child is not disturbing in a social situation, whereas the quarrelsome child is. Actually this form of behavior is more difficult to deal with because it is less obvious and overt than quarrelling. It depends primarily on fear for its emotional cast, and withdrawal is its motor counterpart. Instead of assertion, self-negation is the self-tendency which it incorporates.

Conflict is present in both these types of dissociation. In the one case conflict is resolved by attack, whereby one person or one element conquers, establishing itself by defeating the other. In withdrawal the conflict is resolved by separation from the discordant parts of an experience. This is a more serious form of dissociation because it means a progressive impoverishment of the life of the individual. In quarrelling we are at least in contact with other lives and there is always the off-chance that some kind of fusion may result. In overcoming we may incorporate. The person, on the other hand, who meets every difficult situation by withdrawing from it, becomes more remote from life, and more isolated in himself with each such circumstance. If the conflict is within himself, the unity of his life is hopelessly destroyed; if between himself and others a kind of death sets in when the free flow of thought and feeling to and from other lives is blocked.

It is important not to confuse dissociation with detachment. Detachment is never indifference, it is emotional identification with temporary inhibition as regards action. In the mechanisms of dissociation the centre of emotion is in ourselves; in identification our emotions are focussed not on ourselves but on the other person. When we are detached, or objective we preserve this out-going emotional impulse but overt action is temporarily suspended. Thus, when I observe children I am detached or objective in so far as I make my own interests and feelings subservient to a careful scrutiny of what is happening. I do not allow personal interests to deflect my judgment. Again, I may be detached in reference to certain behavior in my own family, not because I am indifferent, quite the reverse, but because I recognize their rights to their own decisions and their own mistakes. Detachment involves a fundamental consideration in not interfering in situations which are outside the scope of our responsibility. It is really a form of understanding or identification.

With this general plan we may turn to look at particular instances of identification and dissociation as they are manifested in relations among children and between adults and children. We shall consider in this chapter forms of dissociation, especially quarrels, and in the next, identification or friendships.

Quarrels among children probably cause parents more concern than any other form of misdemeanor. Probably one reason is the discomfort in family life which such disturbances occasion. Whether quarrelling is equally distressing to the participants we have no way of knowing as children are rarely critical about their own behavior. We as adults are probably much too prone to sit in judgment from our own point of view without stopping to enquire what the meaning is to the child. One can detect also a lack of sensitivity in adults to the range and depth and meaning of children's friendships. It is probably well to remind ourselves that alike in friendships and quarrelling, our first obligation is to understand the child's motives.

We have said that the components of quarrelling are anger, fear and jealousy with self-assertion, or the mastery or power motive. The differing proportions in which these are found will depend on the particular occasion which provokes the quarrel. Friendship, on the other hand, calls into play a different range of emotions, love, sympathy, the desire for identification, the impulse to approach rather than to attack. These may be regarded as social patterns which, while they alternate in the experience of the young child, tend to become fixed in one direction or the other so that a prevailing trend in social relations is discernible in the adult. The habit is formed either of a prevailing friendliness or of a tendency to difference and antagonism. It is as predictive of these sets in adult life that an early fixation may be significant.

In considering quarrelling it is important to recognize differing forms and to understand the variety of motives which cause children to quarrel. Early quarrels should be regarded as a form of *incipient social adjustment*. Green in her study of nursery school quarrels found that the children who quarreled most were also those who had most friendly contacts. Probably such quarrels are due to inexperience and are on the same level of understanding as the behavior of the child who knocks another child down as he would an inanimate object, or to see what will happen. Quarrelling may also be a kind of social experimentation, an interest in the reactions of another child, a desire to test his strength or try his spirit. It may grow out of the child's desire to maintain his rights and defend himself from interference, or it may be a naive expression of the mastery motive which we recognized as a fundamental ingredient. The emotional content is probably relatively insignificant in these early quarrels and there is seldom any carry over to later situations. The intent behind the overt behavior is seldom serious or inherently hostile.

Secondly, quarrelling may represent the fixation of a bad habit of social response. Bickering may arise between two children where there is no serious anti-social intention. If, however, such behavior is fixed by habit, that which was trifling in its early stages may take on a serious complexion. Again, if children live in a home where quarrels are the accepted procedure they will become conditioned to them and will naturally resort to the same procedures. Even if the strife between adults is smoldering beneath the surface, the tension of the situation may provoke quarrelling in children who are not fully conscious of why they are disturbed. Emotional disturbances dominate in quarrels of this type.

Lastly, *compensatory motives* may produce quarrelling. The child who feels neglected and overlooked in a situation may start a scrap as a bid for attention. Jealousy, even if unrecognized, will provoke bickering. This may be seen in the rivalry engendered in school situations or in the more deep-seated persistent jealousies among members of the same family where competition for the favor of one member may be a constant source of friction. Quarrelling may be a form of compensation for feelings of inferiority, or, if inner conflict is present, the resistance generated may be projected on some perfectly innocent bystander. Adults are particularly prone to vent their spleen on children when the real cause is an unresolved conflict within themselves.

It is flattering to ourselves to picture quarrelling as confined to children. Actually, of course, adults and children quarrel as bitterly if less overtly than children with one another. The dice are always loaded in such a conflict because the adult holds the trump card of parental or school authority. Because we do hold this card we are obligated to renounce our hostile impulses. Actually adults may cloak vindictive motives under the cloak of justifiable punishment. Until we reeducate ourselves into habits of identification we are powerless to change the behavior of children in any fundamental fashion. Punishment may coerce outward behavior by fear, but it inevitably generates resistance which defeats the purpose of an inner harmony.

How should quarrelling among children be dealt with? First of all, the cause must be determined, whether inferiority, jealousy, the will to power, or merely the lack of a better pattern. This may involve observation over an extended period and the picking up of apparently unrelated bits of evidence which may be clues to the child's fundamental needs. It is useless to ask children *why* they quarrel, or to approach the situation by exhortation; the causes lie deep in the child's needs. Where one child quarrels persistently only an emotional identification which makes possible an understanding of the lack in her experience can enable the teacher to interpret the situation and seek a remedy.

The adult who has gained insight into the causes of which quarrelling is a symptom is then in a position to talk the whole matter through with the child. Very often this process affords the needed relief, enabling the child to resolve conflicts and establish a new integrity of purpose which protects him from assaults and irritations from outside himself. *Security* either in his affectional life or through achievement will undercut the need for quarrelling. We are defensive only when we are unsure of ourselves.

To provide adequate outlets for the young child's energies, and play situations which depend on cooperative effort will help to overcome quarrels at a simple level of behavior. Routine removal of a quarrelsome child may be a necessary disciplinary procedure. With older children quarrelling may be a by-product of idleness, and opportunity for play, games, organized sports, together with coaching in how to play will direct into constructive channels energies that otherwise would leak away in futile disputes and horse-play.

In families quarrelling often persists as an inverted kind of affection which cloaks itself in teasing, in the desire to "get a rise" out of a susceptible member. Or it may be present as an inadequate method of settling disputes between young children. In this case, isolation of the offending parties may be necessary to convince them that this method is not acceptable. The family has a right to peace, undisturbed by such outbreaks. The intimacies of family life make conflicts almost inevitable. These can be met only on the deeper level of understanding and identification. The member who has learned to live at peace with himself, neither withdrawing nor attacking, will be the means through whom peace may be mediated to the household. Positive projects calling for cooperative activity often unite a family on a positive basis which is better therapy than a direct attack.

Parents are often harassed by neighborhood quarrels which, beginning between children may infect their elders. Unless one child is obviously at the mercy of the others it seems wiser to stand aside in such situations. To refuse to quarrel is to isolate the disturbance and allow it to die. In some cases, however, it may be necessary for parents to come together and talk out frankly and without rancor the causes of the difficulty. It is hard to be objective about our own children, we tend either to defend or to blame them. If we can combine love with an honest appraisal, both for them and for other children, we may be able to create a better understanding of their needs along with a better relation with our neighbors. Only genuine honesty coupled with real courtesy can accomplish such a result.

Quarrelling is, after all, a fairly obvious form of behavior. The quarrelling child gives himself away so that we may discover the causes of his difficulties. The shy, reclusive child who shuns social contacts is a more difficult problem. The direct approach, in an effort to "draw him out" is bad tactics; when we advance, his impulse makes him retreat. We must leave him alone, watching all the while for symptoms which point the way to diagnosis. Is it fear, repression, a sense of inadequacy and failure, the determination not to give other people the chance to hurt him, which explains his attitude? In relation to a child of this type one must develop an attitude of patient, relaxed waiting; he must sense that we are available and trustworthy Then when the opportunity comes and some incident unlooses the stopper of his repressed personality, our silence may draw his confidence like a spiritual vacuum, and his hopes, disappointments and fears come tumbling out. We are then in a position to help the child to reconstruct his life in relation to a positive purpose so that he directs his energies positively towards this instead of living on the negative basis of withdrawal.

This is probably the most delicate and difficult service which one human being can perform for another. It involves freeing the individual from repression and redirecting his life towards a positive goal. Only people who have learned how conflicts may be resolved in their own lives can perform this service for others. We must use our imaginations creatively for the child to find activities which will satisfy him, reinforce his personality and supply outlets for the energies which otherwise are repressed or turned in on himself in futile reveries.

Whether we deal with quarrelling or with reclusiveness the positive emphasis is necessary for a satisfactory adjustment. It is not enough to prevent quarrelling, we must work for peace. In the reclusive child the hidden conflicts must be brought to the surface and resolved and a new synthesis of creative effort achieved. Such a positive adjustment means unity in the individual life. Viewed objectively this unity is usually in terms of concentration on some accepted goal or purpose. This may be collecting stamps, or learning to roller-skate, or managing a paper route, or mastering the rudiments of algebra, or learning a new language, or writing poetry, or building a boat, or a thousand other things. If we can discover the one thing that the child most desires to do or be, and then help him to work effectively towards that end we will have put him on the way towards unification of his personality. This may seem to overlook the need for a distinctively social adjustment, but the assumption is that social adjustments are secondary to personal adjustment and will follow more or less naturally when the other has been achieved. The person who is at peace with himself has learned the how of relationships with others. His own stability makes him tolerant and ready to contemplate with equanimity differing attitudes and desires. Intolerance, meddlesomeness, and the reforming spirit are usually the products of some lack in ourselves which we seek to compensate by converting others to our side. Balance in ourselves is the subjective aspect of tolerance towards others.

What are the means by which we work positively for adjustment? Honesty is the fundamental one; willingness to face ourselves and an equal willingness to face the truth about other people. This undercuts the sentimental attitude which allows us to excuse and to defend others. It is realistic in always compelling us to look all the facts squarely in the face. Love, in the sense of giving ourselves without reserves to meet the real needs of another person is the other instrument of adjustment. These will be more fully explored in the next chapter.

THE DEVELOPMENT OF STANDARDS OF CONDUCT

The Significance of Conflict

Conflict is a persistent experience in human life, and the attitude we adopt to it is bound to be significant. On the one hand we may regard conflicts as undesirable, regrettable accidents which disturb the smooth functioning of thought and behavior. On the other we may accept conflict as a necessary condition of growth, as being, indeed, the critical point in the developmental process. The resolution of conflict in a satisfying manner is a new synthesis of behavior which makes it possible for us to move on to a new alternative. Progress is thus inevitably tied up with conflict as a necessary expression of the movement forward to new aspects of living.

What are the basic conflicts which the child or the adult has to face? Fundamentally conflict is between different kinds of motivation. I may be hungry, but too sleepy or too lazy to want to get up and find food—one appetite or the other yields in the struggle. Or I may be hungry, but afraid that I will be caught if I visit the pantry shelf. Again, I may be determined to carry through some project although hunger or fatigue is interfering with my ability to do so effectively. These inner conflicts between variant motives in our own nature are basic to all other clashes.

External clashes, such as quarrels among children, are rarely important unless they reflect some inner unresolved conflict in the child. The solution then lies in dealing with the inner conflict rather than the outward circumstance. This principle is basic to understanding and adjusting quarrelling among children and has already been discussed there. The treatment lies always in the resolution of the inner conflict.

How are conflicts resolved? First, by understanding what the warring impulses are, by facing the issue squarely instead of refusing to meet it. In ourselves, this usually means admitting motives which we dislike to acknowledge, fear, a sense of inferiority, the desire to dominate others, greed, laziness, and so on. Often to confront the issue is to solve it. On the other hand, where alternatives are nicely balanced, we must be prepared to identify ourselves with *one* course of action or else to find a new, unthought of possibility. Thus if a child faces the conflict between going to a party and going to school with homework done, she may elect to forego the party and do the homework; or she may go to the party and let the homework go. Or, conceivably, she may devise a way of getting up early to work so that both party and work can be taken care of. Where there is a dilemma with no possibility of satisfying both desires then the conflict is resolved satisfactorily in so far as the individual *accepts* wholeheartedly the course which she chooses, with full willingness to take all the consequences, pleasant and otherwise. Like Lot's wife, she must not look back.

The test of a sound disciplinary procedure is how far it enables children to resolve conflicts. This means, first of all, help in *defining alternatives* so that the child understands the choice he has to make. It next involves leaving the child free to make the *choice, without pressure* to sway the decision. Lastly, it means non-intervention in consequences. If we release a child from the results of his choice the learning value of the experience is destroyed. Thus a child who had stayed away from school to spend a weekend in the country, thereby neglecting her homework, asked her mother to write a note to the teacher explaining that she had been away and unable to do the homework. The mother refused, on the grounds that the child could have done the homework had she chosen to do so.

Successful resolution of conflicts should lead us on to new decisions. If I decide to go to college that one choice automatically closes the door on certain other possible courses of action. It also opens the door to a multitude of new choices, what course to take, what dormitory to live in, what friends to choose, and so forth. Each of these is a situation containing the germs of conflict. Development comes in facing such crises, and learning how to resolve them.

Personal standards are developed through the resolving of such inner conflicts. It is in this area of experience that character is determined. We are less menaced by attacks from outside than by the crumbling of our inner defenses. The person who is of two minds is at the mercy of external forces; whereas if we are at one with ourselves we have a poise to meet alien influences. To help children to resolve their inner conflicts is the surest way to making them able to face the world with equanimity.

When personal conflicts are resolved, our lives are then available to deal with the struggles of others. Parents and teachers who are unable to face the difficulties in their own lives, who are frustrated, tense and maladjusted, are not likely to be effective in dealing with children. If, on the other hand, they have the experience and poise which comes from dealing with their own difficulties adequately, they are free and useful in relation to the problems which others face. In this sense creative conflict continues to be the focus of even the most balanced and adjusted life in so far as we lend our experience for the aid of others.

The Clash of Standards

What happens when we are confronted, not with war within ourselves but with differences between our standards of thought and behavior and those of the people with whom we live?

The clash between the generations is proverbial and has often been accepted as inevitable. What are the underlying causes of differences between young and old, especially between parents and children? One common disparity is inherent in the child's immaturity. Because he is less experienced he has tastes and interests which seem crude and even damaging from the adult point of vantage. Much of the concern which parents show over the child's preoccupation with comic strips, with thrillers whether in novels or on the screen, with the lives of movie stars etc., falls under this class. The funnies are adapted to a juvenile sense of humor; the rapid movement of the thriller is probably more significant to the child than its moral content, and the growing girl idealizes herself in the screen stars whose pictures litter her walls.

Parents need to develop a humorous tolerance for such manifestations. They need also to be reminded of the paradoxical fact that it is only in homes where concern is unnecessary that it is likely to be felt. Where the home standard of taste and intelligence is approximately that of the child then everyone will enjoy the funnies and be happy at the movies together. Where child and adult standards are discrepant it is safe to prophesy that the child will ultimately accept the family standard if he is not forced by too much insistence. Parents are the persistent, pervasive influences in their child's experience; other forces are transitory in comparison. When we are concerned about our children's standards, we do well to strengthen and reinforce our own, also, to look to the conformity between profession and practice in ourselves. We can then trust to the indirect force of our example to be the ultimate determinant of the child's tastes and behavior. To forbid books or plays, to insist on conformity to an alien standard, is to use a bludgeon where a rapier is the appropriate weapon.

A more serious form of disparity between parents and children is when children as they grow up respond to new ideas and customs while their parents cling to traditional practices, thus remaining at a stage of arrested development. What is significant here is, of course, neither novelty nor permanence but the willingness, in children and in parents, to look dispassionately at social customs, to recognize the force of tradition in determining acceptances, and to be willing to break old molds of thought and behavior when they hamper new and desirable forms of experience. The ability to revise and revalue custom should come from adults, yet it is an exceptional ability. The force of inertia works against it. Our educational procedures are largely designed to perpetuate accepted forms instead of to stimulate enquiry and experiment. It is, therefore, important to cultivate in a community those forces which favor an intelligent acceptance of change. Adult education, and particularly parent education, should aid us to see familiar situations in a fresh light. Too often movements for social progress remain on the intellectual level. The urgent need of today is for a philosophy of change which is also a practical [word missing] which provides the stimulus adequate to produce new ways of living.

Cultural lag, such as we have been describing, is seen in exaggerated forms in immigrant families where the children learn the new language and assimilate readily the thought forms and customs of the new country. The parents on the other hand, isolated by language barriers, live in the old world while marooned in the new. Special educational procedures have to be applied to preserve, on the one hand, the cultural values of the old life and the respect which they deserve; and, on the other hand, to acquaint adults with the customs and ideas of the new life. While it is interesting to contemplate the extreme case, it is important to realize that in practically all families the gap between the generations will form and widen unless it is deliberately bridged by intelligent awareness and a willingness to preserve a common ground. In order to do this, however, we must recognize that the difficulty, while real, is not inevitable and that we have the responsibility of finding a solution.

Another clash may be between the standards of the parents in a family. There is less inherent reason for difference here, because the relationship is between two people of the same generation who have presumably a common basis of interest and ambition otherwise they would not have chosen to live together. The initial choice may have been unsuitable; but even presuming two people apparently well-adapted to one another, their rates of development may be very unequal, or new influences may deflect their courses away from one another. Sex interests are probably overemphasized as the causes of such differences—business, religion, intellectual interests, social activities, sport—all these and others may be causes of disparity. The repercussions of conflict, or of alienation and indifference, are bound to react unfavorably on children.

One special form of such disparity of attitude calls for comment here. Frequently a mother attends child study classes, and develops a new set of ideas in child training which she proceeds to put into effect in the home. The father, meantime, has not experienced this educational process; he may cling to traditional methods of child training and be skeptical, derisive or antagonistic of what his wife attempts. Or he may retreat from the family drama leaving the management of the children entirely in her hands. The lack of cooperation between husband and wife is damaging to them, but disastrous for the children, who are unable to respond adequately in a conflict situation which centres around them but in which they have no true part.

The resolution of such a situation must rest, as always, with the person who has insight into the forces operative in it. The challenge is to those who offer courses of training to see that with new ideas there is conveyance to the parent some understanding of how human beings react to novelty and of how novelty may be made acceptable. We have to get parents past the point where they interact by collision. Clarence Day has admirably characterized this state of things.

> Now to say "hush" to father was like pouring kerosene on a fire. I repeatedly saw mother try to quench his flames in this way, and every such effort only made him blaze higher—far higher. Yet she tried it again the next time. Neither she nor father seemed to study the other one's nature. They each insisted the other one's nature should work in some way it didn't. I never once saw either of them observe the other in a calm, detached spirit, to see how his or her ego operated, and how to press the right button. Instead they invariably charged at each other full tilt, and learned unwillingly and dimly —if at all—by collisions.

A third arena for difference is that between the individual home and the community. Children are particularly sensitive to difference in standard between their homes and those of their friends. To deviate widely from the accepted standards of a given community, economically, socially, religiously is a grave hazard for the mental health of the children reared in such a home. They are compelled to rationalize their divergence as superiority, whereas secretly they feel inferior because they are different.

Yet to hold a family to a dead level of conformity is plainly to cramp development and frustrate progress in the art of living. Carlyle somewhere remarks that it is well to wear the same kind of hat as other men do if we want to be permitted to differ in what is inside the hat. This rule of conformity in minor matters is probably a sound one.

Much difficulty between family and community standards lies in not having determined clearly what the true family attitudes are. Thus in the matter of spending, parents may be torn between the desire to live within their means and the desire to let their children enjoy all that their children's friends are able to have. This conflict must first be resolved in the life of the parent, otherwise a vacillating discipline is bound to ensue. When the conflict has been solved there the matter can be discussed dispassionately and the facts of the family circumstance explained to the children. When this is done honestly and sympathetically there is usually little difficulty in getting children to accept a reasonable plan of expenditure. Difficulty arises when facts are not squarely faced, either in the individual or in the family.

Social difficulties usually reduce thus to unresolved inner conflicts in some one member of the family. When our own responsibilities are clearly defined we can usually act with conviction in relation to others. It is when we are unaware of our own conflicts, unsure of ourselves, divided between discrepant desires that we fail to act convincingly in relation to others.

Methods of Social Adjustment

Nowhere is social invention more called for than in finding ways to adjust such differences of standards as we have been describing. Certain traditional ways may be dismissed as ineffective or, at most, interim stages towards a complete adjustment. Of these *repudiation* of alien standards is probably the worst. In rejecting another person's *modus vivendi* I automatically cut myself off from relationships with him; the thing of which I disapprove is set up as a barrier between us. The isolation thus established is seldom restricted to one form of behavior but tends to spread to all others. Thus in a group of adolescent girls the familiar instance was cited of a mother who disapproved of her daughter's smoking. The girl, old enough to make her own choice, therefore smoked when she was out in company but never at home. The group interpreted this as social consideration on the part of the daughter, accepting the mother's attitude without even discussing it. They entirely missed the deeper meaning of the psychological alienation between mother and daughter which such an attitude involved. Repudiation inevitably produces alienation in the timid or antagonism and defiance in the strong. A boy, confronted with a like situation, would probably have been defiant. Of the two defiance is probably a less damaging attitude than concealment as by keeping the difference a point of controversy some working agreement is more likely to be found than when it is tacitly avoided.

The obverse side of the shield of wrong attitudes is insistence on our own standards, attempting to force our ways of thought and action on others. For example, the father of a child has graduated from a certain college; therefore, when the child is ready for college it is assumed that he must go there also. All kinds of professional choices are determined in the same way by the naive assumption of parents that because they have experienced a given value in a situation it is necessarily there for their children to appropriate.

When we repudiate the behavior of another we thrust him outside our life, thereby putting the full burden of responsibility for action on him and debarring ourselves from opportunities for intelligent suggestion and criticism. When we insist on our standards we rob the other person of the experience in making his own choices and abiding by them which alone can produce psychological maturity. In the first instance too much is expected, especially of a young person, as he must not only make his own choice, that is, resolve his own inner conflict, but he must also defend that choice in a clash with adult opinion. If, on the other hand, we supply the child with our standards we deprive him of practice in making his own choices. In the first case we force maturity unduly; in the second we retard it. How difficult for the little bear to find the chair that is just right!

In contrast with these ineffective methods, what are effective principles for the regulation of conduct? No one will deny the privilege, indeed the obligation of adults to influence the behavior of children. The question is to find legitimate and effective ways by which this may be done.

The first principle is that of *loyalty* or genuine, whole-hearted acceptance of a mode of behavior arrived at by personal decision. This implies usually the resolution of an inner conflict. It puts on adults the responsibility of accepting a course of action on the basis of examination and determination rather than because it is traditional or done in a certain social group. Actually to do this in every area of life would be quite impossible; our habits of thought, of social behavior, our religious convictions and practices, our political alignments—all and much more would have to come under review and meanwhile action would be paralyzed and our whole working scheme of living thrown into confusion. The most that can be expected is that, when moot questions are forced on us, we should learn to look at them dispassionately and try, as far as possible, to face them on the basis of understanding rather than of prejudice.

Two extreme types of character appear in relation to such crisis questions. On the one hand we have the person whose mind is so overcast by customary opinions that new attitudes seem impossible. She has so violent a set against the Germans, or the Jews, or Communism, or what have you, that any matter is prejudged before it is stated. At the other extreme are those people who cultivate the judicial attitude, who are always open to all sides of a controversy, but who never make up their own minds because they are too busy holding everyone else's opinions in solution. Of these extremes the latter is easily the more dangerous. Violent prejudices are easily recognizable and usually a little ridiculous; they betray themselves by their intemperance. There is, on the other hand, among would-be intellectuals, a respect for impartial, objective thinking which can easily betray one into a paralysis of action. Deliberation, the weighing of alternatives, is never an end in itself. Unless it is a step towards action it betrays the whole process it was intended to serve.

Perhaps finality in standards is what we should most guard against. Most of us are products of a society in which certain sharp distinctions of behavior were accepted once and for all, as not to be called into question. We are learning now to live in a society which is at least attempting to substitute dynamic for static concepts. This involves the view that no decision is fixed, final and unalterable but that revision in the light of experiment is the condition of social progress. Instead of bringing every act to the yardstick of an unvarying rule, we evaluate our standard in the light of how well it helps us to adjust to each new situation. The standard is then amended in action. The one unvarying rule is to test all things in the light of experience.

If we accept for ourselves the obligation to formulate and then to live by our own principles of action, we have a corresponding obligation to allow a like liberty to other people. That is, *toleration* of other standards is the converse of loyalty to our own. This does not mean agreement or acceptance, but recognition that others are responsible for their own decisions in matters of personal behavior. Tolerance is sometimes regarded as an insipid virtue, but this is because it is confused with a too easy agreement. Actually to maintain our own position and allow others to do the same requires a nice blend of confidence in ourselves and forbearance towards others. It is as difficult as walking a tight rope.

It is inherently hard for adults to acquire these two attitudes of loyalty and tolerance; it is doubly hard because it removes them from the sphere of direct influence in many phases of their children's behavior, substituting for direct control the subtler forces of indirect influence or example. It is hard to free ourselves from pressure methods, especially with those who are so much at our mercy as children are. Yet a scrutiny of our own past experience should convince us that resistance is the inevitable response to pressure, and that we are really influenced by those people who let us go free.

This brings us to the very heart of the question of social method—the alternatives of pressure and of attraction. Are other people to be coerced into accepting those standards of conduct which we regard as valid, or are they to be attracted towards them by the demonstration afforded by us of the principles to which we adhere? Obviously there are certain aspects of our life where we accept coercion—in respect of murder and theft, for example, as well as other lesser crimes. Definitely anti-social conduct is regarded as subject to force in the interests of all. The segregation of people who constitute an active social menace will be generally accepted; how far our penal system aids such people in adjusting to general social demands is another question. It need not concern us here, as we are thinking not of major social differences, but of those smaller differences in custom and manner about which we do not legislate but which constitute powerful and intangible barriers between classes and social groups. How are these to be overcome?

We believe pressure methods to be useless because they are always external to the person influenced; they can compel conformity but never create the desire to conform which alone gives meaning to behavior. Pressure is likewise damaging to the person who exerts it as it gives him a sense of mastery due to adventitious circumstances. Mastery is safe only when it is the control and discipline of ourselves; when it is personal security developed in the process of our own learning or when it is skill exerted on material, a project of ourselves on the things which surround us. In the social setting responsibility rather than mastery should be the motif, because this leaves the other person a right equal to ours to accept or reject our overtures. It lifts matters of discipline to the level of consequences not of personal compulsions.

An intermediate stage between pressure and attraction is that of concession. Frequently where two people, two parties or two nations are at variance the procedure becomes that of each giving up something to meet the demands of the other party. This is always a *quid pro quo*—the spirit of bargain and barter, not the generous surrender of a right, determines it. The sphere of barter is in exchanging materials, not in social relations. We rightly object to this principle in the training of children. We refuse to put a premium on good behavior by naming its price, whether in terms of rewards or punishment. We are less ready to extend the same insight to adult relations and to see that concessions and compromises approached in the barter spirit are full of difficulties. To begin with, it is always difficult to decide what is a fair exchange. Suppose, for example that a wife agrees to live within her allowance if her husband in return will spend more of his evenings at home in her company. How many evenings is a balanced budget worth? How much extravagance would be justified by a night out on the part of the husband? Secondly, compromises of this sort are external to the situation and leave the root of the difficulty untouched. In this example the real need was for a common purpose for both husband and wife—some end greater than their personal enjoyments to which both would learn to subordinate themselves.

How do we reach such common values in social life? The adequate principle is the one we have described above as attraction. In the illustration just used the wife would have to keep her husband at home by making the situation so pleasant that he preferred to stay. Any other motive is really unsatisfying. Conformity exacted is surely as unwelcome to the person who requires as to the one who gives. Similarly, she would have to see her extravagance as a function of some larger social aim—the good of the family, her husband's respect, or what you will—if any genuine economy was to result.

If people like the way I think and the way I act they will be drawn towards that same way of thinking and acting. This means that social progress comes through the heightening of my own insights and my own standards of behavior. This is a hard doctrine as it means that I myself must accept ultimate responsibility. It means also an act of faith on my part to believe that the indirect influence of my own faithfulness to the standards which I profess can really tell with other people. Can I really trust that my children grow up to be honest if I am honest with them? That they will love knowledge or beauty because they see my devotion to some form of study or of art? That they will become religious because they see the fruits of religion in my life? The answer is, of course, that there is no assurance that any of these things will happen. It is simply our best bet that the odds are in favor of this rather than of the desired results on a basis of coercion.

There are few people who are in complete agreement with one another, and yet a *modus operandi* must be found even while we are seeking for more complete understanding. I must develop, first of all, tolerance and a sense of humor towards those people who are not wise enough to see eye to eye with me. Secondly, I will recognize that mistakes may be made, in child training, in committees, in national policy, without destroying the child or the organization or the country. Life has a resiliency which makes it able to withstand many well-meant attacks. Lastly if my own inner conflicts are resolved, I can function in a difficult situation, content to wait for the opportunity for social agreement and acceptance. While unity through the acceptance of a common goal is the desired result in social relations, the resolution of personal conflicts must be kept steadily in the forefront as the direct means by which we proceed to such an ultimate goal.

TRAINING IN RESPONSIBILITY

No subject is more often raised by parents concerned for their children's development than that of training in responsibility; and none is harder to deal with in any conclusive fashion. This is because responsibility is not a specific form of behavior but an attitude manifesting itself in many forms of behavior. The child does not learn to perform isolated acts of responsibility; he learns instead a general attitude of responsibility which finds expression in a varying range of social actions.

A second complication is that a responsible attitude has a dual reference. It characterizes the individual who is thought of as being responsible in a given situation, but it also refers to the social situation in which the developing individual is finding himself. Unless these distinct though related aspects of responsibility are clearly envisaged our thinking on the subject is bound to be confused.

THE PRIMACY OF THE GROUP

Responsibility functions through the group before it develops in the life of the young child. He is born into a family, that is, into a group of people tied together in a biological unity. The infant is nourished, protected, trained within this group; its organic relationships are prior to all others in his experience. Of all forms of social organization, the family has the most genuine stake in cooperative enterprise or mutual responsibility. It is therefore the prototype of all later forms of cooperation. How far it furnishes real training in social relations depends on the patterns which it evolves in face of its needs. Within the family the child may be either a chattel subject to absolute disposal by his elders or a contributing member whose preferences are respected and his suggestions welcomed. In so far as the family evolves workable designs of social cooperation it will influence other social institutions, the school, the state, economic and religious forms. Because social adjustment is largely a neglected art, and because it is being seen more and more as the fundamental need for peace, whether in the family, in economic life and among nations, the importance of the home as a field for experiment in social adjustment is

of prime importance. As soon as the family is recognized as an experimental station where individuals may learn to live together, its function
becomes one of dignity and importance, a contribution to human integration. These patterns of family adjustment will be worked out in the sphere
of work, in common undertakings and achievements in which all members will play a part. They will also find expression in shared enjoyment,
in entertaining, in excursions, in all leisure and recreative activities. The
opportunities offered by the family for cooperative living change from
age to age. Because our present system has shorn the family of many
industrial and educational functions people sometimes speak as if family
life were disintegrating. Actually the exploration of the social functions of
the family is only just begun.

Competence of the Individual

While the developing individual gets his first experience of responsibility in a social setting where he is first helped, and later expected to do his
part in turn, he also learns responsibility in a more limited but equally
important sense through the development of his own capacities. At first,
responsibility in this sense is limited to the response which he makes to
food and to care. As he grows older he learns to distinguish himself as a
person from his environment; in this development of the "self" responsibility for the regulation of his movements, impulses and emotions plays a
part which increases in significance till the child has learned to manage
himself. The daily routine is the preschool child's area of responsibility.
Along with competence to satisfy his bodily needs goes a growing ability
to manipulate the material objects around him and to manage himself in
relation to a world of objects. This involves motor development increasing
in complexity with age, and ranging all the way from learning to walk,
finding one's way on the streets, going and coming to school, driving a
car, and all complex forms of motor control.

Social competence, developed through participation in group life, is
interwoven with these patterns of personal and material activity and from
the interrelations of these emerges the characteristic form of the personality. Every phase of experience has its own contribution to make to the
development of responsibility in the sense of the creation of an integrated
person.

Developmental Levels of Responsibility

When we talk in terms of training in responsibility we are thinking on a fairly high level of social complexity, responsibility being the tie in of the individual with intricate patterns of social relationships. It is important to see this already complex system of action and interaction in its developmental reference, for essentially the same impulse manifests itself at all levels in the biological series. Thus, when we think in terms of the physiological organism we call this principle *integration*; it is what gives unity and coordination to organic behavior. On the psychological level of infancy and early childhood, it may be recognized as the principle of *individuation*; the young child learns to manage his own bodily appetites, to distinguish himself as a person from the objects and people around him, to coordinate his movements, become self-reliant. We measure his development by this growing capacity to care for himself in these elementary ways, to take responsibility for his own needs. Yet when we talk of people as responsible or irresponsible we have passed beyond this level of appetite; we are thinking not of whether they can dress and undress themselves and refrain from knocking down someone whom they dislike; we usually reserve responsibility for the sphere of *social obligation*. The responsible person is the one who will discharge obligations, keep promises, play his part in the network of human activities in which he is involved. Just as the smooth functioning of the physical organism depends on the nice adjustment of motor response to nervous stimulus, and just as the child becomes a person in so far as he learns to control and direct his energies, so the social group becomes a unity in so far as its members learn to relate their actions to one another.

FACILITIES OF HOME AND SCHOOL FOR TRAINING

It will be seen also that in social life there are many concentric circles of relationship. In this book we are concerned with the two nearest the center which are of special importance for the growing child: that is the home and then the school. The family has a unique function in developing a sense of social interdependence and obligation because it is primarily a biological as well as a social unit. It has a permanence which no other social unit possesses; its forms may change but the bonds between husband and wife, between parents and children are generally the hardest to escape from. We may hate and repudiate the members of our family but we can seldom become indifferent to them; the emotional linkage holds. This is true despite the constant changes in the configuration of the family pattern both within itself and in relation to the culture of which it is a part. In the family the familiar sequence of growth, dissolution and rebirth involves a constant adjustment in the relations among its members. In relation to the background of general social organization family life is constantly adapting itself to new demands. The rate of change will be dependent on the degree to which a given society is open to new ideas and impressions. A primitive society will change relatively slowly unless disturbed by some alien influence. In a sophisticated society family sanctions will change with rapidity and a greater degree of individual difference among families will be tolerated than in more static organizations. If change is sudden it often results in a conflict between two sets of loyalties belonging to the old and the new cultures. Responsibility is then harder to define and parents and children may entertain different ideas of obligation within the family group.

Whatever the form of family organization, the definition of responsibility is one of its major problems. Because permanence in change is the distinctive characteristic of the family situation it offers a unique field for social experiment and training. One sees the family in perspective when it is regarded, not as an end in itself, but as a school in which the young immature individual is at first sheltered so that his physical survival is possible, then trained so that he knows how to care for his physical needs, and lastly given an introductory course in the difficult business of related living. We are all familiar with the type of inbred family where the individual is exploited for the sake of perpetuating a family pattern; we have to create instead the type of extraverted family life which trains each individual for larger experience of social responsibility. It is the social institution most naturally interested in training its members for cooperation, but cooperation should be a means to larger social adjustments.

In contrast with the intimate relationships of home life, the school typifies those more impersonal types of social organization of which the state is the complete expression. In the child's experience the state is seldom experienced directly except as the school represents its authority in the field of education. The state has, of course, not always assumed this function; only in modern times and in highly organized societies has it seen fit to relieve parents of certain parts of the educational task. In doing this the patterns set up are seldom those of the home. In reaction against the ideas of individual instruction which governed private tuition in the home, public instruction has been on the analogy of mass production of the factory. Whether a swing back to the less standardized, more intimate procedures of home training within the school is possible or desirable in an open question.

The School and Competition

How far the school offers opportunity for training in responsibility will depend on the type of school and on its conception of its function in relation to the child and to society. One might question how far the typical public school in America is adapted for training in responsibility. Competition is generally accepted as the ruling motive in school progress; such an assumption rules out, automatically, training in social integration and interdependence. Patterns of individualism and rivalry are accepted and children are even penalized for helping one another.

If one asks why the school as an institution accepts a standard which must be lower than that of most members of its teaching staff the explanation would seem to lie in a wrong interpretation of the conditions of our organized society, or perhaps in the persistence of old patterns which were an accurate reflection of the competitive motif in a developing industrial society, but which are becoming obsolete in the more complex coordination of social and economic life today. To understand the interdependence of interests in social, economic and international affairs is the need of the present. The school will not contribute to this until it is willing to drop the competitive motif and study cooperation instead. This implies an understanding of cooperative methods in its own organization and curriculum planning as well as in the enterprises of the school room. Then mutual help among children in common undertakings may become the rule and not the exception in our schools.

Till the school recognizes this obligation the child's training must necessarily be incomplete. The home cannot substitute for the school because its cooperative area is necessarily limited by the peculiar conditions of family life. The home is the instrument of *inequality* in experience; as such it has its unique part to play in the harmonizing of differences and the adjusting of divergent points of view. Because the public school represents the community it should be the prototype of relations of *equality* for the child; its distinctive function is to teach him to get along with his peers. Till it accepts this responsibility it is sending children into the world unprepared for the demands of life situations.

A Plan for Training

Accepting that the adult, whether parent or teacher, provides the most significant environmental control in the child's life, what is his part in creating a situation favorable for the development of responsibility?

First, we may posit that he or she must exhibit in some measure adult attitudes of responsibility. First among these is *willingness to let the child grow up*. This involves a constant revision of our attitudes and practices in relation to his stage of maturity. It means a willingness to take hands off. But its very essence is to free the child from our possessive attitude, which means freeing ourselves from the satisfactions of maintaining someone in dependence on us.

Secondly, adult adjustment requires ability to *plan* in relation to the child's capacities and needs. Such planning to be effective has to be based on recognition of the child's *interests*. This point has been so repeatedly discussed in preceding chapters that it should not need labouring here. One needs only to realize that interest is the bond which ties the individual to some selected part of his environment, to grasp its significance for training in responsibility where the problem is that of relating the individual in the context of his material and social surroundings, as well as of consolidating his personality through self-development. The young child is unselective in his interests, he reacts indiscriminately to a great variety of stimuli. Change alone is enough to capture his attention. Education makes us progressively selective. Variety tends to be sacrificed to strength. Because social consolidation as well as personal development depends on the strength of the interest bond, it is important to focus responsibility at the points in the child's experience where there is genuine interest. Too often parents think of responsibility in terms of *their* interests or needs, rather than those of the child. Then they are surprised when they succeed in evoking only a lukewarm response. "It *is* interesting, isn't it" said one mother trying to cultivate some enthusiasm for bed-making in her seven year old daughter. "*You* may think so" was the reply. One might hazard the guess that a dog might be a better place to begin than a bed. Even here the difficulties are great enough; to get consistent performance in the way of care for a pet from a child is not always easy. But the initial advantage is always in the situation where there is a genuine interest.

Besides discovering or cultivating interests as suitable fields for the growth of responsibility, adults must be alert to meet the demands of maturity. At a certain point in the training process children will become exceedingly restive and resistant to control; they will demand to be allowed to go to school alone, to drive a car, to stay out at night. These requests usually seem to parents to anticipate the child's competence in these areas in which he is eager to take responsibility. We have to remind ourselves continually that we learn by doing and that learning is usually attended by certain risks. We have to weigh these against the risks of *not* learning and decide which is greater.

Lastly, planning for responsibility involves in other cases forcing development by urging the child to take responsibility which he is unwilling to assume. The girl of fourteen may insist on buying her own clothes; if so, well and good. On the other hand, she may be perfectly willing to let her mother make all her choices for her—in which case responsibility should be placed on her—not suddenly without preparation, but as fast as she can be schooled to take it. Recognizing the demands of maturity is governed by our knowledge of the individual and is tuned to individual differences; forcing development is in terms of norms for a particular age group—the performance of the individual is adjusted to the standards of performance of his peers. Only observation, experiment, adjustment of the situation, and constant checking and re-evaluation of our procedures can make adult control minister adequately to the needs of the developing individual.

Learning responsibility is like any other learning and as such is amenable to the same laws. We may expect early *initial success* while the child is strongly motivated by the novel factors of the situation. Lapses must be accepted with equanimity as *irregular performance* characterizes learning. The slowing up of the rate of progress is often baffling alike to the learner and the teacher. Actually it represents a period when habits are being consolidated and fixed. A final level of *satisfactory performance* will be reached provided the subject does not become discouraged and give up the attempt. In most cases performance is below the actual capacity of the individual. To increase the demands of the task progressively so that it is neither too easy nor too difficult, but just hard enough to be interesting will provoke the most satisfactory response. Some measure of successful accomplishment must temper failure if the learner is to want to persevere. Thus in training in responsibility we must feed out more and more as the child demonstrates his ability, luring him on to ever fresh achievements. We must see that he derives real satisfaction from his performance; that is, that he succeeds in his own objectives, thereby consolidating his own personality, not merely serving as a convenience for realizing our desires. As in all learning patience is the beginning and end of successful guidance.

Steps in Development

Learning seldom proceeds under its own impetus without assistance from the adult. Certain stages of guidance may be delineated. The lowest of these is *helping*. The small child learning to take responsibility for dressing himself will need help, especially at critical points. Here the adult will endeavor to have the child identify himself with the task, helping unobtrusively and exploring the child's reliance on his own efforts. She will, however, be alert to give aid at critical points rather than have the proceeding stall, or the child become discouraged. Dawdling, a form of passing up responsibility, is probably the result first of our failure to place the onus of responsibility on the child, secondly of lack of judicious help at critical points.

The second stage, that of *direction*, consists in allowing the child to initiate and carry through the operation in question under his own steam, so to speak, but with adult oversight. Dining room procedures in the nursery school demonstrate this level of accomplishment. In the school situation much work should be at this level rather than on the level of help. Children will often use help rather than supervision if they can get it. Thus a school child with homework to do may appeal for constant adult assistance instead of doing the work independently and bringing it to be looked over afterwards. To allow the former procedure is to encourage dependence.

When a child is further *emancipated* he may take the management of a particular function in his own hands, with only an occasional check up on his performance. Elimination functions soon become established and can be left without regulation except when some indication of disfunction stimulates an enquiry into the regularity of habits presumably automatic. Children given an allowance should be allowed to spend it without constant interference and suggestion. It is wise, however, when the new allowance is being paid to ask for a statement of expenditure for the previous period. This is not to establish a system of espionage but to encourage the child in the laudable habit of checking up on himself. Similarly, constant supervision of the state of order or disorder of a child's own room may prove exceedingly irksome, especially to the adolescent. A periodic checkup in the sense of an objective comment on certain agreed parts of performance minimizes friction and is an aid to order.

The final stage is reached when the growing individual has demonstrated his competence to manage some areas of his life alone. He can be "trusted," we say, to drive the car, to stay out at night, to handle his own banking account. Such privileges are the correlatives of responsibilities adequately discharged. They are reached through a period of probation and learning in which the child is progressively emancipated from external controls as he demonstrates competence to exercise an inner control.

Attitudes to Responsibility

What are the attitudes which indicate the lack of such a consistent program of training as that which we have outlined? Immature, that is irresponsible behavior, whether in child or adult, is characterized by either of two attitudes with their emotional counterparts: one, that of retreat, regression or evasion; the other of aggression or attack. It is important to identify these unsatisfactory forms of adjustment in order to recognize and deal with them in ourselves and in others.

The aggressive impulse expresses itself through inadequate attack on any situation. Meddlesomeness is its characteristic sign. The person wishes to have a finger in every pie, but not to make the pie himself. He wants to pull the strings to make the puppets dance, but not himself to be acknowledged as the source of their movements. He wishes to direct others while at the same time repudiating responsibility for the results if things go awry. Nagging, giving gratuitous advice, making promises and failing to keep them, are incomplete expressions of the impulse to dominate. They are incomplete because the self-assertive or power motive is not frankly acknowledged and fully expressed, but rather hides furtively behind a specious kind of deference. We have here responsibility divorced from acceptance of consequence. No person is more to be pitied than the one who is protected by a too favoring environment from experiencing the results of his actions. Power without the discipline of consequences is the most dangerous of all experiences. Young children, when they are allowed to dominate a social environment, are victims of this kind of discipline; adults who are protected from the results of their mistakes remain on the same level of childish behavior all their lives.

The contrary pattern of regression expresses itself in all types of evasive behavior. These in turn are rooted in fear. A situation in which we are involved seems to be turning out badly; our first impulse is to place the blame on someone else. We ourselves fail and we are full of alibis and excuses. We project our own inadequacies on other people; we blame our associates in the enterprise, our parents, our education—or lack of it, or else we say that the dice were loaded against us. Nowhere is self-knowledge more difficult than in this matter of accepting our mistakes. It runs counter to the ideal picture which each individual constructs of himself to admit that he may have been deficient in judgment, in foresight, in *savoir faire*. Yet precisely this willingness to accept ourselves is the first condition of progress.

How may children learn to accept mistakes and use them constructively in redirecting their actions? By living with adults who have this realistic attitude; who are not saving their "face" but are frank in admitting when they are wrong, who are free from emotionalism or stereotyped patterns in regard to their mistakes, who can be objective in judging their behavior and in looking for better designs for living.

When a child is persistently evasive, the parent or teacher should recognize in such a tendency not an isolated act which can be dealt with directly, but a habit of mind which is symptomatic of some deeper difficulty. This may be retreat in the face of a situation too difficult for the child to cope with; it may be unwillingness to face himself. Fear underlies the flight from reality. Gently but inexorably the adult must bring the child to an acceptance of himself and of his situation. Her ability to do this will be conditioned by her insight into her own processes of feeling and action and by the fundamental honesty of her own life.

A complex form of evasive behavior is the attempt to "put something over" whether on parent or on teacher. In this way the child hopes to escape consequences and at the same time to assert his superior cunning. Such lesser forms of deceit, implied in the term Smart-Aleck, are as damaging to the personality as the more obvious forms of lying and stealing.

The inability to stay with a decision and accept its consequences is seen in its most annoying form in the adult who is forever reversing decisions. The hat is no sooner bought than it must be returned; to settle on one plan is to make the alternative seem more desirable. We need to teach children that our decisions are often less important than our willingness to abide by them after they have been made.

Lastly, the habit of side-stepping obligations is a mark of immaturity which must be early recognized and dealt with on the basis of pleasant but unwavering firmness till the demands of the situation are met. Example of living with people who scrupulously discharge their promises is the best way of overcoming evasive attitudes in children.

Mature Attitudes

What constitutes a responsible attitude to living, or psychological adulthood? First we may posit *emotional stability*. This is not lack of emotion, but that our feelings and attitudes should be predictable and dependable. The person who blows hot one day and cold the next, who is liable to explode emotionally in the face of a difficult situation is useless for a position of trust. We all know people who are handicapped for any position of responsibility, not through lack of intellectual ability or achievement, but just at this central point of attitude and emotion. They are undependable, they are unsure of themselves, or too sure of themselves, they change their minds about people and values. These seeming shifts in opinion are really reflections of changes of feeling. They have never learned stable emotional reactions to the world in which they live.

How may children learn to react steadily? Normally the child's first and deepest emotional bond is with his mother, the source of his nourishment, comfort and security. Attention has been drawn so insistently to the dangers of this relationship with its possible involvements of fixation and dependence that we have tended to overlook its values, notably its stabilizing influence in the child's life. It is the original, profound fact of his social belonging. With growing experience the father and other members of the family circle enter into the drama of emotions and attitudes. Insight on the part of the parents should see that there is no violent disruption of these early affectional bonds, but that the child is not bound by them. While secure in his unique place in his parents' regard he is free to experiment with new friends and interests. A habit of emotional permanence is thus set up.

Secondly, a responsible attitude is expressed in the ability to make choices and decisions. Our response to the world around us is bound to be selective; that is we react to some parts and disregard others. These parts to which we react, we describe as interests—there is an inter-esse—or a "betweenness" of us with them. The young child has a bewildering host of interests, he reacts indiscriminately to many parts of his environment—competing factors engage his attention and he is the prey of the latest novelty in his surroundings. With adulthood we learn progressively to limit our reactions, to *choose* the parts of the world with which we wish to be in relation. Involved in the experience of choice there are various stages. First we deliberate or weigh the probable results of possible courses of action. The child acts impulsively, without reflection or consequences; but the responsible attitude is distinguished by the desire and ability to *forecast consequences*. Having decided, imagination is translated into overt behavior. Here the *acceptance of results* becomes of prime importance to the mature person. It is never possible, in the complexities of social relations to forecast consequences as we do in the physical world. There is no equivalence of cause and effect in organic behavior. But the responsible person, having envisaged the results of action as accurately as possible, will then accept the consequences of his decisions. He will revise and evaluate the outcome in the light both of his original motive and of the results and will then use this final judgment as a guide for future behavior. This ability to reinvest past experience in the interest of the future is commonly attributed to intelligence. This seems to us too narrow a definition. Emotional reactions and the set of the individual towards action are involved as well as processes of reflection to make the past creative in relation to the future.

Lastly, a responsible attitude involves a recognition of the limits of responsibility. If we learn to accept the consequences of our own actions, we should learn also not to infringe on the rights of others in this respect.

We delimit authority in two ways; by respecting the responsibilities of other people and by knowing how to delegate responsibilities to others. Many of the minor annoyances and frustrations of life are caused by failure to recognize the first situation and to refrain from trying to manage what is really someone else's affair. Nowhere do families sin more against one another than in this kind of unwarrantable interference; backseat driving, gratuitous criticism and advice, unwanted help—all forms of interference with situations which properly belong to the other person to make or mar as he chooses. In the school situation the counterpart is the teacher who does the work instead of leaving the child free to learn by his own experiments. Burnham's prescription for the child's needs—a task, a plan and freedom—indicates the positive procedure in such a situation. The adult's part is to help the child to form a plan which will lend itself to successful accomplishment, then to refrain from unnecessary interference. This ability to detach ourselves from a situation, not in unfriendliness but out of respect for the other person's right to learn is as serviceable for our own mental health as it is for his. It is likewise the condition of a sound respect between two people. There is still room in social life for the old-fashioned virtue of minding one's own business.

The second ability, that of delegating responsibility, is the mark of successful management. The person who has not learned this, be he teacher, parent or business executive, is in some sense immature. An emotional factor often underlies unwillingness to trust responsibilities to others. Suggest to the harried business man or to the over-burdened mother that some sharing of tasks might be desirable and you will be presented with an array of reasons why he or she must continue to stagger on under the burden alone. One suspects that in such a case the person feels unsure of her own place, power or authority and that she is compensating in a multiplicity of assumed responsibilities for this sense of inadequacy. Only when we feel secure in the integrity of our own position and of the contribution which we make in any situation are we free to share the responsibilities which it involves. We have already discussed how parents and teachers may delegate responsibilities to children; we desire only to underline what has already been said by calling attention to this fact that willingness to share is as much a mark of maturity as willingness to take responsibility.

Values in Corporate Responsibility

What has such a training as we have been envisaging to contribute to the development of patterns of social living? First, it supplies the necessary balance between subordinate and directive behavior, between what one might call "followership" and leadership. Only the person who has served his apprenticeship as a follower is adequately trained to lead. Followership involves, not blind obedience but intelligent, progressive adjustment to the needs of the situation. It is as socially useful a form of behavior as leadership. The things that matters are: whether leading or following, we are reacting appropriately to the demands of the social situation; and, that no person assume the role of follower or of leader all the time but that we know when to defer to superior knowledge and experience as well as when to assume control when we are fitted best to supply the governing element in a situation.

Secondly, such a training implies a flexible rather than a rigid authority, in which duties and privileges are nicely adjusted to individual capacity while at the same time every effort is made to develop the individual in new abilities. Thus no child is thrust unprepared into the strange world of school; neither is he at twenty-one handed the franchise, or a fortune, or control of a business without adequate schooling for such duties.

Thirdly, such training means interchangeability of function. The person who has developed progressively through different levels of experience can always slip easily from one to another. Thus the father can sit back and let his son drive; the mother can go away while her adolescent daughter manages the household. The teacher can leave the classroom and know that the children can manage in his absence; the executive can delegate his duties to another.

Akin to such flexibility and interchangeability is the diffusion of responsibility among the members of the group. In the old conception of authoritative control in the family the father's word was law—authority was centred absolutely in him. The modern pattern of family life seeks to distribute responsibility among all members of the family. This does not mean that all have an equal vote in decisions, but that as far as they are able to appreciate issues and contribute to their solution children as well as adults will be expected to do so. This kind of group responsibility broadens the base of family life and contributes to the solidarity and to the efficiency of the family as a social unit. Exactly the same principle applies in other social organizations.

Lastly, such training in responsibility should provide a means of identification through common interests. In so far as children in school are interested in the same things they tend to be in unity with one another. This is true of sports, clubs, games which children initiate. The teacher who wishes to be at one with her class accomplishes this best by participating in their activities or interesting them in hers. Similarly, in the home, children find a stake in home life in so far as they share in the interests and activities of the home. Parents enter into the lives of their children when they share with them objectives and responsibilities which make them an integral part of the social whole.

TEAM WORK BETWEEN HOME AND SCHOOL

Up to this point we have been discussing rather empirically special interests, activities and problems of the school age period. It remains in conclusion to attempt a more comprehensive view of what home and school are trying to do, in other words, to state in some fashion a philosophy of education. This may be done most simply and directly in a series of questions with attempted answers. These answers may not chime with any recognized theory of education, but they are offered, not as final or conclusive statements but rather as tentative formulations which may stimulate in others like attempts to express a concept of the meaning of education. If we believe that education is the concern, not of a small group of specialists but of the intelligent citizens of a democratic community, then the more general such reflections on education become the more hopeful the outlook for educational progress.

Whose Responsibility is Education?

Fundamentally and ultimately, responsibility for education rests with citizens. This not only because the children who are to be educated are theirs, but because *they are the state*. In the modern community the habit of delegating authority has become so powerful that the administrative powers thus vested in a part of the whole have taken on an independent prestige and tend to monopolize authority. We come to think of government as a separate entity, existing apart from us and independent of our will. This is fatal, not so much because of the bureaucratic power which it allows to public administrators as because of what it does to us as citizens. It allows us to side-step responsibility. We dissociate ourselves from our inherent obligations by projecting them onto law makers and executives. Thus our thinking about education as about other public services is in terms of *someone else making us do something*. We blame the system, not ourselves, for what we disapprove of. Our ideas are out of focus until we accept that responsibility for government rests with us, not with the prime minister or the policeman. Ours is the original, theirs the delegated and derived authority. Translate this into terms of the school and, as citizens first and doubly as parents *we ourselves* are responsible for education.

Does this mean that teachers, superintendents and boards of education are to be mere tools in the hands of a dominant electorate? Are the evils of a bureaucratic administration as great as those of a subservient one, where programs are determined in terms of the lowest common factor of public opinion? The answer is that both alternatives are undesirable and unnecessary. Few situations are really determined by a show of hands or a count of ballots. Such obvious forms only register the opinions inspired by the *intelligent minority* who have ideas and are prepared to give leadership. Conviction about educational needs and policies is what counts and such conviction may come from any of us who has the insight to receive them and the courage to give them expression. Such leadership of clear-cut, original thinking reinforced by a genuine commitment to the cause of education may arise in any quarter and should be welcomed from wherever it comes.

Leadership in Education

If leadership in education is to come from that intelligent minority, within or without the system, who feel conviction about education, how is such spontaneous leadership to find expression in action? We can make the way straight for constructive leadership by freeing ourselves from the idol of institutional thinking, recapturing the personal note in education. Great movements draw their inspiration from persons; the history of education is written around certain individuals whose lives become the embodiment of a new educational motif. Our tendency to put faith in systems makes us discount the prophetic note in education. Yet, to give only two examples in modern times, it was the persistent demands of one woman on the Governor and legislature of the State of Iowa which led to the present program for child study in that State. The folk schools of Denmark, which have done so much to preserve and create national culture, were the expression of one man's view of the meaning of education in relation to his country's life. Certain people have the responsibility of focussing in their experience the needs and gifts of their generation. Educational leadership should have the marks of such a vocation. It need not be professional, it may arise wherever one person or group feels the obligation to create new forms in response to the needs of the time.

The genius of present-day leadership expresses itself through a group rather than through an isolated individual. This does not mean that individual enterprise is less necessary but that it finds its most effective expression in relation to a group of like-minded people. Our increasing awareness of the significance of social relations inclines us to work together and is giving us increased knowledge of how this may be done. When, instead of the dominance of one individual, there is created a union of people with diverse experiences and a common purpose, we have a more powerful instrument of social change. How such a group functions is of the greatest importance. We are familiar with the action of pressure groups in public life; such groups cohere in relation to some external situation which they are formed to change. In contrast with the pressure group is the fellowship which is united, not so much towards some special point in the environment as through sharing the like emotions, attitudes and intentions. Such a group becomes the visible expression of a common direction or purpose. Its vitality depends on the free interchange of ideas and on the participation of all its members in a common experience. The actions of its several members, while taking place within their several areas of responsibility, will tend to express in concrete form those ideas which are the common deposit of the group as a whole. It is a community not an association.

How may such a group function within the field of education? A small group of parents and teachers, spontaneously related around some person or interest, might devote itself to formulating its views of the meaning of education. When people thus begin to examine and relate their convictions this leads inevitably into some form of action. Here the greatest care is necessary. Whenever we formulate a theory it takes on emotional warmth and we tend almost insensibly to believe that our feeling about it proves it true. We then become advocates of a program, protagonists of a cause. Instead we should accept the responsibility of testing our new ideas in practice. Between invention and advocacy should be inserted the intermediary stage of experiment.

What does educational experiment involve? It means that the problems we accept are related to life situations. It means, furthermore, our willingness to put such ideas to the test. This may be done in a variety of ways. It may involve establishing small private schools with freedom to try new methods; it may mean study and observation in the more standardized but more representative situations of the public school system; it may involve work in voluntary organizations such as home and school clubs; or it may mean accepting public office on school boards or commissions, or serving in the administrative or teaching branches of the school system. No one phase of work is more important than another, but the integration of such efforts through the common policy of a small, voluntary group such as we have been describing seems of great significance. If the group can be kept informal, free from the rigidities of organization yet coordinated for action, it can become a perfect instrument for educational change.

What is Education?

What is the task to which those people who feel responsibility for education must address themselves? The meaning of education can never be encompassed in a definition; one can perhaps indicate by description what its province is conceived to be. Education involves both a backward and a forward look; it is concerned with conserving and transmitting the values of the past and it is also concerned with pioneering the future. When we look towards the past we see its values so deeply embedded in the life of the present that it is impossible to disentangle them; our customs and morals are the products of our history, and a large part of education consists in making us aware of these traditional values. This is the more informal part of the educational task and it is shared by several institutions other than the school, notably the home and the church.

What is the attitude of the School to the inculcation of morals? Certain schools, such as the English public schools, have a traditional life of their own which is so closely identified with that of certain classes in the nation that they are regarded as the only adequate preparation for the life of that class. In Canada certain private schools maintain the same social and professional affiliations though with a much more attenuated relationship. In the United States the army and naval academies are probably the outstanding examples of the type of education which builds itself into a particular professional code. In general, however, in the new world the type of school that exists to maintain and develop a particular kind of character is the exception. Compulsory education produces a more universal form. The common school, because it is necessarily unselective in its clientele, applies the principle of selection by limiting the task which it is prepared to accept.

Thus the common school has singled out from the whole mass of traditional values those more developed parts of the social heritage which are described as *skills* and has concentrated its efforts on teaching these. Skills are highly evolved values; they are the products of the social milieu from which they arise and are the instruments through which a culture realizes itself. We tend to accept as sacrosanct those which are characteristic of our own culture; there is, however, nothing inevitable about them but their relevancy to that life for which they have been designed. Other situations preferred other skills. Thus the Parthians desired that their young men should be trained to ride, to shoot straight, and to tell the truth. Plato made music the basis of his ideal system of education although he gave it a content somewhat different from what the word suggests to us. It might be argued, however, that today music might really be more relevant to our needs than, for instance, arithmetic, first because it does more to contribute to our enjoyment and secondly because skill in music is becoming, thanks to the radio and the depression, one of the marketable commodities of our present life.

If we scrutinize the three R's it is hard to justify the exclusive emphasis placed on them in terms of relevancy for the present needs. We learn arithmetic at the expense of much time and greater effort, but how much do we use it? The elementary skill required in buying and selling, in making change, is mastered readily even by unschooled people. Actually when involved calculations are at stake we resort to a machine. The more significant questions of value, such as we have discussed under the Use of Money, are passed over by most schools and most homes. Similarly with writing; children are required to acquire a standardized handwriting with infinite care and pains. The child, whose ideas flow readily finds his writing ability an inadequate vehicle for his ideas and too often the ideas are lost because too high a standard of performance is demanded for their expression. Actually, most adults write illegibly and resort to a typewriter when they are anxious to be understood. The parallel with arithmetic is an exact one; the free, spontaneous flow of ideas is the important thing rather than a particular mold in which they are cast. What of reading! Here, certainly, we must concede a necessary skill, both for personal enjoyment and for social intercourse. The elaborate techniques by which reading is often taught seem to us, however, to obscure the issues of understanding the printed page and being able to transmit effectively the ideas which it gives. Again the thought and not the form is what matters. Given an adequate incentive children learn to read almost unwittingly. Teaching should focus on the motivation, that is, the relation of reading to the child's interests and needs. Since most adults fall far below their possible maximum ability in the mechanics of reading we have a right to expect more genuine efficiency on the part of schools in such teaching.

It seems, therefore, that a critical revision of skills may not be amiss in determining educational policy. We are concerned here only to point out the fundamental principle that *mores* determine skills. We may have to make some allowance for cultural lag, but is not the time overdue to bring our procedures of common education up to date? Also, what provision can we make for a closer integration of skills with cultural needs so that we shall not forever be attempting to close a widening gulf between education and life?

Another aspect of skills deserves consideration, that is, their relation to the persons acquiring them. Beyond the minimal essentials of basic skills we do allow some leeway in the choice of skills. Obviously no one person can acquire all the skills practiced in a complex civilization, therefore selection is inevitable. Vocational guidance for children is an attempt to relate the interests and abilities of the child to the needs of the community. Such attempts are largely empirical and neither the theoretical assumptions nor the generalizations from current practice have been clearly formulated. The one thing that seems to stand out clearly is that a too early channeling of interests is undesirable. The idea inherent in our discussions in previous chapters has been that children should be exposed to a wide variety of interesting activities in order that *they* may select, on the basis of experiment, those which most completely satisfy their needs.

This kind of vocational choice presupposes that activities to be meaning-ful must be related to the desires of the individual. Home and school share the responsibility to watching over and guiding such an adjustment.

If this view is accepted it will be seen that the learning of skills will become increasingly a matter of selection and individual preference. Skills represent the highest evolution of our social life. They both reflect and define the social matrix from which they emerge. Therefore they are susceptible of nicer discriminations, of degrees in excellence. Morals function on the all or none principle; we apply judgments of good or bad; the sheep are divided from the goats. We exact conformity to social cus-tom and a breach is regarded as more than an error in the learning pro-cess—it sets the person who commits it outside the pale. With skills, on the other hand, we recognize nice differences of performance and our examinations and tests are designed to register these. This difference in evolutionary status has important implications for education. We are apt to treat as differences in kind what are really only differences of degree.

If skills are recognized as the more sharply defined and specific aspects of common culture, the futility of teaching the one without reference to the other should be at once apparent. The common schools, for instance, usually accept as their task the teaching of intellectual skills, with some extras of physical, manual and aesthetic training, but they regard the realm of values as apart from their responsibility. To make children dili-gent, honest, fearless, what you will, is the province of the home. In prac-tice this distinction breaks down. The very way in which we do our work is a clear indication of character. Many an adult looks back on the painstak-ing faithfulness of a teacher in science or mathematics, on the meticulous accuracy of a classical scholar, or the enthusiastic interpretation of a teacher of literature or history as a crucial influence in their educational development. Such are the deposits of value which persist after specific information has been forgotten.

Conversely, it seems futile to attempt to convey values except through the media of concrete skills. Moral admonitions and so called "character education" miss the point through attempting to convey attitudes by those specific rules and instructions which are appropriate to skills. Such teaching puts on the immature learner the responsibility of selecting the situation to which the rule applies. Values are conveyed by implication rather than by direct teaching.

It seems, therefore, that skills and values must be regarded as distin-guishable but always coexisting in a living experience. Effective learning will mean progress in both aspects of experience. The director of the Yale Glee Club recently gave an address in which he emphasized the social and personal values of part-singing. Solo singing, he commented, sometimes did shocking things to one's ego, but it was impossible to take part in choral singing without learning to subordinate oneself to the whole. Both discipline and enjoyment were the products of such a training. This illustrates rather nicely the interdependence of skills and values. The skill depends on value, that is on a certain affective adjustment of each individual to a specific task; but equally value is most adequately conveyed when it is acquired through the concentration of attention on a specific skill.

This suggests a fundamental difference in method in learning skills and values. We learn skills by selecting a precise objective, by concentrated attention, by practice directed accurately to the end in view. Values seem to be learned indirectly, as by-products of the educational process. Thus in the home children learn routine skills by direct teaching, that is by verbal instruction and by being shown how to do the thing required. This is the area of direct control or training. Indirectly, however, they learn infinitely more from the examples and attitudes of their parents. These are the unwitting influences which form the halo which surrounds direct control. Together these comprise discipline, or the art of making disciples, that is, of initiating children into the ways of life accepted by the family. Harmony between these two spheres, the central and the surrounding one, is essential to effective training. It is not otherwise in the school situation. Beneath all the skills which the child learns is the re-enforcing or detracting influence of the teacher's personality. "I wish Mr. B. were not so emotional" a child remarked of her teacher. As both parents and teachers we need to remind ourselves that our mental states, cloudy or serene, are more significant formative influences in the lives of the children for whom we are responsible than are our direct instructions.

One important corollary of this fact should be noted. Children get their attitudes to the subject matter of their studies from the likes or dislikes which they feel for the teachers of these studies. The quality of the teaching is, of course, a part of this system, but in general children react to persons rather than to ideas; or to ideas through the medium of personality. Thus a child gets a slant towards history or mathematics or natural science because of the teacher who is responsible for the particular subject, and a child's future and destiny is often swayed, not by some native inclination, but by the attractions and repulsions in the social relations between pupil and teacher.

CREATIVE THOUGHT IN EDUCATION

So much for that phase of education which is concerned with conserving and transmitting the values of the past. What of the forward look? How can our educative procedures become a guide towards the future, a precise and trustworthy pathfinder for better forms of living? We believe that in providing the conditions favorable for creative thought we may make experience richer and more meaningful for the people whom we try to guide.

One blushes to use the expressions creative thinking or creative experience because they are often bandied about so carelessly that they signify little more than a rosy emotional vagueness. If one believes that the experience is a real and valid one it should be susceptible of at least some definition and description. We wish to attempt to state clearly what we mean when we use this phrase because we believe it to be the most effective instrument for progress in education. It can only be used effectively as the experience is identified and the laws of its operation understood.

To think creatively about any task or situation involves not recapitulating current accepted ideas but forging ahead to what is new. There are two common attitudes to novelty in thinking which seem to us to represent errors, though at opposite extremes from one another. First is the assertion that there is nothing new under the sun. This could be true only if by new we meant the absolutely different. The variety of our heritage of experience makes novelty of combinations inevitable and inexhaustible. The other error is to recognize novelty but to regard it as uncontrollable, unpredictable, almost cataclysmic—the mad genius theory of inspiration. We believe that this quality of "a"—of the fresh, unpredictable emergent, new thing is characteristic of our thought when it is inventive in character, but we believe that the *conditions* of creative thought can be studied and regulated even when in the very nature of the case the *outcome* cannot be forecast.

What, then, must we do if we wish to learn to think creatively? The first step is to surrender our customary thought forms, to clear our minds of mental junk, to be willing to break old molds of opinion. This is for most of us as painful an exercise as a cross country run or horseback riding would be for the person who for years has avoided strenuous physical exercise. A good many of us have to break away from sedentary habits of the mind even more than of the body. A few preliminary stretchings may indicate what is meant. At present we commit the work of formal teaching to the hands of inexperienced young people, whose knowledge of their craft has been drawn largely from a professional training school, who are mostly of the female sex and whom we then insist must remain unmarried thereby either making their interest in their profession transitory or, if they choose to stay with it, cutting off automatically their access to the enriching experience of marriage. Let us suppose that instead of limiting the task of teaching to the professional class that it were made both an obligation and a privilege for those people, men and women alike, who have achieved honorable distinction in any community to assume as a service of their mature years, the teaching of the young. Should we gain or lose? The point is a debatable one, but it is interesting to speculate. Actually this is what happens in primitive societies when the wise men of the tribe are responsible for initiating the young in the mysteries of tribal skills and customs. To them it would be unthinkable to leave the instruction to the callow young. Do we or they take education more seriously?

Let us try another stretch of the imagination. Suppose that, instead of building schools in the analogies of factories, designed for mass production, that we should copy the more informal, more individualized pattern of the home. Then our schools could be neighborhood institutions in our urban centres, where children in relatively small groups and under free, unconstrained conditions, could make their first acquaintance with education. Such schools, of course, do exist but they are pioneering exceptions.

It is unnecessary to pursue the fancy further; anyone who wishes can prove to himself the freeing effects of such stimulating exercises of a dormant imagination. To surrender our cherished beliefs and points of view, our faith in the saving efficacy of some particular discipline or technique of teaching, is extremely difficult, and cannot be done all at once; but the *willingness* to give up preconceived ideas is the first step to seeing the world in a new light, and this is the prerequisite of thinking creatively.

Anyone who is willing to submit his imagination to this kind of discipline will come some day to experience a *release* from the binding force of old thought forms. Such a freeing may be gradual, it may come with all the suddenness and conviction of an experience of religion to which it is closely akin. It usually grows out of a new view of the world. A distinguished professor of education, as the climax of a series of public lectures, described to a smaller group of people how, through realizing certain social implications of the present economic situation he was set free from fears and released into effective activity in relation to educational reform. This seems an oddly intellectual way to save one's soul, but undoubtedly there was an emotional reorientation bringing with it an exhilarating sense of freedom which made possible constructive action. The man thus freed was able to assume a prophetic role in education.

Fear is perhaps the most deadly deterrent to educational reform. The child is afraid of the teacher, the teacher of the principal, the principal of the superintendent, the superintendent of the Board of Education, the Board of Education of the electorate—and so the vicious circle completes itself in the home where it began. What is needed is for someone—at any point in the circle—to break the conduction; to act with confident assurance instead of being subservient to the powers. Only when we are released from educational inhibitions, fear of not passing, fear of losing our jobs, fear of speaking boldly what we believe to be true, will we be able to express new life in education.

The third stage in creative thinking is that of *waiting* for the new form to emerge. In the western world we do not like to wait; we distrust the values of the contemplative life and place our trust in activity as if to be busy were an end in itself. We have to learn the virtues of the "wise passiveness" which Wordsworth extolled—a passiveness which is not empty, but directed yet relaxed. It is the search for an answer but a search which expects the answer to be given, not evolved through the pressure of our overburdened minds. It depends on clearness, singleness of purpose and receptivity, and essentially on the seeking attitude and direction of our minds.

All this may seem visionary and remote from the processes of ordinary living. It is, but only because people are unwilling to experiment and test such procedures. Those who are really willing to open their minds to the operations of the creative power which governs our life and thought may find for themselves the reality of such experiences of fresh thoughts and feelings.

The fourth stage is that of *action*. To be willing to put new ideas to the test of experience is the mark of our taking them seriously. The acid test of thought is in action. There is a fundamental rhythm of reflective thought and vigorous initiative in which each is dependent on the other. Reflection supplies the direction for action, action in turn purges thought and gives it a new bearing. The failure to have a steady flow of fresh ideas is often due to our failure to act on those ideas which we already have. The springs of inspiration become choked when thoughts do not pass easily and directly into acts. Practical experience in them is the best test of the quality of our ideas.

If the task of education is to combine a discriminating selection of the skills best suited to present needs with a forward thrust into the emergent new values of the future, the practical question remains to be faced of how the individual, child or adult, is to *find himself* in such a process. How, in other words, are we to learn to live?

The first step in such a process of learning seems to be to start with those needs which are both personal and universal. To live effectively we need to know first of all how to manage our bodily appetites. Here the home still bears the weight of training, supplemented in some cases by the nursery school. To lift the discipline of the appetites to the level of individual responsibility the school contributes in the fields of hygiene, and more especially of physical education. The latter supplies a nice blend of discipline and enjoyment, essential alike for physical and for mental health. It is thus basic content for any educational program. The responsibility of the school for both satisfying and stimulating the appetite of change has already been considered from many angles. This is a distinctive function outside the sphere of the home to fulfill adequately. It calls into play all the resources of widening experience which the development of the growing child demands. It expresses itself characteristically in manipulations of the environment, both physical and mental. The great danger, both in home and school, lies in the discouragement of the tendency to experiment and explore which is natural to young children. Too early crystallization of habits, even though they be ultimately desirable ones, such as neatness, order, punctuality, manners, social consideration, may be unfortunate if the child's natural curiosity is thereby checked. Paul Prys and Meddlesome Matties, uncomfortable as they are from the adult point of view, are essentially normal children. To react vigorously and in original ways to our surroundings is the beginning of educational progress.

In addition to satisfying the appetitive needs of children, a sound education must provide for their emotional education. This involves training children to react powerfully and effectively to the people and things that make up their world. Certainly not suppression, not even control, but rather educating or the leading-out of the emotions should be our goal. Such emotional training is closely allied with the development of attitudes. Together they should foster in children a sense of confidence, of assurance based on knowledge, of persistent attack on problems, of judgment in relation to situations, and of an adventurous approach to life. Such training must command the resources of parents and teachers alike if it is to be adequate.

Again, the growing individual, in order that he may learn to live, needs abundant early experience in social adjustments. Nowhere is our education more pitifully inadequate than in the fundamentals of social relations. There are two main reasons for this. One is our lack of knowledge, especially accurate observation in regard to social behavior. Such observations should be forthcoming from school situations where social organization can be studied in its incipient form, as in gangs, the emergence of leadership, etc. From such studies we may hope in the future to assemble a body of dependable information as a basis for training in social living. In this way the present haphazard character of our social learning may yield to the ordering influence of the understanding and application of principles. The second reason for our social inadequacy is the postponement of social learning to too late in the learning process—a defect as serious as its incidental character. Nursery schools are a first step towards remedying this defect. The creation of a natural social setting in school from kindergarten on would do much to overcome this lack. While the home implants the basic social attitudes, whether of prejudice or of tolerance and acceptance, the school alone can supply a wide enough opportunity for social learning. For this reason alone it is of the greatest importance to have our schools more informal both as regards physical conditions, seating, size of rooms and classes etc., and, more especially, in regard to discipline. Instead of rigid uniformities of behavior and insistence on arbitrary rules governing speech and conduct, children must be allowed to move and associate freely, constrained by interest in what they are doing and by developing consideration for one another.

Four Areas of Experience

What have we a right to expect from such a plan of training? First of all, that the child finds his *vocation*. At present children drift into occupations without adequate consideration of their adaptation for the jobs which they attempt. Conversely, schools and colleges turn out professionally trained experts, doctors, teachers, lawyers, etc., with little attempt to regulate the supply in relation to the needs of the social situation. A haphazard method which guarantees neither individual fitness and enjoyment nor social demand is surely in need of intelligent revision. In the present confusion the best we can do is to expose the child to a wide range of activities and help him to select that which he *likes* best—on the assumption that what we like we generally do well. Such a procedure is admittedly inadequate as it disregards the need for social integration which is at least of co-importance with individual preference in the matter of vocational adjustment.

Secondly, education should provide, or at least help us to find, avocations, i.e. interests and activities which are subsidiary to our main business or occupation, related by relief and contrast and valued for their recreational powers. Here larger freedom of choice in relation to *personal* needs, with less deference to the social milieu is possible. We may become stamp collectors, may do *petit point* or shoot big game, design jewelry or paint pictures—in short do anything it pleases us to do provided our activities are not anti-social. The main point here is the release and development of the personality through enjoyment which such activities make possible. Recent years have seen a great surge of interest in leisure activities by reason of unemployment. Such a movement has focussed attention on the importance of avocations for mental health.

Thirdly, an adequate scheme of education will provide for the development and expression of social intimacies, first in the home, then at school among children of the same sex, and lastly between those of opposite sexes, leading to courtship and marriage. For such intimacies to flourish we require social opportunity as discussed above, emotional training and especially a meaningful significant relationship between adults, parents and teachers alike, and the children in their care.

Lastly our education should provide us with a view of life as a whole—a philosophy of life if we regard its intellectual aspects—a religion if we are concerned primarily with practice. *What* such a view of life should be can not be dictated; only that the experiences of the developing child should be such that he is able to formulate some coherent interpretation of the sum total of his experience.

If we look at these four areas of experience it will be seen that they differ greatly in degrees of precision and nicety of instruction. Thus vocations are taught with accuracy and are subject to a high degree of regulation from society at large and the special professions organized within themselves as guilds for the maintenance of their professional standards. Avocations we learn more freely, either by independent effort or by ourselves initiating our search for teachers. The selection is ours and we determine for ourselves that degree of proficiency which we find satisfactory, conforming to our own personal standards not to any outside requirements. In intimacies, regulation enters through providing adequate opportunity and favorable conditions for social experience; education is less a matter of instruction than of indirect control through environmental adjustment and through example. In the sphere of life values, we are farthest removed from the center of direct instruction, based on any body of accepted principle and practice. Here example, implication, are the methods pertinent to effective training. We can share our attitude to life with another, but we cannot impose it.

Methods in Education

We are thus face to face with the crucial question of educational method. How are we as adults to impart to children the skills and values which we have tested and approved? It should be clear that the question of method is more than any matter of techniques of teaching in a formalized sense. It involves the vital matter of the transmission from one person to another of certain ways of thinking and living.

Our first answer to the question of method is that we as adults must train ourselves to think in terms of learning rather than of teaching. We must envisage ourselves as learners along with our children rather than as teachers who speak from high places of authority. This means that we are not finished products, but are learning along with our children. We learn by exactly the same processes that they follow. This is not the place to discuss the learning process, but merely to point out how vital it is for all of us to understand it and use it to illuminate the proceedings of our daily lives. Learning is the one perennial interesting pursuit in life; it needs to be released from its academic context and set in relation to all experiences of life. Only when we share with children this enthusiasm for learning will we be effective teachers. Thus, if we want our children to be mathematicians we must do mathematics with them, not in any perfunctory, overseeing manner, but with enjoyment and enthusiasm. If we want them to be painters we must paint with them, and so on. We may be farther along the way, and capable therefore of guiding them, but to share in the learning process is essential. *Participant learning* is now as always the secret of successful teaching.

Secondly, we will recognize the relatively small area in experience which can profitably be occupied by rules and formal regulations and the immensely wider area where example and indirect influences have sway. This is not to abolish rules and regulations but to reduce them to the minimal essentials. That some rules are needed will scarcely be denied. It is interesting to watch an educational system which begins without rules gradually develop them in the interests of the community concerned. Thus a children's art school where there had been no formal rules developed two: one, that children must be there by a certain time; the other, that they must not go out to play at recess till the materials in use were put away. In the first case the rule was made because otherwise the morning's work was disorganized by children coming in at all hours. The second was because the children rushed out to play and left the teachers with all the tidying to do. It should be noted that in this case the reasons for the rules were clearly appreciated by the children. The rules were means for more effective communal living not ends in themselves, with some hypothetical moral value as discipline.

If we scrutinize the less defined but more pervasive influence of example it becomes apparent at once how profound is the influence of both parents and teachers on the educational development of children. Such influence is exerted not consciously or deliberately but often most profoundly when we are least aware of it. It is the impact of the *whole* personality on the child. An understanding of health, physical and mental, as this wholeness of personality, is fundamental to the equipment of parent and of teacher. This means that we will be less concerned with what we do directly with children; we will learn to relax the pressure of our conscientious efforts at training. We will, however, become increasingly concerned with the soundness of our own lives, with our satisfaction and enjoyment in our work, with the cultivation of adequate recreational interests, with the balance of our emotional life, with our ability to get along well with other people and with a dynamic and progressively enriching outlook on life. To have a rich, full, satisfying personal life which we are able to relate effectively to the lives of others is the second requirement of an effective teacher, whether in home or school.

Lastly, to be effective, parents and teachers must combine in the sense of making friends with one another because of their common interest in child training. Any lesser objective bifurcates the child's experience and makes the integration of his life increasingly difficult. As we see it, the whole-hearted cooperation of parents and teachers in a genuine attempt to understand themselves, one another and the child is an urgent present need. Such a need can best be met, not by creating new organizations, of which we have now too many, but by an inventive use of those we already possess such as home and school clubs. It is perhaps most adequately realized when a small group of parents and teachers are drawn together through a common interest in education to think through their common task. Knowledge and friendship are the ingredients for such a successful cooperation. It is in the hope of stimulating such attempts to assess anew the task of education as the common responsibility of home and school that this book has been written.

THE RELIGIOUS TRAINING OF CHILDREN

In the preceding chapters we have been discussing the child's learning in relation to the world around him—his adjustments to people and to things. In this chapter we are to look at his learning to know God—the conditions of such learning, its values in relation to all kinds of life and experience.

What is Religion

When we talk about learning to know the world in which we live, or coming into relation with people it is clear what we mean, but how do we come to know God? Our knowledge of God belongs to the realm of attitude and emotion rather than to perceptual experience. The religious attitude is hard to describe because it is a direct and original form of experience—as distinctive and as ineffable as is a color or a sound. James tried to express it years ago; it will be noted how largely he deals in negatives in his definition.

> Religion, whatever it is, is a man's total reaction upon life, so why not say that any total reaction upon life is a religion? Total reactions are different from usual or professional attitudes. To get at them you must go down behind the foreground of existence and reach down to that curious sense of the whole residual cosmos as an everlasting presence, intimate or alien, terrible or amusing, lovable or odious, which in some degree every one possesses. This sense of the world's presence, appealing as it does to our

peculiar individual temperament, makes us either strenuous or careless, devout or blasphemous, gloomy or exultant, about life at large; and our reaction, involuntary and inarticulate and often half unconscious as it is, is the completest of all answers to the question "What is the character of this universe in which we dwell?"

But so very broad a use of the word "religion" would be inconvenient, however defensible it might remain on logical grounds. There are trifling, sneering attitudes even towards the whole of life, and in some men these attitudes are final and systematic. It would strain the ordinary use of language too much to call such attitudes religious…. For common men religion whatever more special meanings it may have, signifies always a *serious* state of mind…. It favors gravity, not pertness; it says hush to all vain chatter and smart wit…. But if hostile to light irony, religion is equally hostile to heavy grumbling and complaint. The world appears tragic enough in some religions, but the tragedy is realized as purging, and a way of deliverance is held to exist.

There must be something solemn, serious and tender about any attitude which we denominate religious. If glad, it must not grin and snicker; if sad, it must not scream or curse. It is precisely as being *solemn* experiences that I wish to interest you in religious experiences…. The divine shall mean for us only such a primal reality as the individual feels impelled to respond to solemnly and gravely, and neither by a curse nor a jest.

We may describe the essence of religion thus by a general description of attitudes and emotions or we may borrow from the level of everyday experience a homely figure to represent what we mean by the religious attitude. This method of portraying a supra-sensible reality in concrete terms is not peculiar to religion. Every science uses it when it seeks for a metaphysics to explain experienced facts. In religion one of the best expressions of the religious attitude is that of the *confident* approach of a child to his father. We live in a world which is only partially known and still more partially controlled. When we seek for an adjustment to the power that makes that world alive we can assume an attitude of trust and obedience—of putting ourselves in line with this fundamental power—learning its nature—willing to be used by it. This attitude of acceptance instead of resistance or attempted evasion or escape is intrinsic in the religious attitude.

But religion goes farther than this. It assumes, or rather, the more highly developed religion assumes that the power which governs the world and regulates human life is a friendly power—that *love* is the quality which determines the relationship. "Religion," someone has said recently "is a way of living in relation to other people and to God which is a way of love." Thus religion is not a way of explaining why the world and life are as they are; it is rather a way of relating ourselves to the realities of our experience so that our lives reach their fullest possibility. It is concerned less with the *why* than with the *how* of life; not with the inscrutable but with the practical and unavoidable.

If the individual's attitude to God is one of childlike confidence and acceptance, the response of God is best described in the terms of the Father, who gives his child what is good. Other figures have been used— god as King, as Governor, as Creator. But the homely, intimate figures of family life are the best description of what God means—because they are the ones that we understand best. They are the deepest expressions of the sense of God in Hebrew literature, and Jesus employed and intensified the sense of the child-parent relationship between man and God which was the heritage of his religious training.

Learning to Know God

How do children learn to know God? We need not speculate as to an independent access to and relation with God for the individual because actually we all begin with *knowledge about* God. Children hear about God inevitably whether we tell them or not— just as they hear about sex. For this reason, parents cannot ignore the responsibility of taking some attitude to religion; they must be prepared to answer their children's questions. As in other spheres of experience, evasion is never a satisfactory way.

Knowledge *about* is, however, different from knowledge *of* God. Children learn about God by hearsay, but how do they experience Him. Such knowledge is almost invariably mediated by some person who has direct experience of God. We learn to know God by our contacts with people who learn, love and obey Him. Knowledge about can never be a substitute for this intimate contact through the medium of another personality.

The implication of this is very clear for parents. If they wish their children to know God they must themselves know Him and transmit that knowledge to their children. Many parents want their children to have religious training while they themselves are indifferent or skeptical in matters of religion. There is an inherent contradiction in this attitude—in assuming a value for our children in something which we regard as valueless for ourselves. Children take our *real* estimate of religion from what they see of it as a force in our lives, not from our insistence that *they* should go to church or Sunday School.

A child needs explicit teaching and practice in getting to know God— he needs help through the sharing of such experiences with Him and their interpretation by an adult who is at home in such experiences. The form of this intimate, personal training will depend on the religious experience of the parents; but certain general principles may be laid down as to the form which it should take.

First, it should be *honest*. Nowhere is there more pretense and camouflage than in the fundamental teaching of religion to young children. Parents who have learned to be honest about sex, and to admit their ignorance about astronomy will blandly make statements which they neither believe nor have tested in practice. The child's religious life is thus unreal from the start. Better, if parents recognize no knowledge or experience of God to say so honestly at the start. *Then* they may refer their children to those who have, if they are uncertain as to the limits of their own ignorance.

The more urgent problem, however, is for parents who have religious convictions to know how to make these available for the needs of the young child. This involves our second principle of telling simply and clearly what the young child can understand and use. As in sex education parents are warned not to try to tell the whole story of sex, but only so much at one time as a child needs and can assimilate, so in religious teaching simple answers to the child's first questions are usually the most adequate. One child of six who asked his mother what God was told that He was the good in people—in the child's father and mother and sister and so on. No theologian would accept this as an adequate description of God, but it met the child's need and gave him a point of departure in learning to know God.

The third principle is that the child should be taught to seek God for himself—to turn to God and to expect God to speak to him in response. Much of religion is learned by implication, but the core of experience has to come by putting ourselves in the way of cultivating that experience. This is true of any discipline—we learn through practice and attention and effort. The individual, child or adult, can only experience God in so far as he is trained to put himself in the way of God's speaking to him. He must learn to listen, to recognize God's response. The story of the child Samuel is the pattern for such experience. It involves an act of humble, attentive listening on the child's part—along with faith in the genuineness of the response. This is the core of the religious experience.

These may be summarized, therefore, as the rules of religious training, that it should be sincere, adapted to the child's understanding and designed to issue in a direct experience of the child himself. This direct instruction forming the core of religious experience corresponds with the area of rules in general discipline. As specific rules embodied in the routine form the centre of discipline, whether in the life of the family or of the individual, so in religious training, the instruction and practice within this small circle of an intimate personal relation lies at the heart of the religious life.

In discipline the small area of specific rules is surrounded by a larger, less sharply defined circle of what we may describe as example. In this area learning is not by direct instruction as with routine experiences, but is by suggestion and implication. The reinforcement of rules by example is the most potent force in discipline; harmony between the two is absolutely necessary if discipline is to be effective. Religious training shows an exact parallel. The rules are represented by specific religious training, simple, direct, leading to the child's own relationship with God, just as the rules in discipline aim at the child's assuming responsibility for his own action. As in discipline the rules are reinforced and impenetrated by the subtle forces of example, so in the religious life it is the parents' religion, their own sense of God and the governing of their lives in relation to him which constitutes the child's most powerful incentive to religious experience.

Another point of importance here is the influence of the family pattern on the form of religious thinking. We have said that the parent-child relationship seems to offer the most satisfying portrayal of the relation between the individual and God, while the family of God is the reflection and intensification of the earthly family. If the pattern of the human family is marred or broken it becomes much harder to realize adequately the experience of religion as a life on the family analogy. Conversely, if the child grows up in a home where love, consideration, care, respect for the needs of its members are taken for granted he has a background experience which makes it easy for him to accept the idea of the love of God, and to extend the relation of friendliness which he has experienced within the home to those less intimately related. Again the parallel with sex training is informative. Specific sex instruction, important and necessary as it is, gets its context from the adjustment between parents. The child may never consciously formulate the fact that his parents enjoy and love one another; but he interprets marriage in the light of this knowledge. Similarly, the human virtues which are reflections of the character of God become the strongest incentive towards a further approach to Him. Family life, if it is sound and wholesome, becomes the matrix out of which the specific convictions of religion may most favorably develop.

If the special function of the home is to implant and then to nourish the root experience out of which religion is to develop, what of other institutions, notably school and church, in relation to its further growth? The home is concerned with personal religion, but personal experience of God is only the starting point of the religious life, which remains pale and spindly unless it is nourished by relationships with others of like experience. The direct, experimental, experiential principle needs to be reinforced by the social and traditional life of institutions.

Religion is as much a fellowship with other people as it is a direct experience of God. Or perhaps it is more correct to say that out of the direct experience grows a creaturely feeling for other people because they too are the children of God. What does this mean in the experience of the child? He should learn in his own home to live in relation to the other members of the household, to understand and respect them. Outside he needs to have the same social experience cultivated in a wider group. The church can cultivate this experience of social life, giving it point and reality by bringing the child's social experiences in line with the fundamental orientation of his life to God. Many problems that perplex and baffle children can be met in this way if the children meet in small groups with experienced teachers and talk through their perplexities in the attempt to find a genuine answer for their problems. "How to do my homework," "How to get on with my kid sister," "What should I do when the other boys call me names," "If I fight I am not true to Christ, if I walk away they think I am a sissy." Such questions, expressed spontaneously from the needs of children, bear a curious resemblance to the problems that their parents state in child study groups. They indicate an awareness of social responsibility which we often fail to credit in children. A class in a church school, led by an intelligent, trained and devoted adult, can be come a clearing house for social perplexities and a training in social living.

There is a further reach of social experience when children learn to express together their attitudes and emotions towards God. Worship is the distinctive act of the religious life. The child needs to learn how to express and how to intensify the attitude of confident approach which we posited as the first gesture of the religious life. He needs *forms* to do this in, and the church, as the custodian of institutional religion, can supply the adequate vehicle. Worship is intensified when it is a social act and when it is expressed in the historic forms of the religion in which the child is being trained.

The discipline of the emotional life has always been one of the great functions of religion—a function which modern sophisticated parents tend to overlook. Yet religion elicits the most powerful emotions: love and aspiration towards God and men, anger towards wrong, fear sublimated into awe and reverence. Similarly with the attitudes and self-tendencies. We have dwelt on the attitude of approach, which consolidates with the development of the religious life into one of steady, constant acceptance—a tendency of the whole life rather than an occasional gesture. The person who learns to put his trust in God develops a confidence which carries him through difficulties which would daunt a less disciplined person. "Ability to stand strain" has been suggested as a definition of religion. It is obviously inadequate as a definition, but it expresses one important outcome of the religious way of life. The self negative tendency, often slighted in our analysis of motivation, finds its proper place in religion. Just as it is important that we should learn to approach life with confidence, so it is important that we should know when to defer, when to bow before superior power, experience and authority. Religion becomes a touchstone to test the truth or falsity in claims of authority. It cultivates, too, an ambivalent attitude towards God, so that we both love God and fear Him, approach confidently and bow with reverence. Intimacy is always blended with awe in a complete religious experience. If either is emphasized, then religion becomes lop-sided.

In addition to being a personal and a social experience religion is also an *historical fact* and needs to be presented and grasped in its historical sequence. This means that the child should be taught the history of religions and also, more specifically, the history and literature of that particular religious form to which he adheres. This more intellectual aspect of religious training should follow on the earlier elements. It is particularly germane to the experience of the school child. In teaching comparative religion and the history of civilization, the child should be helped to understand the universality of the religious impulse, and thus to realize the evolution of the more adequate and complete forms of its expression from the earlier, primitive stages. To cultivate a sense of history, of the genetic development of the race as well as of the individual is a fundamental of education too often overlooked by teachers as well as parents.

How should the historical feeling for religion be developed? It seems unfortunate that our thinking on religious issues is so beclouded that we have failed to discriminate between instruction in the doctrinal aspects of a particular faith—the task of the church—and the teaching of the history and literature of religion, the proper function of the schools. If the history of ancient civilizations is to be taught in our secondary schools, it seems absurd that the history of the Hebrews must be passed over as though it did not exist—solely because we derive our religion from that source.

The similar neglect of the Bible as literature is equally absurd and equally damaging. The English bible is still the great source book of the English tongue—its sayings and illustrations impregnate the thinking of our writers regardless of their religious convictions. Yet we teach derivative works but refuse to recognize the English bible as a literary source book. The inconsistency of these attitudes is manifest.

Our ideal program, to sum up, would be of the home as the custodian of personal and family religion, the church as responsible for the social and traditional aspects of religious experience and the school as the teacher of the historical and literary aspects of religious tradition.

Having looked thus briefly at the possibilities of religious training it remains to ask what values are to be served by such a plan? The Why as following the How of the religious life? What can religion give us which is a plus value beyond the usual program and incentive of education and mental hygiene?

Discipline or the Regulative Principle

All students of child study are thoroughly familiar with the idea of discipline and its place in training. To bring man's appetitive nature into harmony has always been an ideal of education. Plato gave pointed expression to this need and from his time onward the regulation of instinctive tendencies first among themselves within the individual life, and then in relation to the social setting in which our life is oriented has been a main objective of education. Religion has always accepted and addressed itself to this problem. Its mode of regulation has not always been a wise one; asceticism, or the denial of appetite has often been accepted as the ideal rather than control and use. More pervasive and insidious than the ascetic ideal is the negative conception which placed the distinctive characteristic of religion in prohibitions and restraints rather than in positive action. Nothing is more damaging to the character of the individual or the cause of religion than this negative concept of goodness.

Yet the element of restraint is inherent in a fully developed religious experience! Wherein lies the difference? It consists in what one may describe as the *regulative value of the higher* principle. This may be seen in a simple illustration. The young child in a nursery school alternates between the use of materials and social activity. He seldom combines the two in one complex act until he has reached a certain development of skill through experience. Once he has achieved this synthesis by which he uses material, not as an independent value but as a function of social play he becomes increasingly facile in using material in a meaningful way. In adult life we seldom give material things independent value, we use them as media of social intercourse. The miser and the glutton represent regressions to infantile forms of behavior. The use of materials is disciplined by social requirements.

Similarly, social life may attain a new richness and significance when it is subsumed under an experience of God. When we are significantly related to God we begin to develop new capacities of relationship with other people. As material activities are regulated by social so social activities are regulated by religious in this hierarchy of controls. This means that control is never an end in itself but a means.

Religious control has practical significance because it accelerates the transference from external to inner or self-discipline which is the goal of education. While our behavior stays on the level of social relationship we are constrained by the opinions of others, by social approval and disapproval, by the conventions of society. Religion, by swinging us into the orbit of God lifts us from the round of conventional behavior and gives us freedom through our response to God. This is a paradox of the religious life freedom through discipline—man finding his completest fulfillment when he is most dependent on God. God is the source of order, and in the train of order comes a heightened sense of beauty, and especially the feeling of purpose and meaning in life. To feel one's life growing daily into a pattern through our response to the orderliness of God is an experience which absorbs and intensifies our own conscious, feeble efforts after self discipline.

The discipline of religion is both passive and active. Passive training is largely ignored in present life. Yet in every age certain people have called attention to its value.

> She has a world of ready wealth
> Our waiting hearts to bless
> Think you mid all this mighty sum
> Of things forever speaking
> That nothing of itself will come
> That we must still be seeking
> That we should tune these minds of ours
> In a wise passiveness.

The cultivation of the listening, waiting attitude of expectancy and receptiveness is a distinctive note of religion. It can counteract the fussiness of thought and action which devitalizes life.

On the active side, religion makes it possible for men to act with decision because they have convictions. It expresses vital action because that action is fused in an experience in which emotional and intellectual aspects are nicely blended.

Learning or the Enjoyment Principle

But religion is more than discipline. In the Westminster catechism the first answer states that: Man's chief end is to glorify God and to *enjoy Him forever*. The note of enjoyment is thus sounded where we should least expect it, from these grim Calvinistic divines of the seventeenth century. It is an authentic note of the religious life. While this has always been recognized the forms of enjoyment have not always been agreed upon. The middle ages tended to postpone the joys of religion to a future life; it was the characteristic emphasis of the modern spirit to insist on the present as well as the other worldliness of religious experience. The sense of enjoyment in religion is tied up with the question of incentives, which brings us to the conception of the religious life as a life in which *learning* is a fundamental need. People suffer boredom in everyday life because of limited objectives which are too easily obtained. Alexander, weeping for more worlds to conquer, has many counterparts in the contemporary world. People are bored, disillusioned, defeated largely because they have accepted casually incentives which are too slight to be of sustaining interest in life. Learning is the answer to ennui and the key to enjoyment. It matters, however, what we learn. Some pursuits are inherently more interesting and more productive than others. God is the final horizon of our experience, a horizon which we never reach but which is always environing our present world and impregnating the newer scene with meaning.

What is the distinctive contribution of religious experience to the learning process? Learning is an interrelation between our efforts and some point in the environment to which action is directed. We have seen in the preceding paragraphs how religion trains and disciplines our native powers so that we can act with resolution. On the external side, religion determines our objectives; it helps us to discover what ends of action are desirable, to discriminate among purposes. This is basically a question of emotional training; learning is too narrowly thought of when we emphasize its intellectual aspects to the exclusion of the emotions and attitudes which determine the direction and the degree of learning.

If God is an objective reality comprehending in His nature all lesser forms of experience, which take their values in relation to Him, then knowledge of God becomes the clue to all other forms of knowledge. In particular, our relations with people become different when they are governed by our relation to God.

It is a commonplace to remark on the need for direction in human learning. Yet education rarely takes account of direction, indeed, regards it as outside its province.

"Now her education made of her mind a two-edged tool able to cut in any direction but not to choose a direction" is the comment of a woman doctor of philosophy from one of the great American universities. This question of the direction of learning is one which education cannot continue to evade. Men, individually and in groups, must come to grips with the question of values if civilization is not to destroy itself.

Because learning is the most inherently satisfying of human activities, and because God is the supreme object of our search it follows that the life turned towards Him and lived in relation to Him has the greatest possibility of rich, full, complete experience. Those forms of religion which have interpreted the religious life in terms of negation, prohibition and privation have falsified the true nature of the experience of God. Joy is the deep, enduring note of an authentic religious experience.

Security and Religion

If religion gives discipline and enjoyment it also gives security to life. Security has two main aspects: a sense of at-homeness, on the one hand, of belonging, of confidence; and on the other, of adventure. If I really feel myself in relation to God I get the sense of belonging, of being a part of a plan instead of an isolated unit, of having a role to play instead of being an outcast. The sense of psychological alienation which is seen as underlying crime, delinquency and many forms of mental disorder is succeeded by an experience of integration which grows with the developing experience of the individual. This is necessary to any real sense of security. The individual can never be secure in himself alone. The doctrine of self-sufficiency is false to the constitution of human life. It is told that when James Whitcomb Riley read Henley's famous lines

> I am the master of my fate
> I am the captain of my soul

he exclaimed, "The Hell he is!" Security means first of all reconciliation with the nature of things—physical laws—human relatedness, and the character of God. The child learns this reconciliation in the adjustment of his desires to the social milieu in which he is brought up; the adult learns it in accepting life in the progressively complex situations in which he finds himself.

Security demands, however, more than adjustment. It is important to feel at home instead of estranged from our surroundings; but this is never a static relationship; it can be maintained only by constant new adjustments on our part to the changes in the world in which we live. In other words, security can never mean safety. Safety is the attempt to maintain the status quo, to avoid the uncertainty and risk of living by doing nothing. Such an attempt destroys the life it would preserve because constant learning is a law of self-preservation.

Security in learning involves a constant effort after the new and undiscovered in human experience. Thus acceptance is never enough; it needs to be reinforced by understanding. Understanding in turn should be the revision of past experience in order to get a new direction for present action. Thus security means always moving forward into new and untried areas of experience—in other words, an act of faith.

When we play safe in life the circumference of our life contracts, we shrink into ourselves and fear becomes the determining force in our relations with things and with people. We become scared off from even moderate risks and we trust people less and less as life goes on. Security, on the contrary, challenges us to live richly and completely—to have that enjoyment and full flavor of life that comes only from the full exercise of our powers. The quality of life, not its duration then becomes important. The attitudes and emotions involved in security are thus those of search, exploration, experiment, a consistent advance towards the unknown, willingness to make terms with the unpredictable in experience. This gives a zest to life which cannot be had on any other basis. It is the security which uses learning as the tool of adjustment and of advance.

What is the genetic development of patterns of security? The young child experiences a security dependent on the care of the family. Gradually he emancipates himself from this nurturing security and learns to act independently—to walk, to talk, to satisfy his physical needs, to care for his person, to go to school. But the fostering security of the social environment is always present to complement the security which he is developing through his growing competence to handle situations. McDougall has sketched this progressive emancipation:

> Thereafter all persons fall for the child into one or other of two classes: in the one class are those who impress him as being of superior power, who evoke his negative self-feeling, and towards whom he is submissive and receptive; in the other class are those whose presence evokes his positive self-feeling and towards whom he is self-assertive and masterful, just because they fail to impress him as beings superior to himself. As his powers develop and his knowledge increases, persons who at first belonged to the former class are transferred to the latter; he learns, or thinks he learns, the limits of their powers; he no longer shrinks from a contest with them, and, every time he gains the advantage in any such contest, their power of evoking his negative self-feeling diminishes, until it fails completely. When that stage is reached his attitude towards them is reversed, it becomes self-assertive; for their presence evokes his positive self-feeling. In this way a child of good capacities, in whom the instinct of self-assertion is strong, works his way up the social ladder. Each of the wider social circles that he successively enters—the circle of his playmates, of his school-fellows, of his college, of his profession impresses him at first with a sense of a superior power, not only because each circle comprises individuals older than himself and of greater reputation, but also because each is in some degree an organized whole that disposes of a collective power whose nature and limits are at first unknown to the newly admitted member. But within each such circle he rapidly finds his level, finds out those to whom he must submit and those towards whom he may be self-assertive. Thus, when he enters a great school, the sixth-form boys may seem to him god-like beings whose lightest word is law; and even the boys who have been but a little while in the school will at first impress him and evoke his negative self-feeling by reason of their familiarity with many things strange to him and in virtue of their assured share in the collective power of the whole society. But, when he himself has reached the sixth form, or perhaps is captain of the school, how completely reversed is this attitude of submissive receptivity! When he enters college, the process

begins again; the fourth-year men, with their caps and their colours and academic distinctions, are now his gods, and even the dons may dominate his imagination. But at the end of his fourth year, after a successful career in the schools and the playing fields, how changed is his attitude towards his college society! The dons he regards with kindly tolerance, the freshmen with hardly disguised disdain; and very few remain capable of evoking his negative self feeling, perhaps a "blue," or a "rugger international," or a don of worldwide reputation; for the rest he has comprehended them, grasped their limits, labeled them, and dismissed them to the class that ministers to his positive self-feeling. And so he goes out into the great world to repeat the process and to carry it as far as his capacities will enable him to do."

Paralleling this social emancipation is the corresponding freedom which comes from skills, physical and intellectual. Each step in the mastery of a given skill means greater freedom and control in relation to the environment and hence greater security in terms of such mastery. Education helps to establish such securities by guiding the child's learning.

Material security is sought in some occupation or profession. The ability to do things has always been highly prized in the new world where security in terms of one's own capability is more regarded than the adventitious security of class or social position. Emotional security is sought in love and marriage. As dependence on parental care is outgrown the need for intimate social relationship finds normal satisfaction in a relationship of equality and interdependence between husband and wife, which in turn develops into the care of children. Thus the cycle of social intimacy within the family is completed in the transition from the position of dependence to maintenance in respect of security.

Adjustments in our physical life in work, in intimacies both within and outside the family, are all made either in conformity to the safety or the security motif, either in retreat from experience, or in learning involving growth and progressive cultivation of new possibilities of experience. What has religion to add to these?

Religion may express the safety motif as well as other aspects of experience. Thus any religion which permanently withdraws itself from the world, which fears examination, which shrinks from contact with unpleasant experiences is a religion that plays safe by avoiding the issues. A religion which is interested in security rather than safety pins its faith on God. From the earliest times the great religious leaders have had this element of adventure—Moses going out not knowing whither is the prototype of the religious life.

Today sees many of our accepted forms of security menaced—economic, governmental, social and cultural. It remains to see if there is a final security in man's dependence on God which releases him from all lesser dependencies in order that his life may swing freely into the orbit of

God's purpose. No other argument can be advanced for such a view of life and its consequences than that of experiment. If we assume God as a real power operating in our lives, are we thereby made at home in the world in which we live, given increasing power to understand that world and relate ourselves significantly to it, and do we experience a quality of adventurous living not possible on a less comprehensive basis?

Children's Friendships

The child's first experience of love arises naturally out of the care which he receives as an infant. Normally his mother is his first friend, though a nurse who plays this role may be the object of this primary attachment. The social organization which allots fundamental responsibility to the nurse is reflected, for example, in the devotion to his old nurse which is expressed in Robert Louis Stevenson's poems of childhood. In our society the mother is usually the object of the child's first love because he depends on her for care and subsistence. Relations with other members of the family are often mediated through her. It is easy to see why mothers tend to be the predominating influences in their children's lives, the arbiters of their destinies. It usually takes a deliberate effort of detachment on the mother's part to allow the child as he grows older to emancipate himself from this dependent relation. In place of it there should emerge a relation of friendship in which each is willing to learn from the other without any presumption of superiority. This establishes a permanent relationship which makes constant growth possible.

The family group, where there are a number of children, may present a complex system of alliances and oppositions. Jealousy is a poison commonly distilled in family life, especially when children contend with one another for a parent's favor. This can be avoided only when each child feels secure of his own place in his parents' regard—a place which no other one can fill. This sense of security is basic to the child's later adjustments, to the confidence with which he faces the outside world. It is the point of rest which stabilizes all later social adjustments.

Relations with siblings fall naturally into place in relation to this central adjustment. The inequality of family relationships are their distinctive feature, inequalities of age and sex with their corresponding differences of experience and status. To keep these relations free from rivalry and antagonism so that children may reap the full fruits of enjoyment from the family situation is of first importance. Those activities which draw the family into a unit in some common enterprise of work or play are vital to a wholesome family life. Equally important is the respect for special alignments within the family circle, the willingness to allow freedom for the development of such attachments without the desire of a third party to invade the relation. The care of an older for a younger child, the devotion of two children near together in age, are examples of such alliances.

Patterns of friendship have thus received a certain form before the child begins to associate with children outside the home. The nursery school has supplied us with a fairly clear-cut picture of what happens when children of approximately the same age are brought together under favorable social conditions. Young children manifest as a rule an indiscriminate friendliness. They have relations with all the children in the group. An element of selectivity is present, however, as one child will usually be the recipient of more social contacts than any other. As the children grow older the range of social contacts decreases, and the tendency to choose one companion becomes more marked. The older children tend to restrict their contacts to those of their own age. Well-knit social groupings of two or three children begin to emerge, as shown reciprocal contacts. These groups tend to be relatively permanent. Occasionally strong friendships develop between two children who become relatively self-sufficient to one another. These may be the result of outside acquaintances or they may seem to be determined by real preferences in the children. What governs such preferences we cannot at present say. What will be the influences of such early friendships on later development is hard to say. Children forget early experiences quickly; on the other hand, certain friendships begun in nursery school show a remarkable vitality when opportunity for renewing the acquaintance is provided. Data may some day be available in regard to the persistence of such early associations.

School friendships show as a rule increasing emphasis on the principle of selectivity; the growing child has usually a "best friend" with whom a fairly intense relationship develops. These friendships, although intense while they last, yet form and re-form with almost bewildering rapidity; perplexed families sometimes find it difficult to be *au fait* with the "friend of the month." This tendency to change friends need not cause concern, indeed a too early fixation of a childish friendship may be a less desirable occurrence. Children need practice in choosing friends and these kaleidoscopic relationships are necessary phases of social experimentation.

The "gang" becomes a distinctive form of children's friendships, meaning by this a fairly cohesive group centred around a leader. With girls the same tendency takes the form of cliques, clubs and secret societies. An elaborate paraphernalia of rules, initiatory rites, meeting places, passwords may grow up with apparent spontaneity around such an organization.

Children during the school period rarely form close friendships with those of the opposite sex. One should beware, however, of generalizing from this in regard to innate sex differences. Even if children are not segregated in school, the force of social custom tends to discourage associations. When these intangible barriers are removed, children of opposite sex associate naturally provided they enjoy the same things.

Common interest is probably the soundest basis for friendship with children as with adults. Enjoyment of the same types of activity, whether these be physical sports and games, aesthetic interests, or intellectual pursuits, forms an enduring bond. The friendship is firmly rooted in a common experience, not merely in accident or propinquity.

The fabric of friendship is a delicate thing, and adults should recognize this and exercise insight and forbearance in their attitudes to children's friendships. Certain principles may be outlined which bear on adult regulation. First of all, children need practice in choosing friends; it is much better to let them make early choices freely and learn from experience than to choose their friends for them. A mistake in childhood is easily recognized and corrected with little emotional cost; mistakes in later life such as business and professional associates, and preeminently the choice of a mate, are important and a mistake may be irretrievable or very costly. Trial marriage has its advocates and its opponents, but the importance of trial friendship has not been sufficiently recognized. Parents are often unwisely critical of their children's friends because they feel that they have not been chosen according to the canons that they themselves accept. These canons may not be worthy; they may reflect social snobbery, race prejudice, class consciousness. The child's choice may be more democratic and humane. We should beware of infecting children with our prejudices. A catholic taste in friends is an advantage rather than otherwise; in any case, the child has a right to his own choices and his own mistakes.

Secondly, when parents fear the vulgarizing or corrupting influences of certain companions for their children they should remind themselves of the transient effects of these alliances which seem so engrossing while they are at their zenith. Family standards are the permanent ones; these are wrought into the very fabric of the child's being even though he is in rebellion against them. The way to offset an undesirable friendship is not to oppose it but to look again at the family standards to see if they deserve to be perpetuated. To strengthen them is the only legitimate answer to an undesirable friendship outside.

Thirdly, adults have it in their power to set a pattern of friendship which children will want to copy. They do this first of all in the range, quality and permanence of their friendships with other adults. Children may see in their parents the determination of friendships on a negative basis, that of common antipathies, prejudices, taboos and conventions. Or they may see ambition, whether for professional or social advancement as the governing motive. Another kind of friendship is built on the past, on childhood memories and experiences. It is always significant to know whether a person's frame of reference is in the past, the present or the future.

A positive note is struck when friendships are built on common tastes and interests, whether these be golf, music, literature, social or philanthropic work, scientific pursuits. People who work together on the same job usually have a basis of participation and common understanding. There is, however, a deeper basis than this, when friendship is interpreted as availability for another's need, whoever that other may be. This is the adequate expression of the outgoing or identification motive discussed in the preceding chapter.

This is the exact opposite of a sentimental friendship although it may easily be confused with it. Sentimentality is to stimulate the emotions of friendship for our own enjoyment; we allow ourselves to be exploited as friends when we are ourselves seeking the satisfaction of being kind, or generous. Genuine friendship demands insight into the true needs of the person who asks something of us, and a determination to give that rather than what he asks or what we like to give. When such a conviction is accepted and lived out the range of our friendship is measured by our capacity to give and by the demands made on us. We do not pick and choose, neither affinities nor antipathies are allowed to deflect our attitude. This motive is best expressed in professional life at its highest where the physician's response is in relation to need, where the mental doctor, be he priest or clinician, heals regardless of personal likes or dislikes, and where the teacher's willingness to impart is limited only by the student's desire to learn.

These are mature conceptions, which would imply for children a precocious idea which might easily degenerate into priggishness. Without being formulated in words, however, our responses to the demands of other people will be sensed by children. They will see how we handle beggars at the door, how we entertain our friends, how we tolerate visitors who interrupt our work. Unwittingly they will absorb either a selfish or an unselfish motive from our behaviour.

More particularly children will be affected by our attitudes to their friends. Intense preoccupation with our own children often tends to make us overlook or depreciate their friends. Actually we rob ourselves most when we do this. Few adults know how to be friends with children. We have to learn to approach them without feelings of superiority, without talking down or trying to impress them. There has to be a fundamental respect for the child's attitudes and feelings that forbids us to invade his privacy or to exploit his defencelessness against our advances. A kind of quiet attentive waiting that invites but does not compel his response, but lets the child know that we are interested in him is the attitude which establishes confidence. Courtesy, with children as with adults, is the essence of friendship. When this is recognized there are no age barriers.

The adult who takes the trouble to make friends with children often builds much better than she knows. The teacher has a peculiar opportunity to build herself into the life of a child. I suppose most mature people look back on some such friendship as one of the most enriching experiences of childhood. Ideals, interests and ambitions grow from such a relationship; the adult who is outside the family represents another point of view, and children often feel freer to discuss their desires and difficulties with such a friend than with a member of the family. The counselor in schools has this as a professional function in cases calling for special adjustment, but the opportunity is in no sense restricted to one in such a capacity.

The admiration and adulation of a child may assume embarrassing aspects for the adult on whom it is fixed. "Crushes" belong distinctively to the period of adolescence, but probably every teacher has suffered at some time from the child who is always waiting at the gate. The ideology of crushes has probably never been thoroughly understood. That some teachers encourage extravagant admiration because it feeds some lack of affectional satisfaction is probably true. Others in repudiation of such an attitude repel the child's advances, a response just as damaging to the child. The matter needs to be viewed understandingly from the *child's* point of view. Is it a lack of affectional security in home life for which the child is trying to compensate?

It is probably harder for parents to be friends with their children than for strangers. Real friendship calls for detachment, the willingness to know our children as they really are and to be disinterested in our regard. This means being free from possessiveness, or the desire to project our ambitions and desires into our child's life; it means letting him go free to live his own life and make his own mistakes without ever withdrawing our affection from him. Children thrive in the sunlight of sympathy and approval; to have their parents' favor withdrawn is cruelty in its most subtle form. The child should feel that, whatever he has done, he is never placed outside the scope of his parents' love.

Freedom from preoccupation with our own interests is necessary if we are to be friends with our children. We must have leisure to enter into their experiences. This identification involves giving time, attention, interest, understanding to their affairs, courtesy in other words, such as we would give to an adult.

We have said that friendship implies an equal relation rather than one of dominance-submission. This is best realized when we have the meeting ground of a common interest. Many parents, in their desire to be companions to their children, try to cultivate the child's interests, pleasures and companions. This may be a very artificial procedure. Children can find companions of their own age for active sports, and they are usually more embarrassed than flattered if we start back to college with them. It is better to reserve our efforts for the distinctive part that we can play, enlargement of the mental horizon through enrichment, evaluation, comparison. In the last analysis children should be free to take us or leave us as they see fit.

Respect for the child's rights to his own reserves and privacies, to his own friends, interests and activities, coupled with willingness to enter into these activities when he wants us, and to share ours with him when he wishes to, enters into a successful friendly relation. Freedom is as essential as mutual respect and consideration.

EPILOGUE

These essays exemplify how Blatz and his team thought and worked with those responsible for the care and well-being of children. The agenda Blatz had when they were written, and that remained throughout his career, was to explore human consciousness and examine the way the socialization and education of children could both meet their needs and foster their freedom. The path he charted for caretakers—to allow children to face the challenges of life and to learn from the consequences associated with their responses—is illustrated in these essays. Later in his career he elaborated this notion in his theory of personality and labeled the pattern "security." As the world prepared for war in 1939, Blatz wrote that it was vital to remember that although insecurity was necessary for growth, when people do not accept associated challenges they make compensations that collectively create the social turbulence that leads to war. Blatz asserted that it is in the democratic home and school that children learn the cooperation, compromise, and tolerance that may lead to the wisdom to avoid war. The appealing style of communicating and illustrating this message revealed in these essays is missing in today's evidenced based or critically constructionist advice to parents. Blatz and his team did not claim to solve the challenge of parenting. Rather, they provided their readers with a clear enunciation of values and the basis for the development of a philosophy of parenting.

ABOUT THE AUTHORS

Mary Ainsworth attended the University of Toronto, where she earned her PhD in developmental psychology in 1939 under the supervision of William Blatz. Most of her academic career was spent at the University of Virginia. Ainsworth has received many honors, including the Award for Distinguished Contributions to Child Development in 1985 and the Distinguished Scientific Contribution Award from the APA in 1989. One of her important contributions to psychology was her research along with John Bowlby on early emotional attachment. Ainsworth continued as Professor Emeritus at the University of Virginia until her death in 1999 at the age of 86. Ainsworth related that she was introduced to Blatz as an undergraduate student at the University of Toronto in the 1930s when she enrolled in a course he taught in Genetic and Abnormal Psychology. Through his lectures, she learned about his Security Theory—a theory that remained influential throughout her academic career, especially in her contributions to attachment theory. In her chapter, Ainsworth highlights areas where security theory and attachment theory differ, as well as, security theory concepts that contributed to attachment theory. Concepts include a secure base and security itself. Ainsworth asserts that the concept of mature dependent security is one of Blatz's most original and important contributions to an understanding of personality development. She characterizes Blatz as a bold pioneer of the study of interpersonal relations in an era when the academic community avoided scientific exploration of interactions between intimates.

Peter Gamlin received his PhD in developmental psychology from Cornell University. Gamlin is currently professor emeritus in the Department of Adult Education, Community Development and Counseling Psychology at the OISE, University of Toronto, Toronto, Ontario. He was also a professor in the Department of Applied Psychology and the Institute of Child Study University of Toronto. Gamlin's work has focused on educational psychology, child development and adult education (lifelong learning). In his chapter Gamlin explicates Blatz's notion of security as it relates to conceptions of mental health and learning in the work of Heider, Dweck, and Vygotsky.

Michael F. Grapko, completed his PhD dissertation in 1953 under the direction of Blatz, and much of the author's work including the development of methods for measuring security in school-age children has involved the application of Blatz's theory. Grapko was the third director of the Institute of Child Study and the developer of three widely used psychometric measures of human security. The following chapter is based in part on Grapko's dissertation under Blatz and defines some of security theory's basic terms. Concepts elucidated include dependent security—immature and mature; deputy agents; and, insecurity. Effective examples and scenarios are provided to illustrate each idea. Grapko proposes some causes that might explain individual shifts from a state of immature dependent security to independent security. He categorizes possible responses individuals may demonstrate when confronted by a situation of insecurity. Finally, Grapko looks at security under four Blatzian categories of human activity, namely: social life; vocation; avocation; and philosophy of life.

Richard Volpe received his PhD from the University of Alberta. He was a Laidlaw Foundation Post Doctoral Fellow, University of Toronto, Hospital for Sick Children and the Clark Institute of Psychiatry. Currently he is professor and projects director, Life Span Adaptation Projects, the Institute of Child Study, Department of Human Development and Applied Psychology (OISE), University of Toronto. He is also a member of the Graduate Department of Community Health and the Institute for Life Course and Aging, University of Toronto. Previously he was director, Dr. R. G. N. Laidlaw Research Centre, University of Toronto, director of the Laidlaw Foundation's Evaluation and Conceptual Elaboration Unit of their Child at Risk Program, chair of the Institute for the Prevention of Child Abuse, co-chair, Justice for Children and Youth, and an Organization for Economic Co-operation and Development (OECD) Evaluation Expert. His current research deals with applications of prevention science, knowledge mobilization, and the promotion of evidence based practice. Volpe's long-term interest has been in the relation of theory and practice. Volpe's research has focused on the relationship between early experience and later life and how evidence can inform practices that help children cope with major life challenges and transitions. In the first chapter, Volpe introduces the chapters that follow and the unique perspective each of five authors provides regarding the nature of Blatz's conceptualization of human security and importance of this work for policy and practice. Volpe uncovers some of the sources of Blatz's Security Theory, including the Functionalist tradition in Psychology to which Blatz was exposed during his studies at the University of Chicago. Moreover, he examines security theory's root metaphors, focusing on consciousness as well as Blatz's six appetites. Through a selection of Blatz's writings, Volpe shows how Blatz was ahead of his time with still-modern sounding positions on education, reward/punishment, prevention and mental health.

Dr. Sheri L. Winestock, completed her doctorate in the history and philosophy of psychology at York University, Toronto, Ontario in 1994. Her dissertation was titled "William Emet Blatz: The Development Of A Developmental Psychologist." Winestock begins the chapter with a definition of "presentism," a concept that she uses in the retelling and analysis of Blatz's life and contribution. She describes and considers Blatz's career changes in the context of contemporaneous changes in developmental psychology. In doing so, she divides Blatz's life into four periods reflecting the focus of his work as follows: child study; child science; child psychology; and, developmental psychology. Winestock asserts that Blatz's ultimate alienation from developmental psychology was attributable to his adherence to functionalist and mental hygiene perspectives that fell out of fashion by the middle of the twentieth century.

Mary Wright received her PhD in psychology from the University of Toronto. Currently she is professor emeritus, University of Western Ontario, London Ontario. In 1942, Wright was one of five members of the Institute of Child Study's staff who accompanied Blatz to Birmingham, England to train reservists to provide care to children of working class families struggling in the bomb-damaged city. Wright's biographical chapter on Blatz describes his preparatory years and career milestones which the author organizes into three fascinating and productive phases reflecting changes in his personal objectives and in the external demands made on him. Wright tells the story of a great man, accomplished and polarizing as a scientist and scholar. His views on child-rearing, including positions against punishment/reward, competition and the paramount place of consistency over love were all considered radical at the time. Wright describes Blatz as an effective advocate and influencer of public policy, crediting him with the development of a province-wide parent education program, as well as the standards for Ontario day nurseries which became legislated as the Ontario Day Nurseries Act in 1946. Wright's chapter outlines Blatz's criticisms of contemporaries including Freud, Gesell and Piaget. She describes concepts he rejected—the unconscious and biological determinism, among them—as well as notions he absorbed into his own body of work, such as maturation. Wright clarifies Blatz's take on functionalism—his view of learning and development as adaptation and, consciousness as fundamental to the process of adaptation. Wright categorizes Blatz in the camp of Dewey, Piaget and Kohlberg in his view of the child as interactive within his environment—at once modifier and subject to modification. According to Wright, education for Blatz should be organized around children's interests and thereby intrinsically motivating. Its aim should be to help children "learn how to learn." As an overall goal, caregivers, both at home and school, should promote children's security as Blatz defined it—serenity based on inner strength rather than safety. Wright elucidates Blatz's position on discipline; she explains the phases of security theory and, concludes the chapter with a description of revisions Blatz made to this theory in the 1950s at the urging of his colleagues.

INDEX

229

Parents and the Preschool Child, 20, 75,
    79. *See also* Blatz, published
    works
Parent's Magazine, 79
patience, 76
patterns
  assessments, 49-51
  behavior, 35, 38, 59, 105, 144, 146,
      148, 152, 184-185
  family, 117, 177-180
  of friendships, 217, 219
  and imagination, 148
  motivational, 106
  response, 104, 105
  religious, 207
  security, 57, 59-61, 67, 214
  social, 163-164, 177-178, 188
peace, 165-166, 177
penalties, 76. *See also* discipline
perception, 31, 63, 98, 103, 106, 109,
    145-146
personality development theory, 2, 22,
    16, 35-38, 43-45, 52, 98, 104,
    181
philosophy of education, 189
philosophy of life, 36, 37, 38, 49, 51,
    56, 61, 66, 201
physiology, 8, 17
Piaget, Jean, 30, 31, 79, 98, 135
play, 31, 59, 63, 66, 82, 118, 125, 128,
    137-138, 145, 148, 154, 164-165,
    202, 210, 217
Plowden Report, 24
possessiveness, 155, 181, 220
poverty, 156
power
  motive, 147, 163, 184
  principle, 137, 155-157
  in religion, 205
pragmatism, 72
prejudices, 173, 200, 218, 219
preparation, phase of imagination, 149
presentism, 5-6, 69
pressure, 156, 168, 174-175
prevention, 6-7, 72
  Blatz's definition of, 10
Preyer, Whilhelm, 73

principles
  of action, 174
  enjoyment, 212-221
  pleasure, 155
  regulation, 76. *See also* discipline
procrastination, 36, 57
problem-solving, 6, 31, 36, 51, 108,
    148
psychology
  Blatz study of at University of Chi-
      cago, 18
  child, field of, 2, 70, 82, 84, 87, 116
  developmental, 6, 70-71, 73, 79-82,
      84-88
  functional, 70-71
public health, 2, 28
punishments, 6, 15, 34, 76-77, 78, 80,
    86, 117, 125-126, 153, 164, 175

Q
quarrelling, 161-166, 148
  adult, 164, 165
  and affection, 165
  anger, 163
  fear, 163
  jealousy, 163

R
rationalization, 36, 57, 99
reasoning, 135-136, 148
readiness, 58, 62, 65,
reclusiveness, 161, 165, 166
redirection, 36
reflective process, 7, 187,
reinterpretation, 36
Regal Road project, 4, 21
regression, 64, 99, 184, 211
rehabilitation of wounded soldiers, 18,
    71
reinforcement, 55
reinterpretation, 36
relationships, 47, 48, 56, 57, 60, 61-62,
    76, 85, 99, 133-134
  family, 133, 217
  friendships, 216-221
  intimate, 52, 103, 179

LaVergne, TN USA
10 March 2010
175504LV00001B/16/P